GCSE BIOLOGY FOR YOU

CW00811960

Clare Smallman

HUTCHINSON

London Melbourne Sydney Auckland Johannesburg

Hutchinson Education

An imprint of Century Hutchinson Ltd
62–65 Chandos Place, London WC2N 4NW

Century Hutchinson Australia Pty Ltd
PO Box 496, 16–22 Church Street, Hawthorn,
Victoria 3122, Australia

Century Hutchinson New Zealand Ltd
PO Box 40–086, Glenfield, Auckland 10, New Zealand

Century Hutchinson South Africa (Pty) Ltd
PO Box 337, Bergvlei, 2012 South Africa

First published as Biology For You Books One (1981) and Two (1983)
GCSE Edition first published 1987

© Clare Smallman 1987

Typeset in Century Roman by Wyvern Typesetting Ltd, Bristol

Designed by Roy Mole

Printed and bound in Great Britain by Butler and Tanner

British Library Cataloguing in Publication Data
Smallman, Clare
  GCSE biology for you.—2nd ed.
  1 Biology
  I. Title II. Smallman, Clare. Biology for you
  574 QH308.7
ISBN 0–09–159751–X

Acknowledgements are due to the following Examination Groups for
permission to reproduce specimen GCSE questions appearing on pages
267–271:
Midland Examining Group, Questions 1, 2, 4, 6, 7, 8, 12, 14;
Southern Examining Group, Questions 9, 19;
London and East Anglian Group, Questions 5, 13, 17, 20;
Northern Examining Association (Associated Lancashire Schools
Examining Board, Joint Matriculation Board, North Regional
Examinations Board, North West Regional Examinations Board,
Yorkshire and Humberside Regional Examinations Board), Questions
3, 10, 11, 15, 16, 18.
Acknowledgements are also due to the following for permission to
reproduce photographs:
Barnabys Picture Library, pp. 11, 47, 151, 164, 172, 177;
Biophoto Associates, cover photograph and pp. 19, 62, 89, 98, 156, 160,
161, 166, 167, 180;
Camera Press Limited, pp. 108, 247 (Guillaume du Pont);
Sally & Richard Greenhill, p. 234;
Picturepoint Limited, p. 57;
Science Photo Library Limited, p. 11;
WHO, p. 53;
C James Webb, p. 98

Preface

Contents

This lively and approachable book is a radical revision of the two-volume CSE *Biology for You* course. The following changes have been incorporated: total reorganization of the contents to reflect the four Themes required by the National Criteria; new contents where GCSE syllabuses indicate that more information is needed; additional questions integrated throughout the text, including more structured and practically-based questions; a section of GCSE examination questions at the end of the book; a larger format to make the layouts more accessible; more photographs and some new line diagrams have been produced to enhance clarity when difficult concepts are presented; figure numbers and captions are now supplied to assist understanding and ease of reference.

Theme 1 is a summary of living things. Many of the descriptions are explained in the rest of the book. You may like to read this theme again after working on other themes.

Clare Smallman 1987

Introduction
What is Biology? 4
Food chains 8

Theme 1 *Diversity of organisms*
Bacteria and viruses 13
Fungi 15
Green plants 16
Animal kingdom 1 18
Animal kingdom 2 20

Theme 2 *Relationships between organisms and the environment*
Life and the non-living world 24
Soil 30
Food webs and energy 36

Theme 3 *Organization and maintenance of the organism*
Food 49
Digestion 62
Photosynthesis 77
Strange feeders 87
Respiration 90
Breathing 97
Movement 108
Senses 131
Co-ordination 144
Transport 154
Waste disposal 173

Theme 4 *Development of organisms and continuity of life*
Growth of cells 178
Sexual reproduction 189
Population growth 218
Variation 230
Genetics 243
Evolution 256

GCSE examination questions 267

Index 272

What is biology?

What is biology? This is my list of things biology is about. It will give you an idea of what to expect in this book.

Biology is the study of life – past and present – and in all its forms.

Biology asks these questions:

A1

What do living things (*or* **organisms**) need to do well?

air

light and warmth

food

A2

How do living things work? What things do they do?

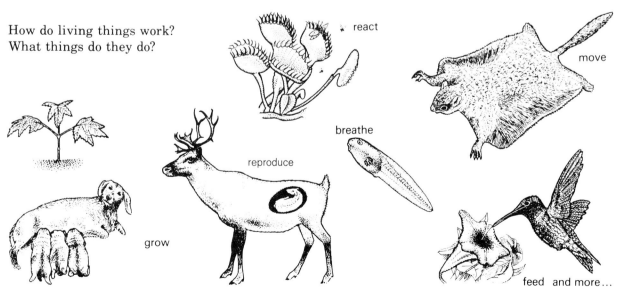

react

move

breathe

reproduce

grow

feed and more…

A3

Where do **organisms** live?

A4

How do organisms get on with
each other?
How do they cope with the
world around them (the
environment)?

A5

What sort of groups can we put
them in?

A6

Can we explain why organisms
are the way they are?

And all the way through – how
do people fit in? How do we
affect other organisms?

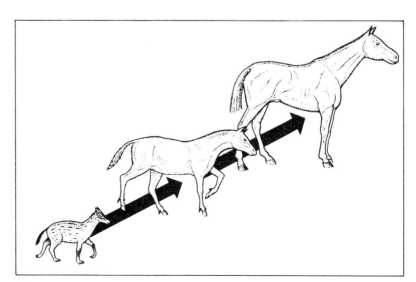

A7

Methods

Experiments in biology often give surprising and unexpected results. This is because living things vary such a lot. So how can we be sure that our ideas are right? The answer is, we can't. In this book, I've included some of the evidence which supports our ideas about life. There has often not been room to explain how each idea has been arrived at and so this page gives a general guide.

Investigations and experiments
Experiments are a way of testing ideas (theories) we have about the world. We can repeat an experiment many times to make sure we are getting a real result. A **control** is an experiment done in exactly the same way as the main experiment but leaving out the thing we are really interested in, or keeping it normal instead of changing it. Because everything else is the same, a control shows that the thing we changed or added is really causing what happens. Experiments in the lab with animals and plants may give misleading results because the organism is out of its normal surroundings.

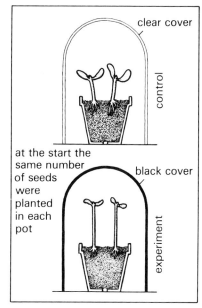

A8 Experiment to find the effect of light on the growth of seedlings

Observing organisms in their usual surroundings helps us to check up on the results of experiments and may give us new ideas. We can only look at a few of all the organisms around – a **sample** of them. Ideas are safer if they are based on large samples and many observations. If an organism does something it can be hard to sort out exactly what's causing it – is it longer days or warmer weather that starts plants growing in spring? Back to the lab to find out.

A9

Close up observation provides lots of useful details but again there are problems. It takes practice to understand the view through a microscope. You may be looking at a dead or dying organism and putting it on a slide will, in any case, cause changes.

By using various methods to sort out one problem at a time, we can be fairly sure of our ideas. A few of the details in this book may change or be added to by the time you leave school because more is being found out all the time.

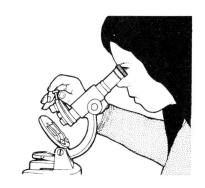

A10

Units

Measuring matters in biology –
just looking isn't enough.

Length
The unit of length is the **metre**
(m).

Many organisms are small –
centimetres (100 cm = 1 m)
and **millimetres** (1000 mm
= 1 m) are useful.

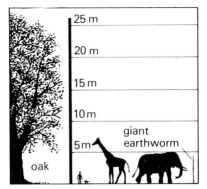

A11

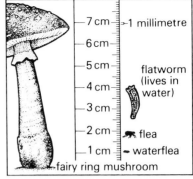

A12

Microscopic organisms are
measured in even smaller
units – **microns** (written μm).
A micron is $\frac{1}{1\,000\,000}$
(one-millionth) of a metre.

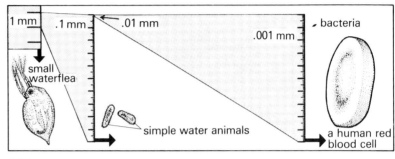

A13

Mass
Mass is measured in **grams** (g).
Larger masses are measured in
kilograms (1000 g = 1 kg).

Time
Scientists use **seconds** to measure time. However, many
biological happenings take a long time and so minutes, hours and
days are used. To get a full idea about what is happening,
organisms may have to be watched for years – and years.

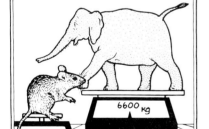

A14

A15

The units of measurement – the metre, the gram and the second –
are called SI units. These are standard units which most
scientists in the world have agreed to use. The SI unit for
temperature is the Kelvin (K), but it is much more common to
measure temperature in degrees Celsius (°C). We have used °C in
this book.

Food chains

A very basic relationship between organisms is food – who eats whom. Food chains are a way of sorting this out. They lead on to questions like 'What is food?' 'How is it made?' 'Why eat?' This book answers these questions. This page introduces the ideas you will meet later in the book.

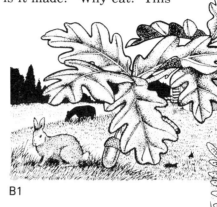

Figure B1 shows a number of food chains. We could write them rather than draw them; for example, one would be:

B1

oak leaf ⟶ caterpillar ⟶ bird

The arrows show the direction the food goes in. They point from the food to the eater.

Describing a food chain
All food chains begin with green plants which are called **producers** as they make (produce) their own food from simple raw materials.

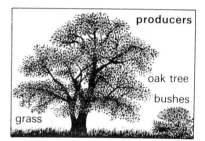

B2 Producers

Animals consume ready made food when they eat other organisms – in a food chain, animals are **consumers**. We divide them into two main groups.

These are all **primary consumers** – the first lot of eaters – the ones which eat plants.

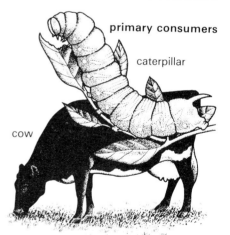

B3 Primary consumers

The **secondary consumers** eat animals – and are further along the chain.

B4 Secondary consumers

Plants and animals which die but aren't eaten are also broken down by **decomposers** – otherwise we'd be knee-deep in dead leaves and rabbits (among other things). Some examples of decomposers are earthworms, fungi and bacteria. The wastes decomposers make can be used by producers as raw materials.

B5 Decomposers

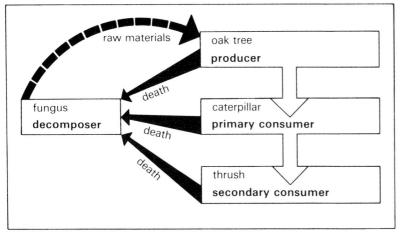

B6 Food chain including decomposers

Decomposers usually work fast, but you may see rabbit or seabird skeletons among sand dunes. This is because the decomposers work more slowly on the bones in dry sand – they need water to work properly.

Adding decomposers to food chains produces a diagram like the one on the left.

The position of an organism in a food chain depends upon what's eaten.
In Fig. B7, the human being is acting as a secondary consumer.
When you eat bread made from wheat, you are a primary consumer.

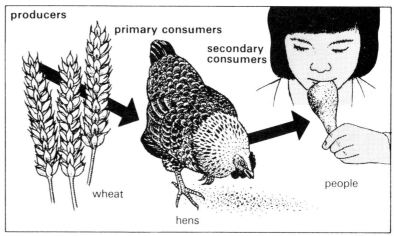

B7

Questions

1. Copy this out and fill in the blanks.
   The first organism in a food chain is always a _____ which can make its own _____. Such organisms are known as _____. Animals feed on other organisms and are known as _____. A caterpillar which eats an oak leaf is a _____ _____. A bird which eats the caterpillar is a _____ _____. Plant and animal remains are broken down into _____ _____ by _____ such as _____.

2. Write down as many of the things as you can remember from your last meal. You were a primary consumer when you ate some of them. Which? You were a secondary consumer when you ate others. Which? Did you ever act as a producer? Give a reason for your answer.

Summary and questions

Summary
Biology is the study of living organisms – it combines laboratory experiments with work in natural surroundings. There are many ways of starting the study. This book begins with food chains – sorting out who eats whom – and goes on to look at food itself.

Questions

1. Write a letter to a young friend who is doing an integrated (combined, general) science course explaining how to sort out the biology from the rest.

2. Explain why it is not enough just to do experiments in the lab.

3. What units would you use for measuring:
   (a) the mass of a giraffe?
   (b) the mass of a mushroom?
   (c) the life span of a man?
   (d) the life span of a mushroom?
   (e) the height of a mushroom?

4. Match up each organism in A with its size in B.

A	B
oak trees	2 m
giraffes	3 cm
tall person	3 mm
flat worm	25 m
flea	7 mm
waterflea	6 m
bacteria	0.0001 mm
red blood cell	0.008 mm

5. Choose two of the organisms (plant or animal) shown on pages 4 & 5. Look them up in an encyclopedia or biology reference book. Write about half a page on each of them – just describe the most interesting thing about them and why you think it is interesting.

B8

6. Figure B8 shows another food chain. Write out the chain using the arrow layout. I have started the chain for you.
   Grass → ········ → ········ → ....
   Which organism produces its own food?
   Which organisms consume their food?
   Which organism is the primary consumer?
   Why are organisms like toadstools (fungi) important in food chains?

Theme 1 Diversity of organisms

Bacteria

Bacteria are found everywhere – they are small and tough.

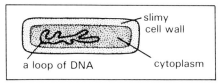
C1 A basic bacterial cell

slimy
cell wall
a loop of DNA
cytoplasm

A bacterial cell has no nucleus (a membrane bag containing chromosomes).

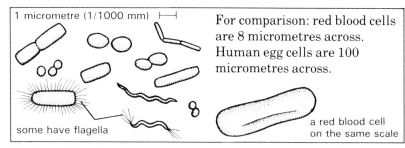
C2 Bacterial variety

1 micrometre (1/1000 mm)

For comparison: red blood cells are 8 micrometres across. Human egg cells are 100 micrometres across.

some have flagella

a red blood cell on the same scale

Bacteria vary in shape and size.

Bacteria reproduce rapidly – usually by splitting in two.

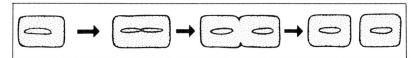
C3 Bacterial reproduction

Their numbers are enormous. It has been suggested that the mass of all the bacteria is 20 times that of all animal life – and that 1 gram of dead skin cells from your head contains 500 million bacteria. They have been found 6 miles down in the ocean, in hot springs at near-boiling temperatures, and floating high in the atmosphere – as well as on and in plants, animals and soil. Some bacteria feed off other organisms, alive or dead. Others make their own food using light or chemical energy.

Helpful bacteria

Most animals cannot digest cellulose. Bacteria live in the guts of cows, horses, rabbits and so on, and break down cellulose for them.

Bacteria help in the breakdown of dead organisms – vital for the recycling of materials. We use them in sewage farms.

Bacteria in the roots of clover (and its relatives) help fix nitrogen – needed for proteins and DNA.

Cheese, butter and vinegar are the result of bacterial action. We use them to make vitamins. In the future, we will be able to use bacteria to make insulin for diabetics, and other useful chemicals.

Harmful bacteria

Some bacteria damage tissues or make poisons (toxins). They are the exceptions.

Bacterial diseases include gonorrhoea, whooping cough, diphtheria, tetanus (lockjaw), leprosy, and typhoid. Vaccines may help to overcome harmful bacteria, and so do antibiotics.

Viruses

Viruses are even smaller than bacteria. They can only 'live' inside cells.

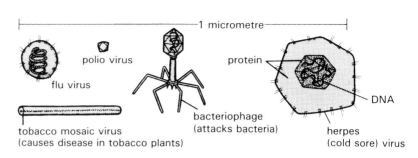

C4 A few viral shapes

Viruses are just a length of genetic material (DNA and RNA) and one or more kinds of protein. They hardly count as life. They do not feed, breathe, grow or move – on their own they do nothing.

However, once they are inside a living cell they take over its machinery and redirect it. Instead of making more cell materials, viruses are produced. The cell eventually bursts and viruses are released to start invading cells all over again.

Viruses are parasites and can do a lot of damage. Vaccines help provided they are used in advance, but antibiotics don't. The body's natural defence chemical, interferon, is normally produced in tiny quantities, but genetic engineering may soon mean that we can make and test interferon in large amounts.

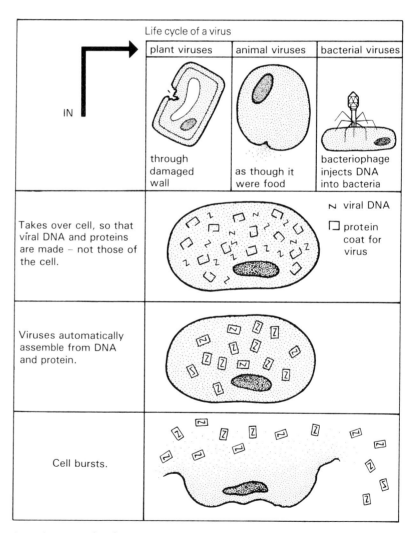

C5 Life cycle of a virus

A few virus diseases

polio
flu
colds
smallpox and chickenpox
measles and german measles*
mumps

*can damage unborn children.

Fungi

Like an iceberg, most of a fungus is below the surface. Its thread-like hyphae weave through the tissues of other organisms, alive or dead, and digest them. Fungi evolved separately from green plants. As they have no chlorophyll, they cannot make their own food. Many are decomposers and, along with bacteria, are mainly responsible for recycling materials. They include yeasts and moulds as well as the mushrooms and toadstools.

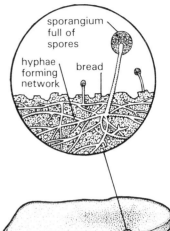

D1 Mucor, a bread mould

Fungi produce spores, sexually or asexually, in enormous quantities. Fungal groups are identified by the way they produce spores. Mushrooms are typical of a group different from the moulds. They produce spores between the gills under the mushroom 'cap'.

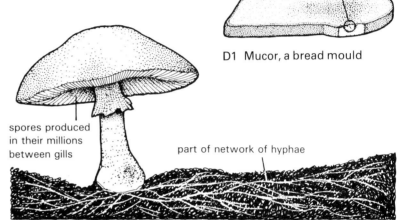

D2 Mushroom

Some fungi have symbiotic relationships with other organisms. One result is a lichen – a combination of an alga and a fungus.

Helpful fungi

Decomposers recycle material.

Some are edible, e.g. field mushrooms.

Yeasts are used in making bread and alcohol.

Many fungi produce antibiotics, e.g. penicillin (discovered by Alexander Fleming).

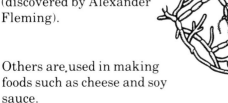

Others are used in making foods such as cheese and soy sauce.

Harmful fungi

Some are poisonous, e.g. death cap.

Some – not as many as bacteria and viruses – cause disease in people, e.g. athletes foot and thrush.

More cause disease in organisms useful to people, e.g. potato blight (damaged leaves mean a ruined crop),

and the smuts and rusts, which cause enormous crop losses.

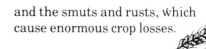

D3

Green plants

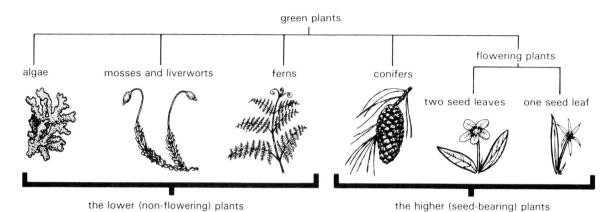

the lower (non-flowering) plants   the higher (seed-bearing) plants

E1

Algae

Algae are a mixed bunch – everything from single-celled organisms to huge seaweeds.

All algae have chlorophyll and can make their own food. Some groups have other pigments which mask the green of chlorophyll, and so they may look brown or red. More on plants and photosynthesis (food making) on page 77.

Their structure is simple. Large algae – lacking support – must live in the water. Many small algae float in the surface waters as part of the plankton, while others are found in soil or growing on buildings and trees. Look for pleurococcus on the shady side of trees. It's a green powdery alga.

Seaweeds are used as manure and as food – especially in Japan. Agar – the jelly bacteria are often grown on – is made from seaweed. Seaweed jellys are used in making beer, cosmetics, paint, ice cream, film and many other things.

E2

Mosses

Mosses and their relatives are the next step for plant life. They live on land, but most prefer damp, shady places to live. They produce spores in a spore capsule, and their 'leaves' and 'roots' are simpler than those of higher plants.

There is a sexual stage in the production of the spore capsule, but the spores are asexual. The plant does not have special cells for transporting food and water, and there are no support tissues – mosses remain small.

Important mosses include sphagnum moss, which is involved in colonizing open water and turning it first into a peat bog and then into dry land able to support trees. Peat is used as fuel in some places.

Mosses help prevent soil erosion, and also break down rocks. They still need water for part of their life cycle.

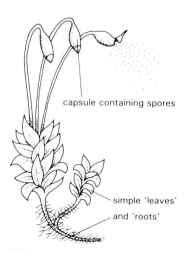

E3 Sphagnum moss

Ferns

Ferns are better adapted to life on land than mosses. They have a transport system and stiffened support in their stems. It is simple, but it allows ferns to grow large.

They still need water for part of their life cycle.

The adult plant grows from an egg cell fertilized by a sperm which swims towards it through a water film. You could say that ferns still have one foot in the water.

Most ferns are looked on as attractive and many are grown in gardens and greenhouses. Bracken, on the other hand, counts as a weed – it grows very well on land that could be used for pasture.

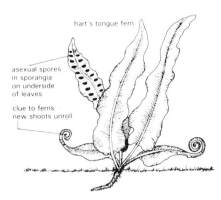

E4 Hart's tongue fern

Conifers

Conifers can grow very successfully on dry land, thanks to an improved plumbing system, and to pollen. Instead of sperm which swim, they have a waterproof male gamete to fertilize egg cells on the scales of female cones. The resulting seeds fall out when the cone opens. (They have no protective coatings as there's no ovary to make them.)

Conifers were fully developed 220 million years ago. Today the group includes firs, pines and yews. Among them are the bristle cone pines, thought to be the oldest living plants on earth. One is believed to be 5000 years old.

Leaf patterns and cone shapes help identify conifers.

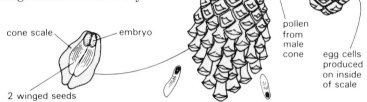

E5 Scot's pine

Flowering plants

Equipped with adaptable leaves, effective transport systems, flowers and double-wrapped seeds, flowering plants have beaten conifers into second place as land plants. They come in two groups, depending on whether they have one seed leaf or two.

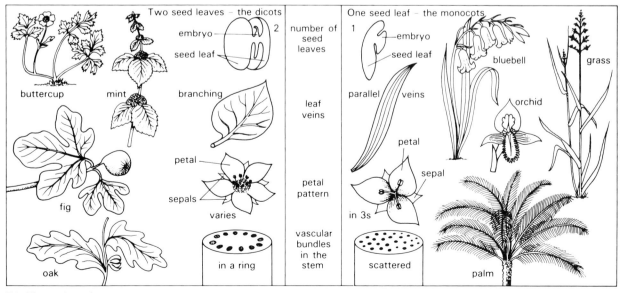

E6 Flowering plant summary

17

The animal kingdom 1

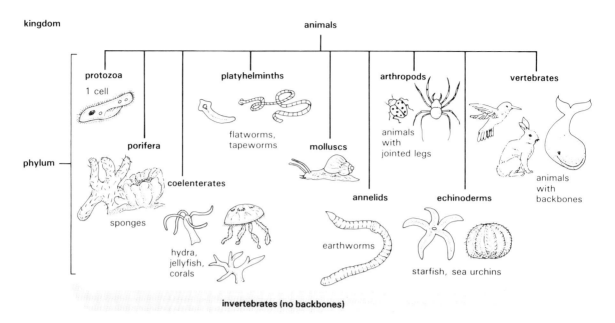

F1 Animal kingdom

The major groups of invertebrates are as different from each other as they are from vertebrates. They make up 95 per cent of all animal species. The diagram above leaves out the smaller of the twenty-five phyla of invertebrates.

Protozoa – the single-celled animals

Some classifiers would like to put all single-celled organisms in one group – the protists. There are not only animal-type and plant-type single-celled organisms, but also some which show features of both. Chlamydomonas, for example, may be described as an alga in one book and be included as a protist in a book on animals. Decide for yourself whether it matters.
Protozoa include Amoeba, Paramecium and Plasmodium.

Protozoa all need water to survive, though some can live through dry times in waterproof cysts. They may be free-living like Amoeba (found in ponds) or live on or in other organisms. Plasmodium is a parasite which causes malaria. Other protozoan diseases include a form of dysentry, and sleeping sickness.

Sponges (Porifera)

A bath sponge is just a skeleton – in life it is completely covered with a layer of loosely organized cells. Sponges lie anchored to the sea floor (or a few in fresh water). They have a variety of cell types, including some with flagella. These beat and keep water moving through the animal. Food particles in the water are trapped and digested.

Other cells make the skeleton of the sponge. In bath sponges this is mainly a protein called spongin (yes, really!), but in others the skeleton is reinforced by 'needles' of calcium carbonate or, in the glass sponges, silica.

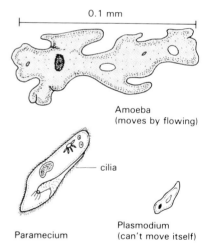

F2 Protozoa

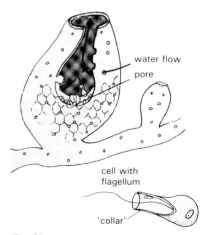

F3 Simple sponge, cut away to show inside

Coelenterates

These include animals whose bodies are based on two layers of cells which work together as a whole.

They have tentacles with stinging cells to paralyse their prey. The tentacles, working together, push the food into the mouth. Digestion is inside the body tube. Coelenterates can all move, or at least move their tentacles, and many can glide or swim. Reproduction is sexual or asexual. They include sea anemonies, jelly fish and the well known (but tiny) Hydra.

Platyhelminths – flatworms

These are simple animals with a body plan which is bilaterally symmetrical. That is, one half is a mirror image of the other, on a line drawn from head to tail.

Planaria is a free-living flatworm.

Other flatworms do more damage – they include parasites like tapeworms, found in guts, and flukes.

The blood fluke Schistosoma harms 200 million people.

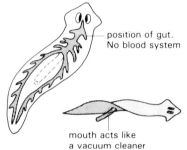

F5 Planaria

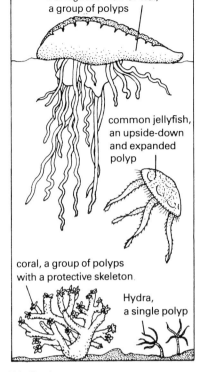

F4 Coelenterates

Annelids – segmented worms

These have bodies which are divided into similar sections, with a gut and nerve cord and blood vessels running through it.

They include earthworms and rag worms (which live in mud by the sea) as well as blood-sucking parasites – the leeches.

Molluscs

The basic mollusc plan is a soft body full of guts, reproductive organs and so on, covered by a mantle – a sheet of tissue which sometimes produces a shell. They include snails, slugs, bivalves (which have two shells), octopuses and squids.

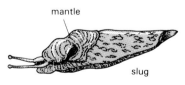

F7 Molluscs

F6 A leech

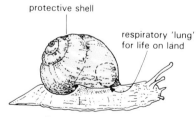

Echinoderms

These have bodies which divide into five equal sections, not two. They move slowly – lacking head or brain – on tube feet powered by hydraulic (water) pressure. Chalky plates under the skin provide protection for starfish.

Roll up a starfish into a ball, add spines and you have a sea urchin.

F8 An echinoderm

19

The animal kingdom 2

Arthropods

These animals with their jointed legs form a huge group. They have a tough exoskeleton, which covers a body which is often in segments. The arthropods show adaptations for many ways of life.

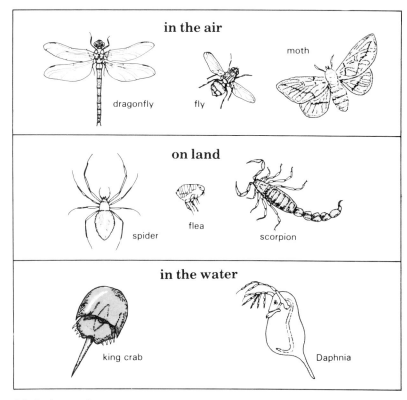

G1 Arthropods

Animals with backbones

The vertebrates, with their brains and spinal cords protected by skull and vertebrae, have done well. These two pages are a reminder of the groups that make up the phylum (phyla is the plural).

Fish

Fish live in water, are cold-blooded and, mainly, breathe through gills. Their muscular, scale-clad bodies are built around two types of skeleton – cartilage and bone.

The bony fish have evolved many forms, from eel-shape to plate-shape and to flying fins.

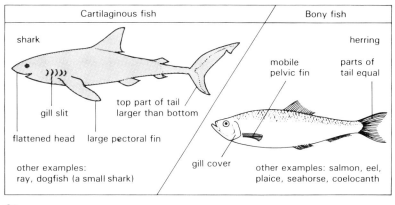

G2

Amphibians

The first of the land-living vertebrates, most amphibians have a thin scale-less skin and must remain in a damp environment or die from dehydration. Their young are tadpoles living in water and breathing through gills, but the adults have lungs. They include salamanders and newts, as well as toads and frogs (tail-less as adults).

G3 A salamander

Reptiles

Reptiles are more adapted for life on land. They are cold-blooded, with thick scaly skins. They lay eggs with leathery shells from which mini-adults emerge already breathing with lungs. They include turtles and tortoises, lizards, snakes and crocodilians.

G4 Reptiles

lizard

snake

turtle

crocodile

Birds

Very early fossil birds are hard to tell from the fossils of some dinosaurs – and it seems likely that birds are descended from early reptiles. Scales have become feathers. Birds are warm-blooded – that is, they have a steady body temperature and a four-chambered heart. They have no teeth. They range from flightless kiwis to birds of paradise, with a lot of variety in between.

G5 Kiwi

Mammals

Mammals started in a small way at the beginning of the age of dinosaurs. They have fur and feed their young on milk from mammary glands. They are warm-blooded and generally have large brains.

G6 Monotreme, a platypus

Monotremes include the platypus and the spiny anteater. They lay eggs but feed their young on milk.

Marsupials include kangaroos. The young start life inside the mother, but there is no placenta, so they are born at an early stage of development and grow in the mother's pouch.

G7 Marsupial, a kangaroo

Placentals have young which are born well developed, thanks to the placenta.

G8 Placentals

bat

dolphin

Theme 2 Relationship between organisms and the environment

Life and the non-living world

Pick a place for a holiday – and you'll probably go south to the sun and a more reliable climate. Climate affects the kind of plant and animal communities in an area. The map (Fig. H2) shows the world's main communities, or **ecosystems**, or **biomes**. The type of ecosystem in an area partly depends on physical factors, including climate.

Physical (non-living) factors such as **temperature** and **water** depend on such factors as distance from the equator or from the sea. Height above sea level counts, too. Walk up a mountain and you may see several ecosystems.

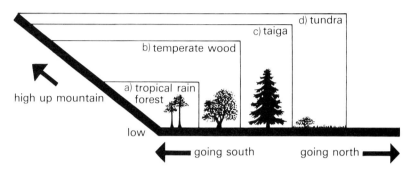

H1 Ecosystems

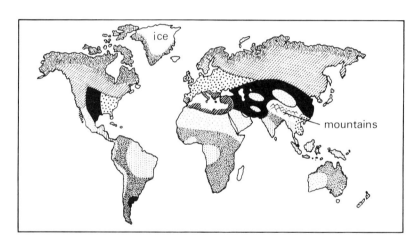

H2 Ecosystems around the world

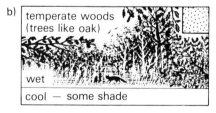

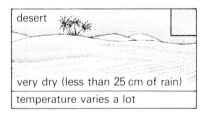

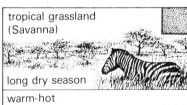

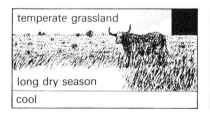

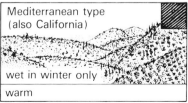

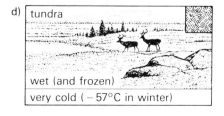

H3 Key to map H2, ecosystems around the world

The non-living world - temperature

Life mostly goes on at temperatures between 0°C and 40°C. Within that range, most organisms live in places where the temperature doesn't vary too wildly. Think of the temperature range you're happy in without any clothes on.

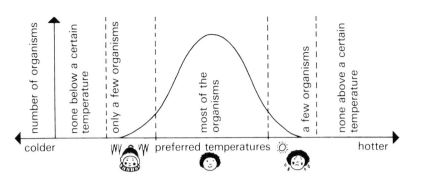

H4 Comfortable and uncomfortable temperatures

Organisms are adapted to the temperature they live in. Here are a few adaptations to very hot or very cold climates. (Fig. H5).

During reproduction and the early stages of growth, organisms are especially sensitive to temperature. For example, madder plants won't grow in places where it's colder than 4.5°C in January, because the cold stops the young shoots being formed properly (Fig. H6).

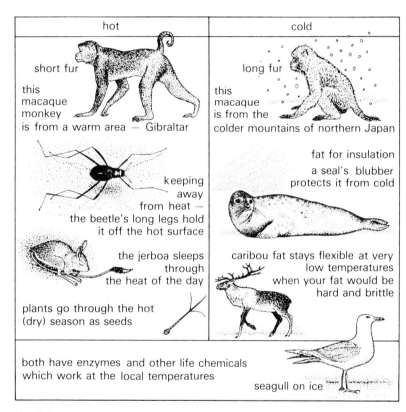

H5 Adaptations to heat and cold

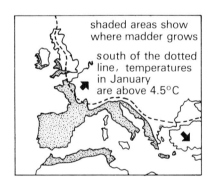

H6 Madder distribution

shaded areas show where madder grows

south of the dotted line, temperatures in January are above 4.5°C

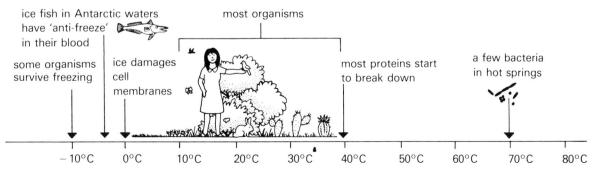

H7 Summary – temperature and living organisms

ice fish in Antarctic waters have 'anti-freeze' in their blood

most organisms

some organisms survive freezing

ice damages cell membranes

most proteins start to break down

a few bacteria in hot springs

−10°C 0°C 10°C 20°C 30°C 40°C 50°C 60°C 70°C 80°C

25

The non-living world - the seasons

In the course of the year, in this country, there are changes in temperature, rainfall and **light** produced by changes in the tilt of the earth relative to the sun. In short – the seasons.

Organisms are greatly affected by the seasons – including people.

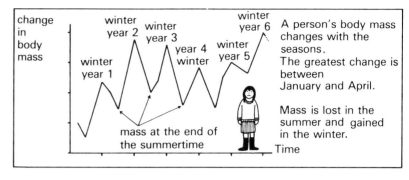

A person's body mass changes with the seasons.
The greatest change is between January and April.

Mass is lost in the summer and gained in the winter.

H8 People are affected by the seasons

Summer

In summer the days are longest, brightest and warmest – great for photosynthesis. Plants grow like mad, and so do the animals that depend on them. This is a time for young animals to grow and for plants to produce flowers.

H9 A summer scene

Autumn

Seeds are produced and go their way. Broad-leaved trees lose their leaves to avoid frost damage. Buds grow, ready for next spring, and then remain dormant. Evergreen trees keep their leaves, which are well protected by a thick waxy cuticle.

scale protects next spring's leaves

scar where leaf fell off

This will be unchanged (dormant) through the winter.

H10 Sticky bud of horse chestnut

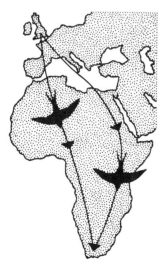

H11 Swallows migrate over 6000 miles, by various routes, to South Africa for the winter

In autumn, animals make a choice. They can prepare for the winter and cope with cold and lack of food, or migrate. As we're on an island, only birds can leave. They often travel great distances.

Winter

The days are cooler and shorter. Plants have slowed down. Trees have protective bark, but many small plants avoid the cold by spending the winter as a seed, or in an underground form (such as a bulb).

The remaining animals may continue to move around. They will have built up defences against cold, such as extra fat, longer fur, stored food and somewhere to shelter. Others spend the winter in an inactive form. A few mammals, such as the hedgehog, go into a long sleep – **hibernation**. Frogs and worms slow down and stay in crevices or deep in the soil. Many insects spend the winter as pupae, but others make it as adults.

bats hibernate from October to April in barns and old trees

hedgehogs under piles of leaves under a hedge can be heard snoring. They may come out on warm days

natterjack toad under a stone

queen wasps and ladybirds hibernate under bark

H12 Techniques for surviving winter

Spring

Plants are triggered into action by the longer days or higher temperatures (just as many organisms were switched off in the autumn by the cold or the shorter days). Chemical processes speed up and leaves grow.

Animals return or become active again. Many mate, and the young are born. Larger animals may have carried their young through the winter, and now give birth.

sheep and lambs

stored food in crocus corm gives plant a quick start

courting great crested grebes present each other with nesting materials

H13 Spring activities

PS: These are overall patterns. Many plants produce seeds in the summer or even in the spring. Some animals produce two families a year – and so on.

Questions

1. Look at the picture illustrating summer (Fig. H9). Make up a food chain based on the animals shown. Which ecosystem will have the most food chains – the desert or the tropical rain forest? Why?

2. What changes are likely to happen in the food chain you described in answering question 1 when winter comes? How could you check your suggestion?

The non-living world - water

Life began in water and still relies on it – especially for reproduction. Water dissolves and transports many life chemicals. It is important in many chemical reactions in plants and animals. Can you remember one? (If not see later on this page.)

The change from living in water to living on land involved solving major problems:
    supporting the body
    preventing water loss (by evaporation)
    reproducing

The problems of life on land are greater in dry areas.
The rule is
'lots of water . . . lots of life
little water . . . little life'

There are many reasons why an area may have little water for organisms to use. These may include:
(a) low rainfall (drought – as in the Sahara)
(b) rain runs away fast (like the sand dunes)
(c) water is frozen and so can't be used (like the tundra, poles, tops of mountains)

Whatever the reason for the lack of water, you will find some organisms living in all but the dryest places. How do they manage to collect and keep enough water?

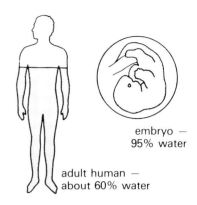

embryo –
95% water

adult human —
about 60% water

H14 Water matters

protected embryo

bones for support

skin - more or less waterproof

H15 Some adaptations to life out of water

Animals

Desert animals have similar problems, but worse (because they move around more and lose more water by breathing). They have many adaptations. Here are a few.

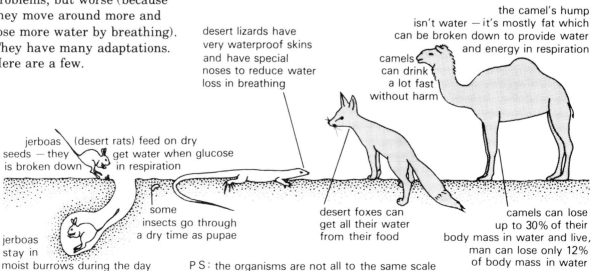

desert lizards have very waterproof skins and have special noses to reduce water loss in breathing

the camel's hump isn't water — it's mostly fat which can be broken down to provide water and energy in respiration

camels can drink a lot fast without harm

jerboas (desert rats) feed on dry seeds – they get water when glucose is broken down in respiration

some insects go through a dry time as pupae

jerboas stay in moist burrows during the day

desert foxes can get all their water from their food

camels can lose up to 30% of their body mass in water and live, man can lose only 12% of body mass in water

P S: the organisms are not all to the same scale

H16 Adaptations to desert life

Plants

The drought dodgers are mostly grasses and small plants. They grow very fast indeed when water is around, and then get through a dry season as seeds.

Xerophytes – the toughies

Xerophytes are plants able to survive drought. They have two main problems: collecting water, and then keeping it. Most xerophytes have large root systems to collect water. They avoid losing it by keeping their surface area as small as possible.

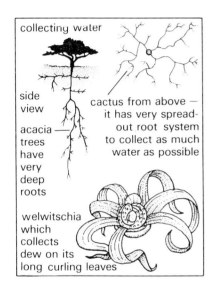

collecting water

side view

acacia trees have very deep roots

cactus from above – it has very spread-out root system to collect as much water as possible

welwitschia which collects dew on its long curling leaves

keeping the water   less water is lost if the surface is small compared to volume

water stored in stem   acacia tree loses leaves in dry season

green stem for photosynthesis

small spiny leaves (help keep away herbivores)

grass leaves roll up (remember marram)   many cacti   leaf spines form a fuzz – it keeps damp air near the plant

H17 Collecting water   H18 Keeping water

Summary
The kind of organisms that live in an area, and how well they grow, depend upon a combination of physical (non-living) factors. These include temperature, water, light and wind. Few organisms live in extreme conditions. The ones that do have special adaptations for those conditions.

Questions

1. What changes in temperature occur as you
   (a) go north?
   (b) climb a mountain?
   What happens to the size of plants growing in a cold area? Describe three adaptations of animals to the cold.

2. Explain the meaning of these words and give an example in each case: hibernate, dormant, biome, migrate, xerophyte.

3. Describe any three plant adaptations and any three animal adaptations to a dry environment.

4. Design an ideal desert organism. It can be a plant or an animal. Add your own ideas to those in this book. Give reasons for your design.

5. Think of an area you know well – like a back garden, a corner of a park, a small wood or a pond. Make brief notes on how it appears in each season. Think particularly about the plants and animals you've seen and how they change through the year.

   Draw a plan showing it as it is now.

Soil - the physical features

Soil provides a base for many plants, and is their source of water and minerals. It is the home of many organisms. The kind of community in a soil depends partly upon the kind of rock it is made from. It also depends on how the inhabitants affect it.

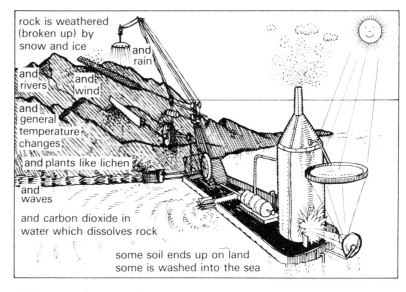

soil as seen by an inhabitant

clay (less than 0.002 mm wide)

silt (0.002 – 0.02 mm wide)

sand (0.02 – 0.2 mm wide)

mineral particles of various sizes

thin water film (contains dissolved mineral salts)

air space (up to 20% of total in loose soils)

humus

I1 Soil as seen by an inhabitant. The type of soil party depends on the particle sizes.

Soil is formed when rock is broken up into tiny **mineral particles**. Lots of things can make this happen: the weather, rivers, the sea, plants (Fig. I2). Soil also contains **air, water** and **humus** (decaying plant and animal material).

Water and air

Water around soil particles has minerals dissolved in it. Both are available to plants as long as there is enough air for the roots to respire. Too much water can mean not enough air, and plant growth is stunted. The air in soil is usually very humid (damp).

rock is weathered (broken up) by snow and ice ...and rain

and rivers ...and wind

and general temperature changes

and plants like lichen

and waves

and carbon dioxide in water which dissolves rock

some soil ends up on land some is washed into the sea

I2 Rock weathers to soil

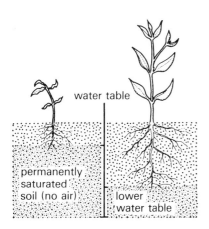

water table

permanently saturated soil (no air)

lower water table

I3 Too much water can stunt growth in many plants

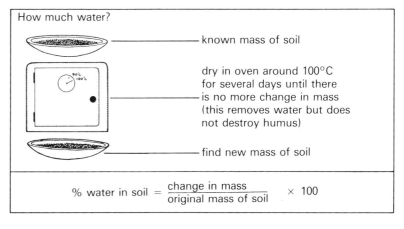

How much water?

known mass of soil

dry in oven around 100°C for several days until there is no more change in mass (this removes water but does not destroy humus)

find new mass of soil

$$\% \text{ water in soil} = \frac{\text{change in mass}}{\text{original mass of soil}} \times 100$$

I4 How much water? Weigh a soil sample, heat to dryness and weigh again to find out.

Humus

Dead organisms decay to produce humus, which gives soil a dark colour. The mineral nutrients released by decay may be **leached** (washed) down to the lower layers of the soil – perhaps right out of it (Fig. I5).

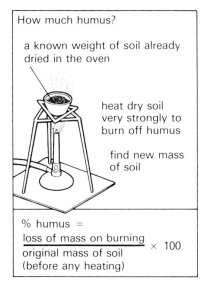

How much humus?

a known weight of soil already dried in the oven

heat dry soil very strongly to burn off humus

find new mass of soil

% humus =
$$\frac{\text{loss of mass on burning}}{\text{original mass of soil}} \times 100$$
(before any heating)

I5 How much humus?

Mineral particles

These come in various sizes (Figs I1 and I6). Their size matters because it affects the amount of water and air in a soil.

Loam soils contain a mixture of sand and clay particles.

This experiment (Fig. I7) compares the way soils hold water. Several different kinds of soil are put into funnels which are plugged with cotton wool. Water is added. It drains through the soils at different speeds.

The kind of rock the particles come from affects the final community. Here are a couple of possible ecosystems on different kinds of base rock. (Fig. I8).

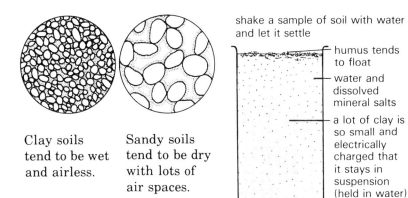

Clay soils tend to be wet and airless.

Sandy soils tend to be dry with lots of air spaces.

shake a sample of soil with water and let it settle

humus tends to float

water and dissolved mineral salts

a lot of clay is so small and electrically charged that it stays in suspension (held in water)

a little clay

silt

sand

I6 Finding out how much of each particle size a soil contains

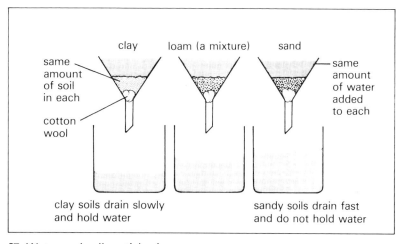

clay   loam (a mixture)   sand

same amount of soil in each

cotton wool

same amount of water added to each

clay soils drain slowly and hold water

sandy soils drain fast and do not hold water

I7 Water and soil particle size

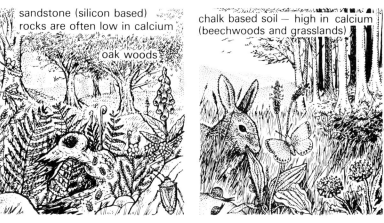

sandstone (silicon based) rocks are often low in calcium

oak woods

chalk based soil – high in calcium (beechwoods and grasslands)

I8

Life and soil

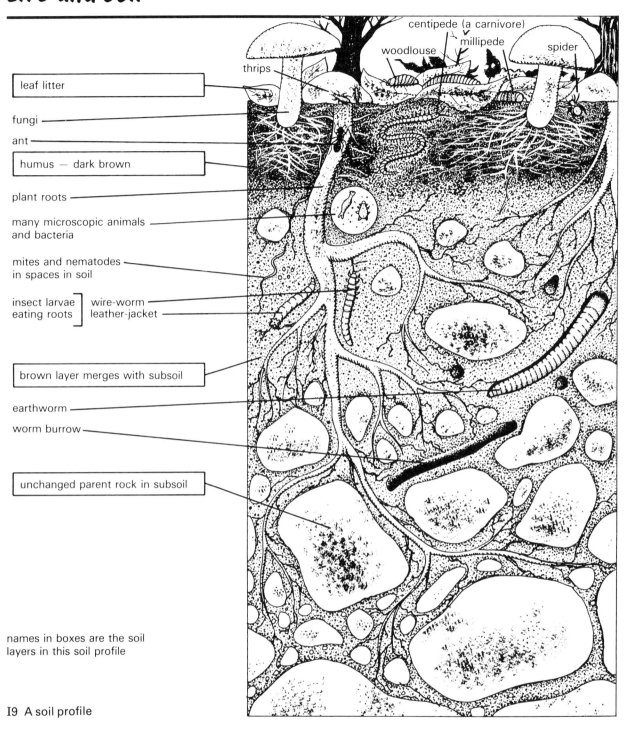

leaf litter

fungi

ant

humus — dark brown

plant roots

many microscopic animals and bacteria

mites and nematodes in spaces in soil

insect larvae eating roots] wire-worm leather-jacket

brown layer merges with subsoil

earthworm

worm burrow

unchanged parent rock in subsoil

names in boxes are the soil layers in this soil profile

thrips

centipede (a carnivore)
millipede
woodlouse
spider

I9 A soil profile

Small warning

This is all about the average woodland (oak wood) soil. Soils vary according to the communities living on them. Beech trees tend to produce a leached soil. Leaves from conifers decay slowly and result in a deep litter layer — and so on.

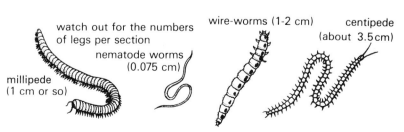

watch out for the numbers of legs per section

nematode worms (0.075 cm)

wire-worms (1-2 cm)

centipede (about 3.5cm)

millipede (1 cm or so)

I10 Soil animals are mostly long thin shapes, ideal for crawling between soil particles

Soil animals

These include everything from visiting rabbits to the full-time microscopic nematode worms. Most feed on plant roots (like wire worms) or decaying material (like millipedes) or other animals (like centipedes).

Large ones (like earthworms) can be sorted from soil by hand. Smaller ones can be collected with a Tullgren funnel. A lamp is set up above a funnel full of soil. The insects crawl away from the heat and fall through the funnel into the jar.

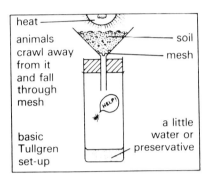

I11 Basic Tullgren set-up

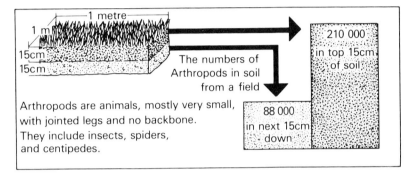

I12 Collecting from grassland

The diagram (Fig. I12) shows the results of a collection made from one square meter of grassland.

Micro-organisms in the soil include bacteria, fungi and single-celled animals – **protozoa**. They live in the water film around soil particles.

Most of the bacteria and fungi are decomposers. The protozoa feed on bacteria and fungi.

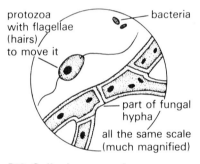

I13 Soil micro-organisms

We can prove there are living things in the soil by testing it for respiration with lime water.

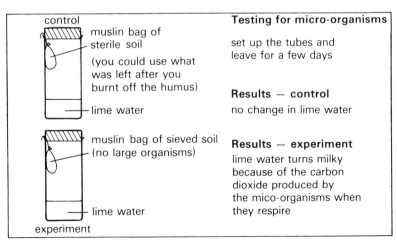

I14 Testing for micro-organisms

Questions

1. What is the difference between the pattern of legs in a centipede and a millipede?

2. Describe a possible food chain made up of soil organisms.

3. Explain what these words mean: humus, water table, loam, protozoan, arthropod, soil profile.

4. How many arthropods would you expect to find in the top 30 cm of five square metres of grassland?

People and soil

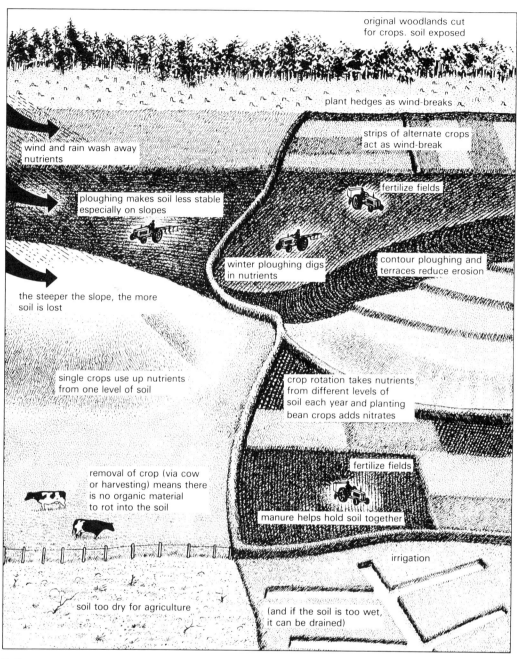

original woodlands cut for crops. soil exposed

plant hedges as wind-breaks

strips of alternate crops act as wind-break

wind and rain wash away nutrients

fertilize fields

ploughing makes soil less stable especially on slopes

winter ploughing digs in nutrients

contour ploughing and terraces reduce erosion

the steeper the slope, the more soil is lost

single crops use up nutrients from one level of soil

crop rotation takes nutrients from different levels of soil each year and planting bean crops adds nitrates

removal of crop (via cow or harvesting) means there is no organic material to rot into the soil

fertilize fields

manure helps hold soil together

irrigation

soil too dry for agriculture

(and if the soil is too wet, it can be drained)

I15

Summary

Soil is built up from mineral material (weathered rocks) and humus (decaying plant and animal material). The properties of a soil depend upon:
   the type of rock it came from
   the size of particles
   the kind of living community which uses it
      and adds to the humus
   the amount of rain in the area.

Soil organisms include many animals (mostly very small), fungi, bacteria and the roots of green plants.

We use soils for farming and in doing so may damage it – but there are ways of avoiding or reducing the damage.

Questions

1. Match up the words in column A with a phrase from column B and write out your answer in full sentences.

A	B
Soil	may be of several sizes; the largest are called sand, the smallest are clay.
Mineral particles	is in the remaining spaces. It is vital for organisms so that they can respire.
Water	is made up of non-living minerals and humus – the rotting remains of organisms.
Air	include fungi, bacteria and the root systems of green plants.
Animals	surrounds the mineral particles and contains dissolved mineral salts.
Other soil organisms	in the soil include many insects, worms and protozoa.

2. Look at Fig. I15.
   (a) List the problems which farmers are likely to cause for themselves as they work the land.
   (b) For each problem, give one way the farmer can avoid the problem.
   (c) For each solution, give one way wild life might be badly affected.

3. The food requirements of two species of earth worms were studied. Five adult worms were kept in one pound jars with one of three foods supplied. Altogether there were 12 jars with species A and 12 with species B worms. After three months the cocoons in each jar were counted. The number of cocoons per jar were:

FOOD	Species A	Species B
Farmyard manure	1	9
Sheep dung	14	76
Chopped straw	2	12

   (a) Draw a graph showing these results.
   (b) Would the Tullgren funnel method be suitable for extracting cocoons? If yes, explain how it would work. If not, why not and how would you try to extract the cocoons from the soil for counting?
   (c) What conclusions do you draw about the way food supply affects the rate of reproduction in these two species of worm?

4. How does air in soil compare with the air just above the soil? In your answer, please include
   light
   temperature
   humidity (dampness)
   carbon dioxide near the surface
   carbon dioxide lower down
   Part of the answer is in the text, part you'll have to work out.

5. Bonsai trees are tiny minature trees. They are kept small by all kinds of tricks, including:
   (a) keeping them in small pots
   (b) clipping off the growing tips of stems and roots
   (c) keeping nutrient levels in the soil low
   Explain how each of these helps to keep the bonsai's growth almost at a standstill.

6. Match each ecosystem in column A with the correct description from column B. Write your answer as a full sentence.

A	B
Tundra is	cool and damp – the trees are mostly broad leaves like oak.
Taiga is	very hot and dry with few plants and animals.
Temperate woodland is	warm, with rain in winter only.
Tropical rain forest is	very cold. The ground is often frozen and only a few small plants survive.
Mediterranean type is	hot with a dry season. It has long grasses and acacia trees. (Also known as savanna.)
Temperate grassland is	cold and damp – the trees here are mostly conifers.
Tropical grassland is	hot and wet. This is the most productive growing system of the lot.
Desert is	cool and dry for part of the year. It has short grasses. (This is also called steppe or prairie.)

Food webs

We are surrounded by food chains – indeed we are part of many of them ourselves. Because we eat so many kinds of foods, if one is in short supply, we can usually find another which will do. Many animals follow the same policy.

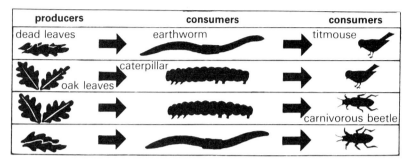

J1 A fox and a few of its prey

Many food chains overlap (Fig. J2)

producers	consumers	consumers
dead leaves	➡ earthworm	➡ titmouse
oak leaves	caterpillar ➡	➡
	➡ caterpillar	➡ carnivorous beetle
	➡ earthworm	➡

J2 Overlapping food chains

They can be put together as the start of a **food web** (Fig. J3). Other organisms can easily be added.

As we add to the food web it becomes more complicated. This (Fig. J4) is still a simple version of who eats what. It is part of a food web studied in an oak wood near Oxford.

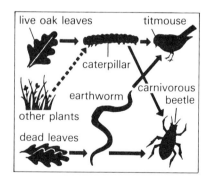

J3 Summarizing overlapping food chains as a food web

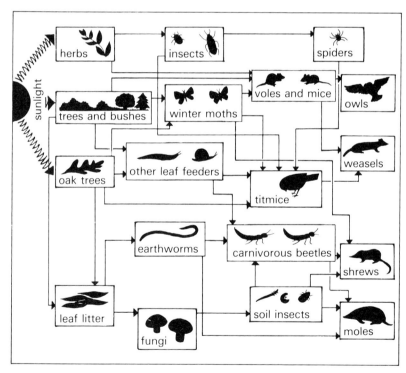

J4 Oak wood food web

Questions

Look at the woodland food web (Fig. J4).
1. Name three producers.
2. Name five consumers – and in each case say whether it is a herbivore, a carnivore or an omnivore.
3. Write out any two separate food chains from this web.
4. The seafood chain (Fig. J7) includes man – where can people be fitted into the woodland chain?
5. Name two top carnivores from the woodland chain and two from the seafood chain.

Finding out what things eat is not always easy.
We can look in guts and watch organisms feed, but this is not all that simple. Small animals may be hard to see and others feed at night. Some animals chew their food to a pulp, so looking in their stomachs doesn't help much.

However, a good many webs have been worked out.

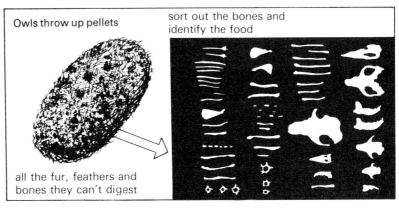

J5 Owl pellets

Owls throw up pellets

all the fur, feathers and bones they can't digest

sort out the bones and identify the food

The more species in a food web, the more stable the community. Small upsets, say in the weather, do not destroy it. Organisms always have alternative foods. Experiments with food webs which contain only a few species show that they break down easily. A change in the numbers of one of the organisms has a devasting effect on the other organisms.

Normally there are as many species as the physical conditions allow. There are lots in the tropics, fewer in tundra – but still enough for systems to be stable.

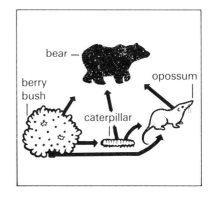

J6 A food web that didn't work

bear

berry bush

caterpillar

opossum

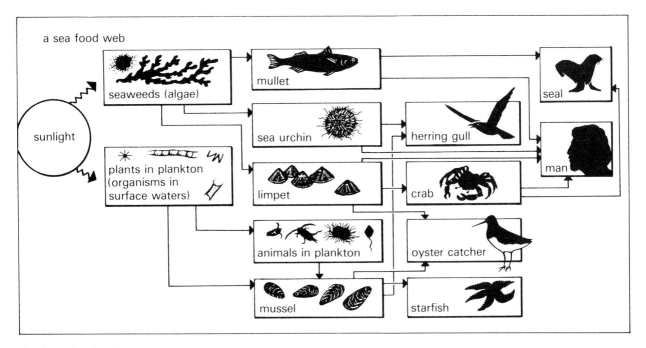

J7 A sea food web

a sea food web

sunlight

seaweeds (algae)

plants in plankton (organisms in surface waters)

mullet

sea urchin

limpet

animals in plankton

mussel

herring gull

crab

oyster catcher

starfish

seal

man

The nitrogen cycle and food webs

Within the food webs of the world materials are passed around. Nitrogen is one example. The problem is to fix (trap) it and hold on to it. There is plenty of nitrogen in the air, but it has to be turned into **nitrates** before plants can use it.

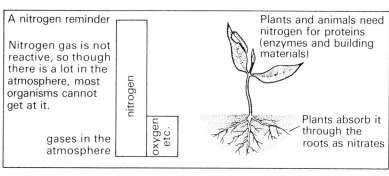

A nitrogen reminder

Nitrogen gas is not reactive, so though there is a lot in the atmosphere, most organisms cannot get at it.

gases in the atmosphere

nitrogen

oxygen etc.

Plants and animals need nitrogen for proteins (enzymes and building materials)

Plants absorb it through the roots as nitrates

J8 A nitrogen reminder

Converting nitrogen gas to nitrates needs a lot of energy. There are three main ways to do this: by an industrial process, by **legumes** (peas, beans, clover), or (in small amounts) by lightning.

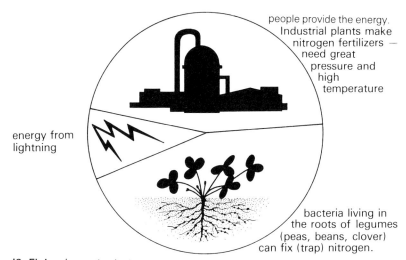

people provide the energy. Industrial plants make nitrogen fertilizers — need great pressure and high temperature

energy from lightning

bacteria living in the roots of legumes (peas, beans, clover) can fix (trap) nitrogen.

J9 Fixing (trapping) nitrogen

Legumes have a way of turning nitrogen into nitrates.

They have **nitrogen-fixing bacteria.** These bacteria live in swellings or **nodules** in the legume roots.

nodules on the root of a legume (a trefoil)

nucleus

bacteria

cell of plant root

Section through a nodule

J10 Nitrogen-fixing bacteria section through a nodule

The **plant** gets a supply of usable nitrogen.

The **bacteria** get energy-rich nutrients from the plant.

Both gain – this is an example of **symbiosis.** See page 88.

Plants can take up nitrates from the soil – they are dissolved in the soil water. They can use the nitrates to make proteins. The consumers and decomposers of a food web get their usable nitrogen by eating plants, or decaying organisms, or each other. Most decay processes result in nitrates being released into the soil.

Farmyards smell of ammonia because that is a step in the decay process.

Some bacteria, **de-nitrifying bacteria**, break up nitrates and release nitrogen gas into the air. Fire does the same. The amount of nitrogen released to the air used to be the same as the amount fixed from the air. Nowadays there is a gain in fixed nitrogen each year because of our activities. (The total amount of nitrogen – nitrogen fixed and nitrogen in air – of course doesn't change.)

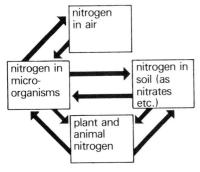

J11 The basic nitrogen cycle – without people

Questions

1. A farmer wants to rotate (plant different) crops in his field each year – partly so that their roots remove different nutrients from the soil each year. He suggests the following plans:

	Year 1	Year 2	Year 3	Year 4
Plan A	potato	wheat	peas	turnip
Plan B	potato	turnip	grass	wheat
Plan C	wheat	potato	lettuce	turnip

What would you recommend and why?

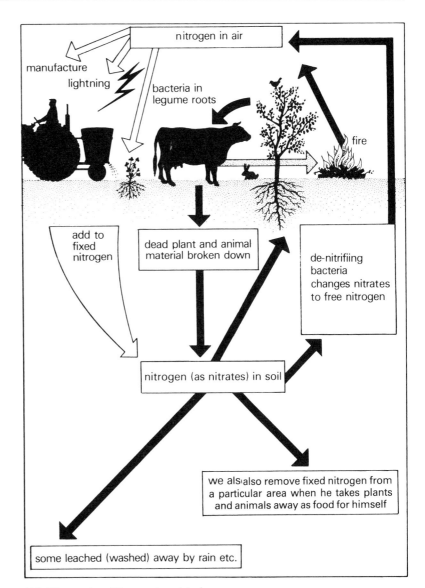

J12 The cycle with people added

2. Explain the difference between
   (a) a food chain and a food web
   (b) producers and consumers
   (c) nitrogen-fixing bacteria and denitrifying bacteria
3. In parts of India, cow dung is dried and burnt as a fuel. What other better use might be made of the dung? Give a reason.
4. Explain what the experiment below shows.

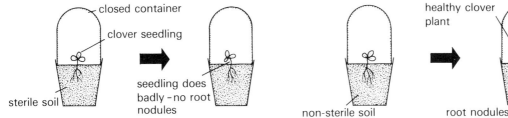

J13

People and food webs

We make many changes in the food webs around us. Here are a few examples.

We **remove groups** of interlocking species to grow one species – a crop useful to us.

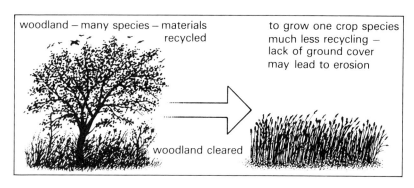

J14 We reduce variety when we plant crops

We **move** organisms to new habitats. Many do not survive, but others increase in numbers explosively and seriously affect the food webs in their new homes.

Grey squirrels were brought to England from America about 150 years ago. They have spread and replaced the red (European) squirrel in many places.

grey squirrel areas today

To protect crops we use **pesticides** of various kinds – at a cost of more than £600 million a year. Many kill other organisms besides pests. DDT is no longer used in many places because it became clear that it caused the death of many birds. They ate DDT-coated seeds, or other organisms in their food web which had themselves taken in DDT.

The grey squirrel eats birds's eggs, young birds, shoots and bark. Red squirrels are vegetarians.

J15 We move species to environments where the normal biological controls are missing at our peril

Today, more people are trying to use their knowledge of food webs. Here is a success story from the world of biological control. An organism from a pest's normal food web was used to control its numbers.

The prickly pear
In 1836, twenty-six prickly pear plants were taken from South America to Australia as garden plants. They did very well. The plant spread all over the country. It replaced plants which sheep grazed on.

10 million plants	58 million plants	60 million plants
1900	1920	1925

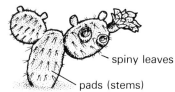

spiny leaves

pads (stems)

After various failures, a moth from Argentina was found whose larvae ruined the prickly pear pads. After 1940 only a few scattered plants survived.

J16 Biological control may be possible

Energy and food webs

Organisms need energy to run their body processes. The energy is trapped from sunlight by green plants, by photosynthesis. Most sun energy simply keeps the world warm but about 1% is used by living things. The energy is passed from organism to organism as animals eat plants or each other (not forgetting decomposers). At each step in a food chain energy is lost as heat. Eventually all the energy trapped by plants is lost back into space.

How does it happen?

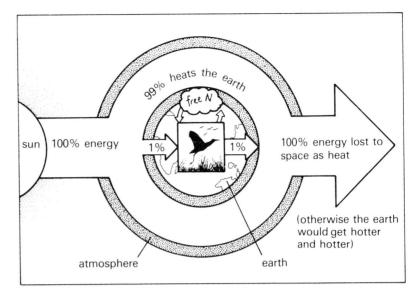

J17 Eventually all the energy plants trap is lost

1. Energy is lost to a chain as food that is not eaten or not changed as it travels through the gut.

2. As the result of **body processes.** This is the energy used in keeping warm, moving and running chemical reactions. All this energy ends up as heat.

3. And the **rest** is **stored** as new living tissue. This is the energy which the next animal in the food web collects when it eats. The amount stored varies for a number of reasons. Here are two:

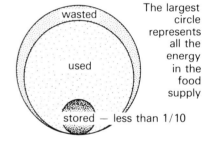

J18 What happens to the energy at each step in a food chain?

(a) A lion eats about eight times as much as a crocodile, which is much the same size. Like all warm-blooded animals, the lion needs a lot of energy to keep its body at an even temperature. Most of its energy is lost as heat.

(b) Animals that hunt food use up a lot of energy while searching for their prey. Herbivores need less energy. So do animals that wait for their prey to come to them.

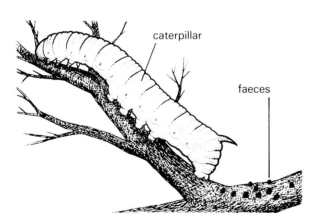

J19 Energy is lost when unused or turned into heat

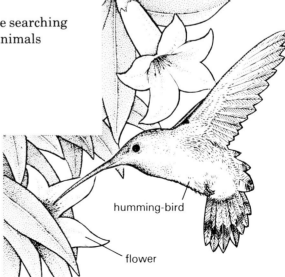

41

Measuring energy in food webs

A great deal of energy is lost to living things every time it is transferred from one organism to another. Because of this, masses of producers must trap energy for any of it to reach a top carnivore. The amount of energy in one ecosystem can be shown as a pyramid. There is a lot of energy stored at the bottom (producer) level, which gets less and less at the levels of herbivore and carnivore.

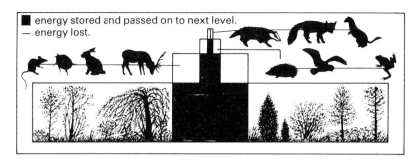

J20 An energy pyramid

Measuring how much energy is trapped by an ecosystem is not easy. The **direct** way is to use a **bomb calorimeter**. This burns a known amount of plant or animal material, and measures how much heat energy is released. It is difficult to do accurately and takes time. Also it kills the organisms involved.

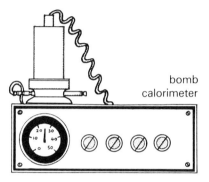

J21 A bomb calorimeter

Usually an **indirect measure** is made. This can be by:
(a) counting numbers of organisms to give a **pyramid of numbers**; or
(b) weighing organisms to give a **pyramid of biomass**.

What you count depends on what you are trying to find out – and how much time you have. Pyramids of numbers are quick and need little apparatus but they can give puzzling results.

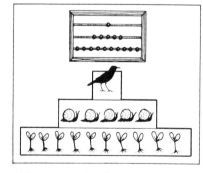

J22 A pyramid of numbers

This is what you get when **one** tree supports many other organisms.

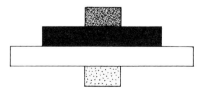

J24

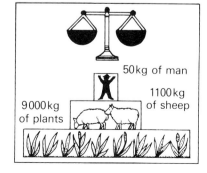

J23 A pyramid of mass

Pyramids of biomass don't have this problem. The mass of the tree or the rabbit is much greater than the mass of the organisms that live on them. However, it matters what **time of year** the measurement is made (Fig. J26).

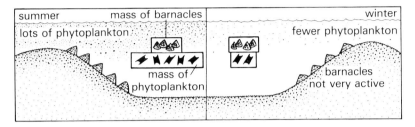

J26 Pyramids of biomass may change with the seasons

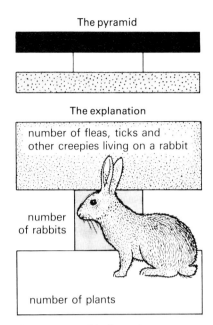

J25 A pyramid of numbers

Measuring something which allows for the whole year gets rid of the season problem.

Productivity is an extra measure – it is the amount of new material made over the year. Productivity can be useful for comparing natural ecosystems and farming ecosystems. Measuring productivity involves lots of samples over a lot of time as you keep track of the biomass made.

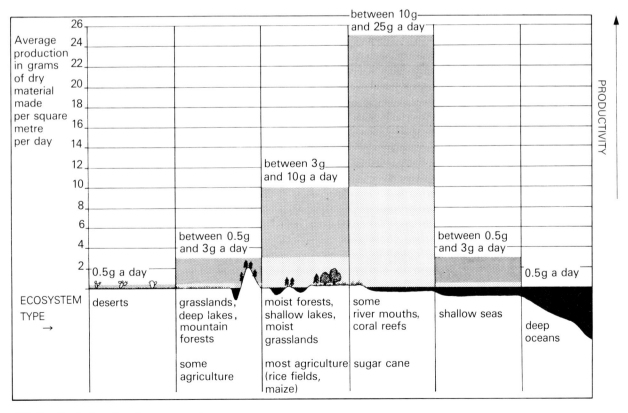

J27 Productivity of various ecosystems

People and energy

Modern agriculture with its pesticides, fertilizers and modern machines can produce a lot of food as well as problems. How do our methods rate in energy terms? This loaf represents the amount of fuel energy used up in getting bread to your plate, which is two and a half times the food energy in the bread.

How about other foods?

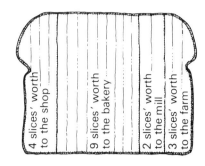

J28 Energy needed to make bread

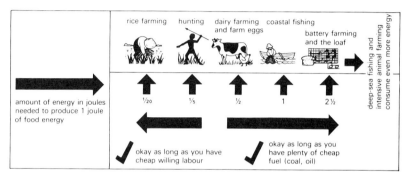

J29 Energy used in farming

The kind of food production we can afford is probably somewhere in the middle. Fossil fuels tend to produce pollution (smoke and heat – look back to the carbon cycle page) and will run out. What will we use then – muscle or nuclear power?

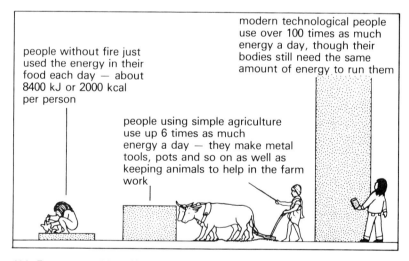

J30 Energy used in different ways of life

Summary

A food web tries to show who eats what in an ecosystem. Usually they are very complicated. The more organisms in a food web, the more stable it is. Man causes no end of trouble to himself and to the rest of the world by greatly simplifying food webs in agriculture. Problems include invasions by weeds and animal pests, as well as the loss of nutrients like nitrogen. An understanding of nutrient cycles and the structure of food webs can be used to produce less damaging ways of dealing with these problems.

Energy is unlike materials in that living organisms cannot recycle it. All the energy trapped by plants in photosynthesis is eventually changed to heat. On the way, many organisms may use it for moving and growing. People tend to use up a lot of fuel energy (mostly biological in origin) to produce food and the comfort they think they need.

Questions

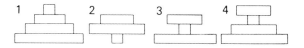

1. Explain (with examples) what the following mean: legume, nodule, symbiosis, artificial fertilizer, biological control.

2. In an experiment, a number of crops were grown on three plots for three years. The chart shows the pattern in which they were grown.

At the end of the time, the plots were tested for nitrogen. What changes would you expect to find in each plot (no gain, some gain or large gain)?

Plot	year 1	year 2	year 3
1	potatoes	wheat	clover
2			turnip
3			

J31

3. From the 'food webs and energy' pages:
   (a) Pick out three animals that use up lots of energy in getting their food (for their size). Add two more that you've noticed.
   (b) Pick out two animals that use up little energy for their size catching their food. Add three more that you know of.

4. Look through the textbook and make your own summary of the ways discussed so far in which people affect the environment.

   Which of those ways are very damaging now?
   Which are worries for the future?
   What can be done to reduce the damage?
   Do add your own ideas and examples.

5. Explain why
   (a) Mice need more food than lizards.
   (b) A centipede which runs after its prey needs more food than a spider.
   (c) An indirect measure of energy is often used instead of a direct method.
   (d) Not all pyramids of numbers are pyramid-shaped.

6. Match each pyramid of numbers with a description.

   1   2   3   4

   a. This is the orange tree in my flat – it is being eaten by aphids so I've added a few ladybirds to eat the aphids.

   b. This is a vegetarian friend – who like the rest of us has lots of bacteria and other organisms living on him.

   c. This is bread being eaten by mice who are eaten by a cat which has round worms.

   d. This is my cat, who eats birds, which eat caterpillars, which eat grass and other plants.

7. Match the words in column A with meanings from column B. Write out your answer as full sentences.

A	B
Energy	shows the large amount of energy trapped in plants in comparison with animals.
Materials	is trapped in photosynthesis and is eventually lost as heat.
An energy pyramid	are very productive systems.
A pyramid of biomass	like nitrogen can be recycled – unlike energy.
Productivity	often gives a better idea where energy is than a pyramid of numbers.
Sugar-cane plantations	is the amount of new material made by a system in a year.

8. The diagram below shows a section through a pond where two samples of animals, sample A and sample B, were collected.

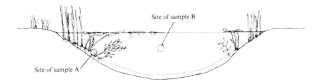

The table shows the animals collected in each sample. The same method was used to take samples at each site.

Animals	*Number of animals	
	Sample A	Sample B
Snails	90	2
Mites	140	80
Leeches	5	2
True worms	80	0
Flatworms	10	1
Insects – Damselfly nympths	30	5
Water boatmen	170	45
Mayfly nymphs	50	100
Midge larvae	120	35
Beetles	30	15

*(Numbers simplified from actual data)

(a) *i* Which animal was present in the largest number at site A?
ii Which animal was present in the largest number in the combined samples, A and B?

(b) Complete the circle opposite right to form a pie-chart of the insects at site A. The circle has been divided into 20 equal parts. The sector for the damselfly nymphs has been completed on the pie-chart to help you.

(c) From the numbers given in the table, which animal is likely to be a secondary consumer?

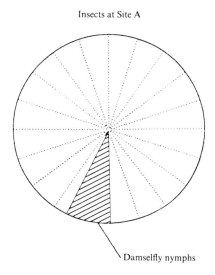

Insects at Site A

Damselfly nymphs

(d) Suggest *two* reasons why there are more snails in sample A than in sample B.

(LEAG)

9. The diagram below shows a food web in a wood.

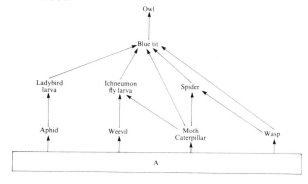

(a) *i* What kind of organisms would be in Box A?
ii Name one secondary consumer shown in this food web.
iii Write out a food chain from this food web. Start with A.
iv If all the ladybirds died, explain what might happen to the number of aphids.

(b) Energy comes into the food web at A.
i Where does this energy come from?
ii How do the animals in this food web use this energy?

(c) Describe *one* method you could use to collect animals from the shrub layer in a wood.

(d) *i* Find out about possible effects of acid rain on a wood.
ii What can make rain acid?

(LEAG)

Theme 3 Organization and maintenance of the organism

Food

Our bodies are built from the food we eat. Think about what happens when a cow eats grass. Some grass passes straight through the cow. But some parts of the grass stay in the body and are made into 'cow'. The grass is changed completely – it doesn't go on being grass within the cow. How big is the change – what is happening?

Imagine you have a lot of different kinds of buildings. They are all made of bricks and glass and wood. They are different because the bricks and so on are differently arranged and in different amounts – the shop might have lots of glass and the shed have no glass.

You could take some of the buildings down, separate the glass and the wood and the bricks. From the pieces you could build a completely different kind of building.

Food when it's eaten is a bit like the buildings. The grass or cow or caterpillar are built up of simple biological 'building blocks' which are in different patterns and different amounts in different foods. The 'blocks' or **molecules** are arranged one way in grass. When the cow eats the grass she breaks it down into these 'blocks' and then uses the bits to build more cow or milk or perhaps as fuel.

The 'building blocks' are the three food types – **proteins**, **carbohydrates** and **fats** – and the next few pages are about them. The diet must also include **vitamins**, **minerals**, **water** and **fibre**.

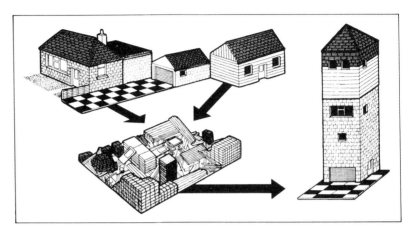

K1 Houses are made of the same simple materials arranged in different ways

K2 Cows and grass are made of the same simple materials arranged in different ways

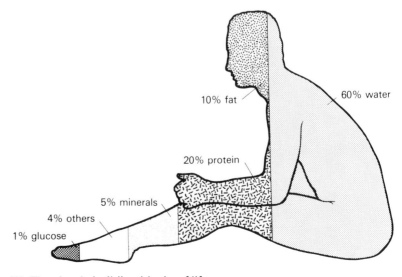

10% fat

60% water

20% protein

5% minerals

4% others

1% glucose

K3 The simple building blocks of life

Proteins

There are many kinds of protein all with different shapes and different jobs. The jobs fall into two main groups.

1. They can control chemical reactions.
Proteins known as **enzymes** control all the chemical reactions in living organisms.

2. They can act as a building material.
Proteins are important for the *shape* of an organism. For example – bones are mostly made of a protein called **collagen** with calcium salts to stiffen them. Collagen fibres (threads) hold teeth in place and skin together.

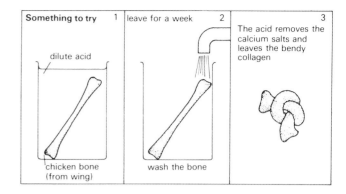

K4 Some proteins are important in giving things shape.

Fats

Fats include things which are fatty, waxy or oily. They have three main jobs.

1. They can be used in chemical processes.
Fats take part in many chemical processes in living things.

2. They can be stored.
Fats are easy to store. They contain a lot of energy.

Fats are a popular way to keep reserve fuel – for example, cod store oil in their livers, olive trees store oil in their fruit.

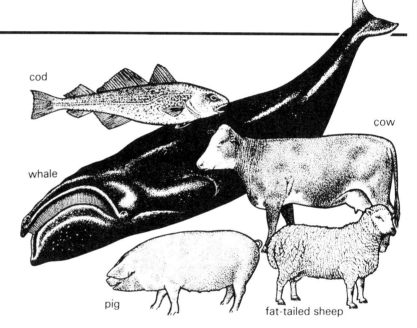

K5 Animals which store a lot of fat

Many seeds contain fats to get them started in life. Later plants make their own.

Stored fats in animals also help to keep out the cold – they insulate animals (including people). Whales, for example, can live in very cold seas near the poles.

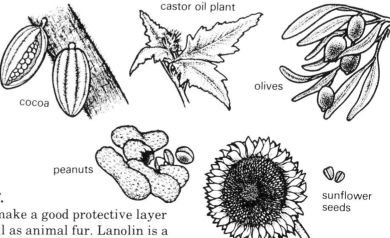

3. They make things waterproof.
Fats don't dissolve in water so they make a good protective layer for leaves and stems of plants, as well as animal fur. Lanolin is a fat which comes from sheep's wool – and we all know about greasy hair.

K6 Plants which store a lot of fat

Carbohydrates

People who worry about dieting will have heard of
carbohydrates. But what are they and what do they do?
Carbohydrates do three jobs.

1. They are used for instant energy.
Animals and plants rely on **glucose** (a carbohydrate) as a fuel
supply. They use energy in glucose and other sugars for growing.
Animals also use it for moving and keeping warm. These
carbohydrates do not stay in the body long before they are used.

2. They can be stored.
Some carbohydrates can be stored and act as a reserve fuel
supply. **Starch** is a carbohydrate which is stored by plants. It is
found in wheat (bread) and potatoes.

3. They can act as building material.
A carbohydrate called **cellulose** is used in plants to give shape
and support. It is strong and tough.

lots of sugars in food

most is used at once to provide energy

a little is kept in the body

K7 What happens to carbohydrates

What do they look like?

The details of the shapes of proteins, fats and carbohydrates
cannot be seen under the light microscope. When purified they
are powders (proteins), crystals or fibres (carbohydrates) or oils or
waxes (fats). Chemical tests using expensive delicate equipment
show that they are all made up of oxygen carbon and hydrogen
arranged in different ways. One very small carbohydrate is
glucose. Many large carbohydrates are made up of lots of glucose
molecules stuck together in chains.

Proteins have nitrogen (remember the nitrogen cycle) in them
as well as carbon, oxygen and hydrogen. they are made up of
long strings of small amino acids. There are twenty kinds of
amino acids and the order of the amino acids decides what
shape a protein is. A protein can be broken up into its separate
amino acids. The amino acids can be put together in a new
order and the result is a new protein.

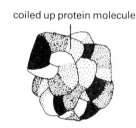

coiled up protein molecule

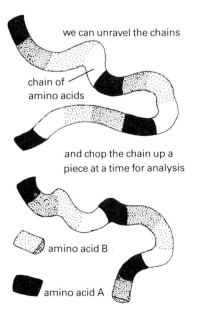

we can unravel the chains

chain of amino acids

and chop the chain up a piece at a time for analysis

amino acid B

amino acid A

K8 Protein molecules are chains of smaller molecules

How do we know they are there?

There are chemical tests to show that foods contain proteins, fats and carbohydrates. The tests on this page are just a few of many. You may know others. Other tests tell us how much protein fat or carbohydrate there is in a food. Starch (Fig. K9) and glucose (Fig. K11) are both carbohydrates.

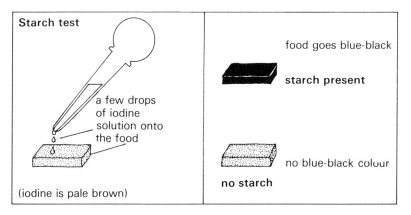

K9 Starch test

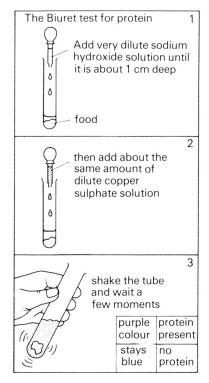

K10 The Biuret test for protein

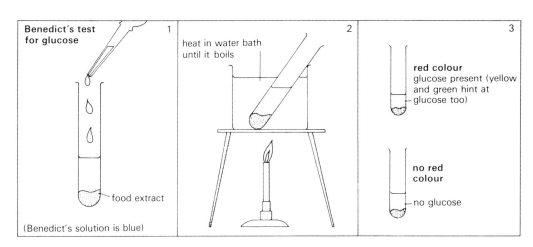

K11 Benedict's test for glucose

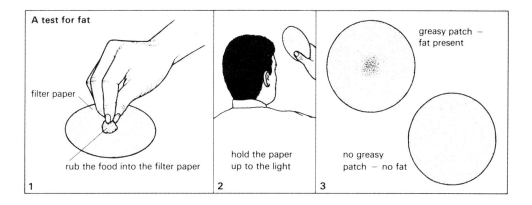

K12 A test for fat

How much?

How much protein?
Green plants make their own protein. Animals get it from their food. Proteins aren't stored in the body. If animals get *too much* protein in their food they break it down. They get rid of part of it and they turn part of it into sugars which they store in their bodies.

If they get *too little* protein, their bodies don't grow properly. Children with too little protein in their food grow very slowly and sometimes develop a disease called kwashiorkor.

Most plant foods contain some protein. Nuts like almonds and some of the beans and peas have quite a lot. Animal foods like meat and fish are usually good sources of protein.

How much fat?
Plants can make their own fats. Animals can make fats from extra proteins and carbohydrates. They also need to have some in their diet.
Extra fat gets stored.

The rat on the right had a normal diet. The rat on the left ate too much. It has a lot of extra weight to move around.

Too little fat
Remember fats are needed in some body processes. A complete lack of fat in the diet often leads to poor skin and changes in behaviour. People on low-fat diets (for slimming) sometimes find it hard to concentrate.

How much carbohydrate do organisms need?
Green plants make their own carbohydrates. Animals get them from food. The amount needed depends on how active an organism is and how large it is.
Extra carbohydrates are stored. Plants store them in roots or underground stems.

Animals may store 'large' carbohydrates in the liver or as fats.

Too much carbohydrate
Carbohydrates which are not used at once are changed into fats and stored in various parts of the body. This is why some diets try to cut down the amount of carbohydrate that is eaten.

Too little carbohydrate
Animals need a constant supply of glucose to keep themselves going. They can turn food stored in their bodies into glucose. This happens when there is not enough glucose in their food. If the stores run out, an animal becomes weak and dies, as in the experiment shown in Fig. K16.

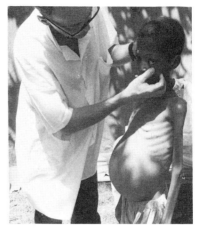

K13 Child with kwashiokor

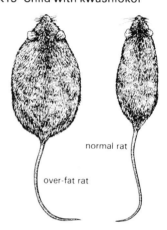

K14 Too much fat

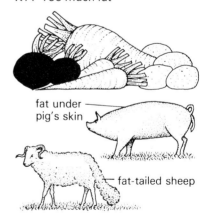

fat under pig's skin

fat-tailed sheep

K15 Spare carbohydrate is stored

K16 Experiment with locust hoppers (baby locusts)

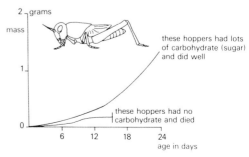

these hoppers had lots of carbohydrate (sugar) and did well

these hoppers had no carbohydrate and died

age in days

Summary and questions

Summary

Food includes materials for body-building and for providing energy – among other jobs.

There are three food types: fat, carbohydrate and protein.

Energy giving → fat
↘ carbohydrate
Body-building → protein

Each of the food types is found in many kinds of food and can be detected with simple tests.

Questions

1. Which of the food types fits each of the following descriptions?
    (a) contains nitrogen
    (b) can taste sweet
    (c) includes oils and waxes
    (d) a solid at low temperature and a liquid when heated
    (e) cannot be stored in animals
    (f) may be enzymes
    (g) forms an important part of bone

2. Describe the chemical tests for the following food types and say what you would expect to see if the food was present.
    (a) protein, (b) starch, (c) glucose, (d) fat

3. Use the information in Fig. K17 to answer the following questions.
    (a) Name two animal foods which contain a lot of protein.
    (b) Which contains more protein per 100 grams, almonds or brown bread?
    (c) Which food contains only 2 grams of protein per 100 grams?
    (d) Name three foods which contain the same amount of protein.

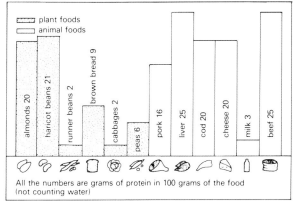

K17 Protein in different foods

4. Name two animal foods and two plant foods rich in each of the following:
    (a) protein
    (b) fats
    (c) carbohydrates
    Name two places in animals where fats are often stored. You have little carbohydrate in your body but you eat lots. What happens to it?

5. Dried locust consists of 75% protein and 20% fat plus some minerals. Some years they swarm in huge numbers in Africa and Australia causing a lot of crop damage. Locusts have a high nutritional value – can you think of any way of making use of them?

6. Here is some information about the change in eating habits in the UK since the Second World War. Read it and then draw simple graphs or diagrams which show the information in picture form. 'Since the Second World War, the proportion of protein in the diet has not changed much. However, more animal protein – meat, milk and cheese – is eaten and less vegetable protein, especially potatoes and bread, although potatoes are becoming more popular again. Carbohydrate makes up a smaller proportion of the diet, because less bread and potatoes are eaten. There has been an increase in one kind of carbohydrate, though – sugar. In 1960, on average 54 kg of sugar was eaten by each person. This however, was the peak level – even sugar intake has dropped and in 1977 we each ate 43 kg. Since the late 1940s, the proportion of fat in our diet has increased as we eat more meat, butter, margerine, cooking fats and cream. We also drink more alcohol. It now provides 6% of the daily food energy intake of the population – twice as much as in the 1950s. These changes are similar to those in wealthy societies all over the world. Few people in the UK have too little to eat today. There is more food and it is more fairly shared.'

Water and fibre

Around two-thirds of the human body's mass is **water** and it matters. The body processes nearly all happen as reactions between substances which are in solution (dissolved in water). If the solution is too concentrated (not enough water) then you die. People can survive for weeks without food but only for a few days without water. Other organisms may be better at holding on to their water while many must live in water or die. For all life it is vital.

Fibre or roughage as it used to be called is all the material in the diet which is not removed from the gut by the body. It is surprisingly important and complex. It adds bulk to material in the gut and helps keep things moving – it really does help you to avoid constipation.

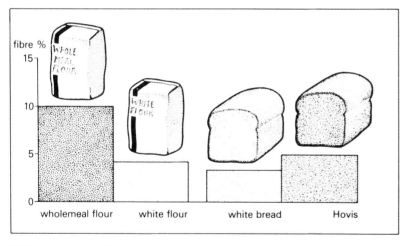

K18 How much fibre?

Question

Use the information in Fig. K18 to answer these questions.

(a) About how many more times more fibre is there in wholemeal flour compared to white flour?

(b) Would you recommend Hovis or white bread as part of a healthy diet and why?

It has been suggested that plenty of fibre in the diet may reduce the risk of cancer of the large bowel and help in preventing diabetes. A good deal of research is needed before we can be more certain. In the meantime there is plenty of fibre in whole cereals and in many fresh fruits and vegetables, but not in white bread or sugar or processed food.

K19 Foods with fibre

Vitamins

Professor Hopkins made up an artificial diet. The artificial diet contained proteins, fats, carbohydrates and minerals. At the start of the experiment he gave the diet to the rats in group B. They didn't do well. The A rats had the artificial diet plus milk. They grew well. After 18 days, he swapped their diets. The B rats now grew and the A rats didn't. The milk provided **vitamins**.

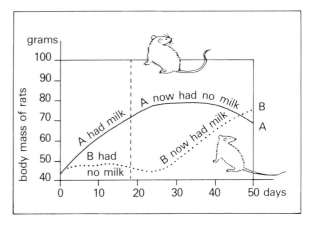

K20 The result of Hopkins' feeding experiments

Animals die if they are fed on nothing but proteins, fats, carbohydrates, minerals and water. They must also have **vitamins**. Vitamins are only needed in tiny amounts. They help control large-scale body processes. There are many vitamins. The ones on these pages are important to humans. Without them we suffer **deficiency diseases**.

K21 Damaged eye of a child with vitamin A deficiency

Vitamin A

Vitamin A is important for healthy skin and good sight (Fig. K21). It is found in foods like cod liver oil, lettuce, watercress, carrots, butter, eggs and liver. Lack of vitamin A produces dry skin and problems of seeing at night. Too much vitamin A does no good, though. A man once died from drinking too much carrot juice – litres of the stuff.

The B vitamins

There are several vitamins in this group needed for good skin and body growth. The Bs help extract energy from carbohydrates. They are found in beans, peas, eggs, milk and whole cereals (like rice and wheat). Anaemia and pellagra (Fig. K22) are deficiency diseases found in people who eat mostly maize, which has no vitamin B. Beri-beri is another deficiency disease. People who suffer from it have wasted legs. They are people who eat white bread or polished rice and not much else. The vitamin is in the husk around wheat and rice grains. If the husk is removed, the vitamin is lost. White bread and polished rice contain no husks and so have no vitamin B.

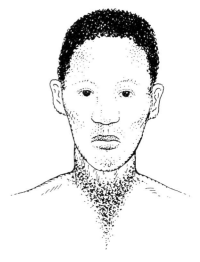

K22 Man with pellagra

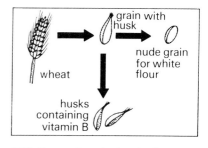

K23 Removing the husks from grain removes vitamin B

Vitamin C

Vitamin C turns up in the news because some people think it helps prevent colds. They may be right. Vitamin C is needed to help make the protein **collagen**. Without it, joints swell, skin is poor and teeth become loose. This deficiency disease is called scurvy. Vitamin C is found in potatoes, fresh green vegetables and fruits like oranges, lemons, grapefruit, limes and blackcurrants. Old people sometimes forget to eat enough fresh vegetables and suffer a little from scurvy. Vitamin C is easily destroyed by air, especially when it is heated. Cooking needs to be as brief as possible.

Most animals can make vitamin C for themselves. Only a few animals can't.

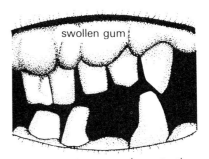

K24 Mouth of a person with scurvy

Vitamin D

Vitamin D helps in fixing calcium in bones. Vitamin D is found in butter, eggs, and cod liver oil. We can make some in our skins in the sun. Children who don't get enough sun or the right foods may get rickets. People with this deficiency disease grow up with bent legs.

K25 Child with rickets

To sum up

This chart shows how many hours' supply of various vitamins there are in each 100 g of some of the fruits and vegetables you eat. In England, most people get plenty of vitamins in their ordinary food.

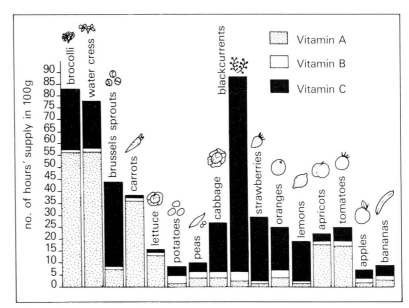

K26 Sources of vitamins

Questions

1. Which contains most vitamin C – brussel sprouts, blackcurrants or potatoes?
2. Which contains most vitamin A – carrots, apricots, or peas?
3. Most of a potato plant – apart from the tubers (spuds) – is poisonous. In the light, tubers turn green and the green areas contain the same poison as the rest of the plant. The poison, solanine, is not destroyed by cooking. Potatoes are a useful source of dietary fibre, starch and vitamin C. What advice would you give a cook about preparing potatoes?

Animals and minerals

Quite a lot of an animal's body mass is made up of minerals. They include ordinary table salt, but there are many others. They do many jobs in an animal's body. Here are a few important ones and what happens if they are missing.

K27 Foods with calcium

Calcium Birds need calcium for eggshells and snails for their shells. Calcium is needed to produce hard bones and teeth. Without calcium animals with bones suffer from rickets. People need between about $\frac{1}{2}$ and $1\frac{1}{2}$ grams a day – you could get all you need from a litre of milk, but calcium is also found in eggs, cheese and dark green vegetables like cabbage (Fig. K27).

Phosphorus is needed for the same kind of things as calcium in the same kind of amount. It is present in nearly all foods.

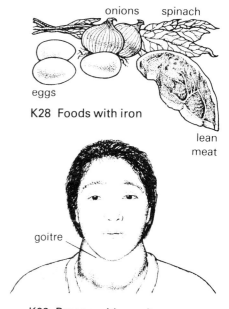

K28 Foods with iron

Iron is needed for blood to work properly. Haemoglobin, the stuff that makes blood red and carries oxygen round your body, is made of protein and a little iron. Lack of iron causes anaemia – animals (and people) become weak and fall ill easily. It's just as well only a tiny amount of iron is needed each day. There is plenty in meat, and other sources are bread, eggs and many vegetables (Fig. K28).

Iodine is needed for young animals to grow at the proper rate. It is found in milk, cheese, fish and many vegetables. Iodine is often added to table salt to make sure people get enough. The adult body needs little but without it a goitre develops (Fig. K29).

K29 Person with a goitre

Common salt is formed from sodium and chlorine. It's needed for nerves to work well and for the body to have the right amount of water. Without it, you get muscle cramps. People like dancers who lose a lot of salt when they sweat eat extra salt tablets.

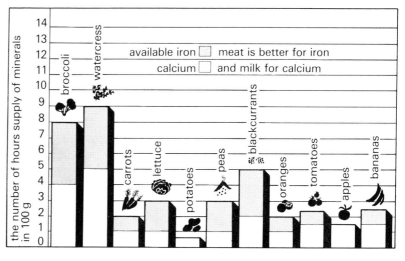

K30 Minerals in various foods

58

Plants and minerals

Green plants make their own food but they do need raw
materials. These include minerals from the soil or water the plant
is growing in. Plants do not need much of each mineral but they
must have the right ones. A few are shown in Fig. K31.

These and other minerals can be washed out of the soil or lost
when plants are eaten. Plants which die where they grow are
decomposed and their minerals used again by other plants. To
make up mineral loss in gardens, people can add fertilizers.

This tomato plant had *no phosphate*. It is very
puny with shrivelled leaves. It has been
unable to grow properly.

A *normal* young
tomato plant
growing in soil
with all the
minerals it
needs.

This tomato plant has been grown *without
nitrogen* (in the form of nitrate).
It is small and yellowed.
Nitrogen is needed
to make proteins.

This one had no *potassium*. It is small
with yellow edges to its leaves.
This plant cannot
make protein
properly, either.

K31 Three minerals important to plants

Questions

1. Which contains most calcium – bananas,
   carrots or watercress?
   What would you recommend as a better
   source of calcium than any of the vegetables
   or roots shown?
   If you couldn't get meat as a supply of iron,
   what food would you suggest as a supply?
   (Information in Fig. K30).

2. Plants make their own food but they do need
   a supply of minerals. Choose two minerals
   and describe what happens to a plant
   growing without them (Fig. K31).

3. Animals like reindeer who drink snow water
   suffer from a lack of salts. They have to find
   salt licks to keep them healthy. Animals
   who drink pond or stream water don't have
   this problem – why not?

4. A hundred years ago, an anaemia called
   chlorosis, in which the skin goes greenish,
   was common among women who worked in
   factories. The women ate mainly white
   bread, potatoes and sugar. When their diet
   included meat, the anaemia disappeared.
   What caused the anaemia, and why did
   women rather than men suffer from it?

A balanced diet

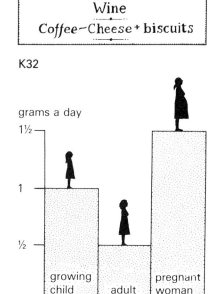

Menu
Sherry
Tomato Soup
Sole
Roast Chicken
Roast potatoes, peas+sprouts
Fruit salad+cream
Wine
Coffee~Cheese + biscuits

K32

What's your idea of a perfect meal? Write it down. How does it compare with the menu (Fig. K32). This menu was the result of a survey made in 1962 in England.

Is this menu a balanced meal? *First*, check for *food types* – are they all there? Make a check-list like this for your own meal.

Food type	In
Protein	fish, chicken, peas, cream, cheese
Carbohydrate	potatoes, alcohol, sugar in salad and coffee, biscuits
Fat	cream and cheese
Vitamins	fruits and vegetables (if not too overcooked) include A, B and C. D in cheese
Minerals	iron and calcium in vegetables, calcium in cheese and cream. More in rest of meal.

K33 The amount of calcium different people need

Next, does your diet have the *right amount* of each food type?

1. How old you are matters. Growing children need more protein, adults need less (for their size), since it's only needed for repair work. This is why deficiency diseases are much worse in children than adults.

2. How big you are matters. A large person needs more energy to move around than a small person like a child (Fig. K34).

Fat people are experts at not moving if they can help it, and that just makes their problem worse.

3. Your job matters. So does how you use your free time. The more active things you do, the more fuel-type foods you can eat without putting on weight.

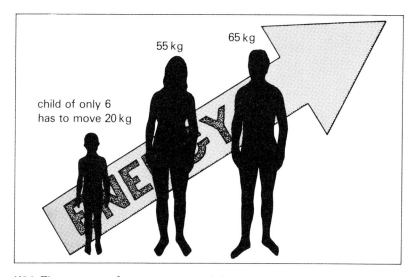

K34 The amount of energy you need depends upon your size

Too much food

Most extra food is stored; you get fat or **obese**. Fat people die earlier. Women tend to have more body fat than men and they become obese even more easily. Too much of some foods can poison you. Your body tries to get rid of foods like this or changes them into something less harmful. For example, alcohol is changed into carbohydrate.

A test to see if you are too fat. Squeeze a fold of skin from the back of your arm. If the fold is more than 2 cm thick, then yes you are too fat.

Too little food
This can happen in several ways.

(a) **Essential food types are missing** – and the deficiency diseases strike. People at risk include old people, poor people and alcoholics who drink and don't feel like eating. Skin problems are a warning sign.

(b) **People deliberately eat too little** for too long – perhaps because they wrongly think they are too fat. You may have read about girls who do this. The disease is called anorexia nervosa and it needs medical help.

(c) **People can't get enough of any kind of food** and starve. The map (Fig. K35) shows parts of the world where many people never get enough food. Land may be too poor for growing much food or there may be too many people. Sometimes food is produced but sold to people like us in Europe and America. We can afford to pay more for food than many others.

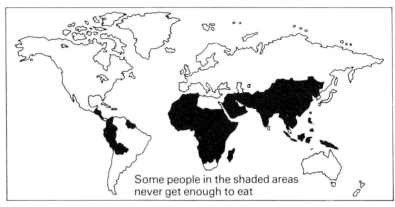

Some people in the shaded areas never get enough to eat

K35

Summary
Animals need the following things in their diet:

Fats ⟶ Energy giving
Carbohydrate ⟶ Body-building
Protein ⟶
Minerals ⟶ Protection, and controlling
Vitamins ⟶ body processes

They also need water (and often fibre).

Plants make their own food – animals eat other organisms for food. The amount of food needed depends on things like age and activity. Too much food produces **obesity** (fatness). Too little food results in **starvation**. **Deficiency diseases** are the result of one essential thing missing from the diet.

Questions

1. A slightly overweight friend decides to go on a crash diet. She/he tells you that she/he is only going to eat grapefruit and drink black coffee for two weeks. What advice would you give your friend, based on the information in the last chapter?

2. Spinach contains a number of nutrients and can form a useful part of an adult's diet. It also contains small amounts of a chemical which makes it less easy to take in calcium from food. Spinach should not be given to babies. Explain why not.

3. Collect information about the world food problem as it is now. Share it with the class. What are the main problems that you have discovered? What is being done about them? What do you think could be done?

4. Choose six common foods in packets at home. You will find the ingredients listed. What would be missing from your diet if you ate just these foods? What has been added which is not a food material and why?

5. Here is a list of ways of changing the way we grow food. (There are more, of course.) Choose one and find out more about it. How easy would it be to produce more food this way? What might the unpleasant side effects be?
   (a) Develop new plants.
   (b) Learn to farm land we do not use yet, like deserts, forests and the Arctic.
   (c) Fish farming.
   (d) Domesticating new animals.
   (e) More factory produced food like protein from fungi grown on petrol wastes.

Feeding and liquid food

What do animals do when they need food? *Taking in food* is the first step. Liquid food is easy to take in, you just suck – or is it? On this page are animals which eat three different kinds of liquid food, each with its own problems.

Nectar drinkers

Nectar is the sugary liquid made by some flowers. It is found at the bottom of the petals.

A butterfly has to reach right into the flower to get the nectar. The mouth of a butterfly is a long tube – the **proboscis**. It sucks up the high-energy nectar through the tube, rather like drinking juice through a straw.

The proboscis is coiled up when the butterfly takes off. Such very special mouth parts mean the butterfly eats nectar – or nothing.

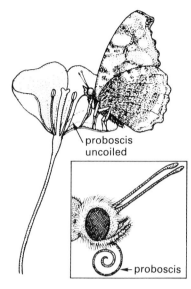

L1 A butterfly's proboscis allows it to suck up liquids

Blood drinkers

Blood makes a complete food if you can get it, and mosquitoes can. Their mouths form sucking tubes with a sharp point on the end. This makes a hole in the skin of the animal the mosquito attacks.

The mosquito can suck up blood as long as it doesn't **clot** (stop running). Think how quickly blood clots when you cut your finger. Mosquitoes make saliva (spit) which stops blood clotting for a while.

They aren't the only ones to stop blood clotting – human head lice (nits) and vampire bats can do the same trick.

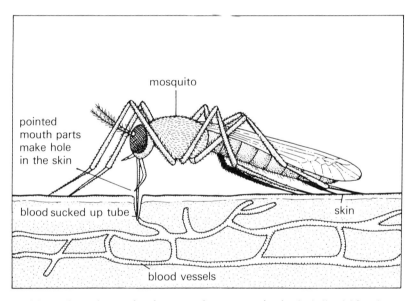

L2 Mosquitoes have piercing mouth parts to obtain their liquid food

Milk drinkers

Milk has everything (though it hasn't much iron). All you need to do is suck. All mammals start on milk and a very good start it makes. The mother eats solid food (like grass or meat) in order to produce milk. Eventually baby mammals must go on to solid foods too.

L3 Young mammals live on liquid

Solid food and teeth

Solid food is harder to take in than liquid food. Animals with bones solve the problem with teeth. These can do several jobs. Solid food may be caught with them, chopped up by them and even mashed up a bit. The shape of the teeth will give a clue to what an animal eats. Incisors, canines and molars all do different jobs, though in humans the differences are not very dramatic.

Teeth sit in sockets (pits) in the jaw-bone which is covered by gum. The bit you can see is the **crown**.

The **roots** hold the tooth in place. Incisors and canines have one root. Molars have more.

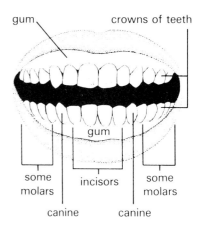

L4 A mouthful

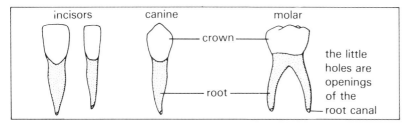

L5 Tooth types

Most of the tooth is made of a bone-like substance called **dentine** (ivory). The outside of the crown is covered with very hard **enamel**. Enamel protects dentine. The root is covered with cement. There is a hollow inside the tooth, with a way in and out – the **root canal**.

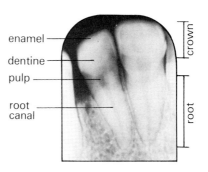

L6 X-ray of an incisor

In the hollow are **nerves** and **blood vessels** which keep the tooth healthy. They are surrounded by jelly-like pulp. Nerves, blood and pulp fill the hollow or **pulp cavity**.

Usually teeth don't jar when you bite. If you've ever bitten on something that wasn't there, you'll know how useful this is. Teeth bounce a bit. They have shock absorbers made of protein threads (collagen). These threads or fibres link the cement to the jaw-bone.

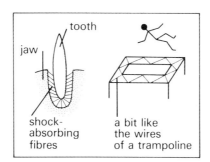

L7 Teeth have their own shock absorbers

Question

Use a mirror to look at your own teeth. Make a plan to show the layout of both jaws. Label the incisors, the canines, and the molars. Have you got a complete set of adult teeth? How many are missing?

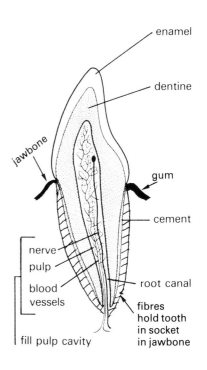

L8 Cross-section of a tooth

Meat-eater, plant eater?

Plant eaters
These are the primary consumers in a food chain. They are also called **herbivores** (herb = plant; vore = eat).

Herbivores' teeth do two main jobs:
(a) to gnaw or snip off mouthfuls of plant, and   (b)   chew it.
Plants make tough eating because they contain so much **cellulose**. The break-up of food starts in the mouth, with a good chew.

L9 Sheep

Meat eaters
These are secondary consumers in a food chain. They are also known as **carnivores** (carni = flesh).

Carnivores' teeth have two main jobs:
(a)   to catch the food (which may be running away or fighting back); and (b)   to slice it into swallow-sized lumps.
Meat is usually softer than plants so chewing is less important.

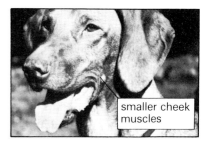

L10 Dog

Humans, of course, eat anything – we (like rats and some bears) are **omnivores** (omni = all). We have average, do-anything teeth. Look at your own.

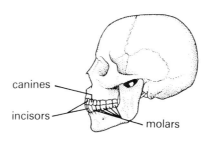

L11 Human skull showing teeth

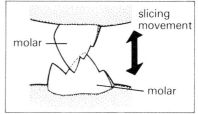

L12 A carnivore's molars slice

Usually you can tell what an animal eats by looking at its jaws and teeth.

Meat eaters again

Carnivores depend on their canines to grab food, so these teeth are large. The big molars slide food up rather like a pair of scissors.

Dogs' jaws go up and down. Their largest jaw muscles are attached to the jaw and the back of the head. Move your jaw up and down and find these muscles.

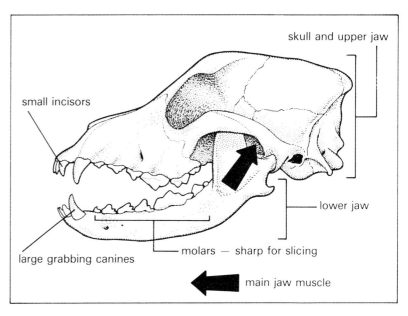

L13 Dog's skull

More plant eaters

Herbivores don't grab, they chew.

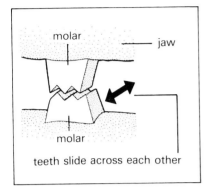

L14 Chewing teeth slice

Chewing is done from side to side. The cheek muscles move the jaw-bone and the molars grate across each other. Try it yourself.

The cheek muscles need to be large (Fig. L9) and so is the part of the lower jaw-bone they are attached to (Fig. L15). Other herbivores have similar jaws.

Questions

1. Draw and label a diagram of a section (slice) through a tooth. Explain what each of the following do: the root, the blood vessels, the pulp cavity, the enamel, the fibres.

2. Look at Fig. L16. What do you think each animal eats and why? Figure L16D may be a bit of a puzzler, but animals do not always use their teeth for eating, do they?

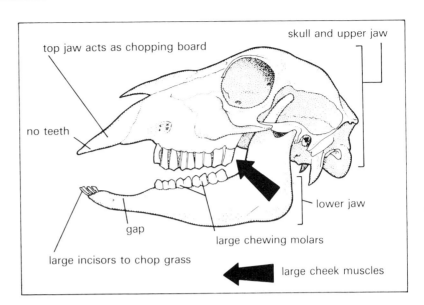

L15 Sheep's skull

Summary			
	incisors	*canines*	*molars*
herbivores	often large	missing or small	grinders
carnivores	smallish	large	slicers

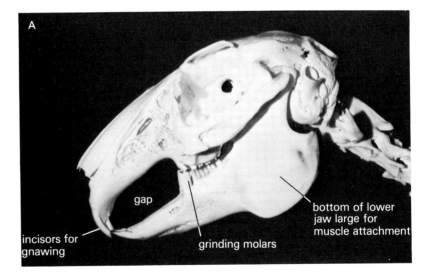

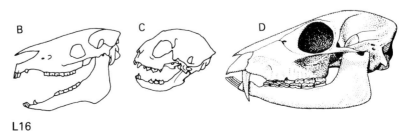

L16

Tooth decay

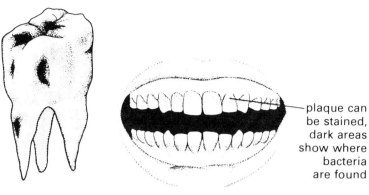

L17

What happens?

Bacteria are tiny organisms living pretty well everywhere. Those living on your teeth form **plaque**. Plaque can be stained to make it easy to see.

Count your decayed (and filled) teeth

Humans get a second chance when their milk teeth drop out. Most people have their permanent teeth by the age of 14, except for the molars (wisdom teeth) in the back corner of each jaw.

The number of teeth most people have at different ages

new babies	3-year-old	14-year-old	21-year-old
no teeth	20 teeth	28 teeth	32 teeth

Keeping them may be a problem.
   cleaning helps
   eating less sugary food helps
   fluoride helps

A little fluoride makes a big difference (X–Y on the graph). Beyond a certain point (A on the graph) adding fluoride makes no difference (Fig. L19).

In some parts of England, tiny amounts of fluoride are added to drinking water. Do you know if it is added in your area?

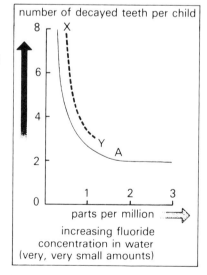

L19 Fluoride and tooth decay

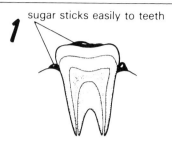

Bacteria feed on sugary foods and make acid.

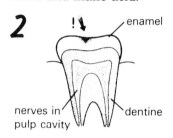

Acid destroys enamel.

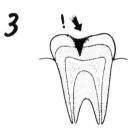

The bacteria, still making acid, arrive at the dentine. Dentine is softer than enamel and the acid soon makes a hole in it.

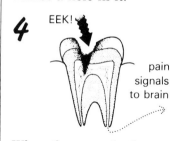

When the nerve in the tooth is attacked it hurts.

L18 Tooth decay

Question

Design a poster or leaflet aimed at getting people to take care of their teeth.

Life without a gut

Very small animals can absorb enough food through their body surfaces. They produce proteins called enzymes to digest their food and make it small enough to absorb. They rely on the process of diffusion to take the food into their bodies.

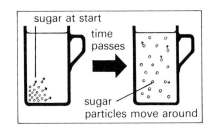

Diffusion

Tip some sugar into a mug of tea and don't stir it. After a while all the tea will be sweet. The sugar particles move around on their own and spread out evenly. This is **diffusion**.

It isn't very far from the outside to anywhere inside a small organism. Soluble food can diffuse in, and wastes can diffuse out, fast enough for the organism to live quite happily.

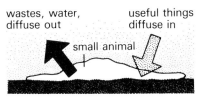

L20 Diffusion

This is a small animal called **Amoeba**. It lives in ponds.

Amoeba's body can flow around small bits of food, such as microscopic green plants. The food is trapped in a food vacuole. A vacuole is a bag of water inside the animal.

Amoeba uses enzymes to digest the food. The food then diffuses out of the vacuole and into Amoeba's body. Undigested food is left behind as Amoeba moves on. Soluble waste diffuses into the water.

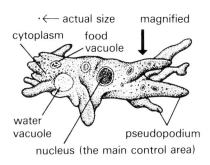

L21 Amoeba

Fungi (the plural of fungus) are an odd kind of plant. They can't make their own food. Some of them digest the remains of dead organisms. If they do, they are called **saprophytes** (sapro = putrid or rotten; phyte = plant). They are decomposers in food chains.

You might find a fungus called Mucor on bread or cooked potatoes – both have lots of starch (Fig. L22).

A close-up view shows that Mucor is made of white fluffy threads called **hyphae**.

Hyphae grow down into the food. They make enzymes which break starch down into glucose. Glucose can diffuse into the hyphae.

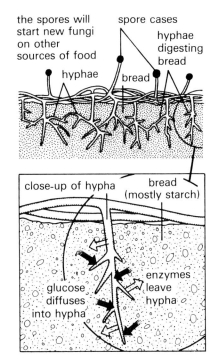

L22 Mucor on bread (magnified)

Digestion

Food particles need to be small to get into the body. Food is broken down in two ways:

A. mechanically. This breaks food into small lumps, for example by chewing.

B. chemically – by **enzymes**. This is called digestion. Digestion turns large insoluble food particles into smaller soluble particles.

We can show the importance of being small and soluble using a model gut. Figure L24 shows such a model – and it is only a model. Real guts do many jobs. Large carbohydrates cannot get through the 'gut' wall – small carbohydrates can.

sugar is **soluble** in tea

grated cheese is **not soluble** in tea

(it might melt but the fats will float. Try it)

L23 Soluble and insoluble

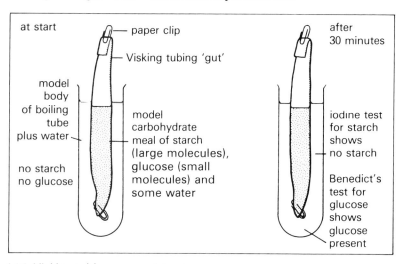

L24 Visking tubing – a model gut

Visking tubing acts like gut wall. It is filled with a solution of starch (a làrge carbohydrate) and glucose (a small carbohydrate). After 30 minutes, tests show there is glucose in the water round the Visking tubing, but no starch.

If we could look more closely at the model gut wall (Fig. L25), we would see it has tiny holes in it. The small glucose molecules can move out of the bag through the holes. The large starch molecules are too big to get through the holes. They stay in the bag.

In a real gut, starch is broken up into the glucose molecules it is made of by enzymes.

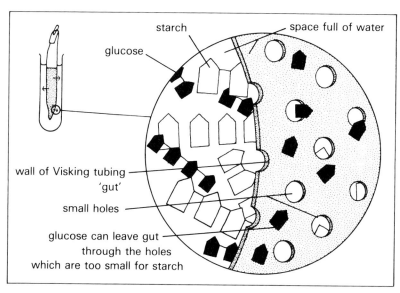

L25 Close-up of gut

Enzymes

There are many enzymes. They are made of protein and each is a special shape. They can break down materials into smaller pieces *and* build them up into larger ones. Most enzymes are found *inside* body cells, and work there. Gut enzymes are unusual – they work outside cells.

Here's one example. Saliva (spit) contains an enzyme called **amylase**. Amylase breaks down starch into sugar. Try chewing some bread for a long time. It will start to taste sweet.

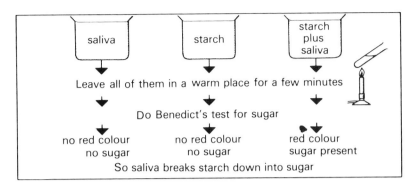

L26 Amylase at work

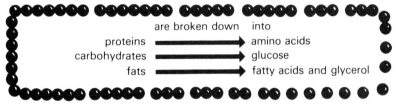

L27

In the gut there are many enzymes. They digest the different food types. Food is broken down into amino acids, glucose, fatty acids and glycerol. These can all get through the gut wall into the body. The table (Fig. L27) shows how each food type breaks down.

The whole process can work the other way – building up large chemicals from smaller ones.

The enzymes of digestion break down large food particles so they can get through the gut wall. Many of the enzymes in the rest of the body then help to build up body materials from the pieces.

Summary
To enter the body, food must be digested. This means it is broken down into small soluble particles which can diffuse through the gut wall into the body. Solid food may first be broken down mechanically by teeth. The type of teeth an animal has gives a clue to the type of food it eats. All food, solid or liquid, is made of large proteins, carbohydrates and fats. These are broken down by enzymes into their soluble sub-units. Other enzymes in the body build the sub-units up again. Very small organisms can take food in all over their surfaces and do not need a gut.

Questions

1. Copy this out, filling in the spaces.

   Food must be broken into _____ and _____ particles to get into an organism's body. This process is called _____. Liquid foods like _____ and _____ can be sucked up. Mammals have _____ to cut up solid food.

   The kind of teeth needed depends on the kind of _____ eaten. A _____ or plant eater has _____ to cut or gnaw at plants, and large _____ to grind them. A _____ or meat eater has large _____ to catch prey animals and scissor like _____ to slice it up.

   Food is also digested by special proteins called _____. These break up large food particles like _____ and protein into _____ and soluble ones like _____ and amino acids.

2. Explain what is meant by the following: soluble, diffusion, digestion, saprophyte.

3. Starch is broken up by an enzyme. What is the name of the enzyme? Where would you get some? What is produced when this enzyme digests starch? Describe an experiment which shows this enzyme has the effect you say.

4. Explain how the following organisms get their food: a mosquito, Mucor, a butterfly, Amoeba. Pictures may help.

5. People who herd cattle for a living sometimes use the animals' blood as food. On journeys, Mongol raiders drank blood straight from their horses as their only food. What makes blood so nourishing? What problems might there be if blood was the only food for a long time?

Moving food along

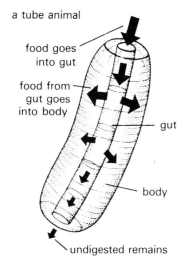

a tube animal

food goes into gut

food from gut goes into body

gut

body

undigested remains

L28 A tube animal

Moving food along

In large animals, diffusion isn't enough. Soluble food can't move to all parts of them quickly enough. Large animals need a gut to digest food, and blood to carry it round the body. The gut is a tube running through the body. Different parts of it do different jobs, even in a simple animal like an earthworm.

Food has to be moved along the gut. The walls of the gut contain rings of muscle which contract (tighten up) behind the food and push it along.

Muscles in front of the food relax (go limp) so that food can easily be pushed into the next bit of gut. This process is called **peristalsis**.

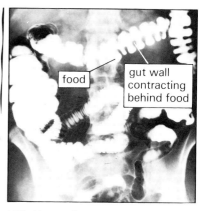

food

gut wall contracting behind food

L29 X-ray of your gut

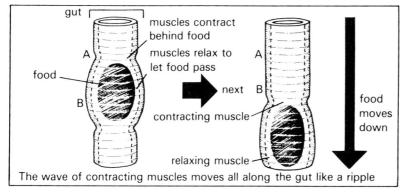

gut

muscles contract behind food

muscles relax to let food pass

A

food

B

next

A

B

contracting muscle

relaxing muscle

food moves down

The wave of contracting muscles moves all along the gut like a ripple

L30 Showing peristalsis

Peristalsis moves food along the gut. There are other gut movements which help mix food with enzymes. You may be able to see some of these movements in yourself.

Something to try

Lie in a bath of water two or three hours after a meal. The water supports your body and makes it easier to see your guts moving under your skin.

this is the bit to watch

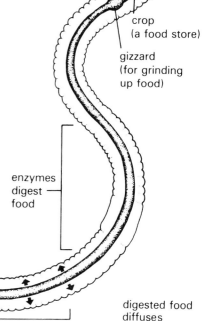

mouth and pump for pulling in dead leaves and soil

crop (a food store)

gizzard (for grinding up food)

enzymes digest food

wastes ready to leave body (mostly soil)

digested food diffuses into blood

L31 An earthworm's gut – different parts of it have different jobs

Gut structure and action

Guts are not usually simple tubes. They've become wider and longer. Pockets, including glands, lead off the tube in places and the whole lot coils up to fit inside an animal.

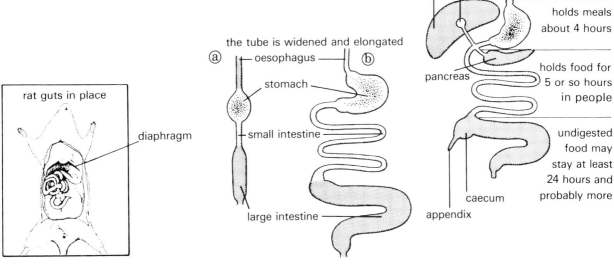

L32 The tube is folded

Digestion takes place in the **mouth**, the **stomach** and the first part of the **small intestine** (the duodenum and start of the ileum).

The mouth and swallowing

As food is chewed in the mouth, it is mixed with **saliva** (spit). Saliva is mostly a slimy liquid which makes swallowing easier. In some animals, like man, saliva contains an enzyme which begins the digestion of starch. Saliva is made by the **salivary glands**.

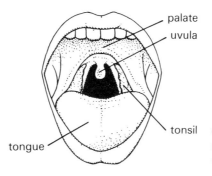
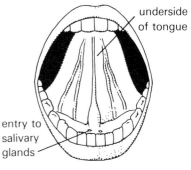

L33 Tongue down and tongue up

Glands

Glands are small pockets of tissue doing a particular job. Some help the body fight disease, some are important in growth. There are several glands opening into the gut which make enzymes.

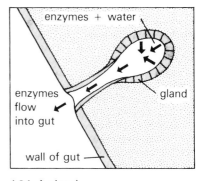

L34 A gland

Journey along the gut

Swallowing and breathing

Air moves in and out through the nose and mouth on its way to and from the lungs. During breathing, the passages from the nose and mouth to the lungs must be open. They are shown in Fig. L35.

If food gets into an animal's lungs, it chokes. For swallowing the arrangement changes.

> The tongue pushes food to the back of the throat.
> The uvula (back of the palate) moves up to close the openings to the back of the nose.
> The epiglottis – a small flap – closes the larynx (entrance to the lungs).

So food is pushed backwards and has to go into the **oesophagus**, the part of the gut leading to the stomach. Food moves down the oesophagus by peristalsis.

Check the changes – trace the solid lines in the left-hand diagram and lay your tracing over Fig. L36.

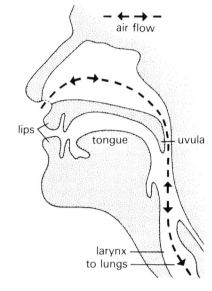

L35 Breathing

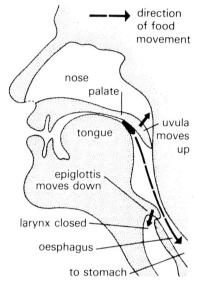

L36 Swallowing

In the stomach

The stomach is a bag in which food can be held for a while. Without it you'd have to eat every twenty minutes or so. With it, the rest of the gut has small regular doses of food to work on in between meals. The strong muscular walls of the stomach help mix and mash up the food (Fig. L37).

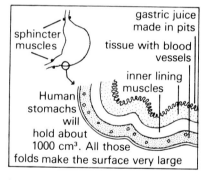

L37 The stomach wall

Pits in the wall produce **gastric juice** which does three jobs because it contains:

1. **Hydrochloric acid** Food contains bacteria, some of which might harm the eater. The acid in the stomach kills these bacteria (usually).

2. **Pepsin** This acid-loving enzyme starts breaking up proteins.

3. **Renin** Especially in young animals, it clots milk into a semi-solid which stays in the gut long enough to be digested.

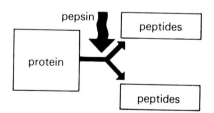

L38 What happens to proteins

The food mixture – **chyme** – is pushed into the duodenum in squirts. Stomach muscles do the pushing. Circular muscles at each end of the stomach – the **sphincters** – make sure it goes the right way (Fig. L39).

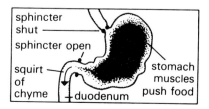

L39 Leaving the stomach

Vomiting (throwing up, being sick) is a way of getting rid of materials which might damage the body. The diaphragm, which divides the body in two, pushes down hard on the stomach. The sphincter near the oesophagus opens and up it all comes. Already digestion will have made changes in the food.

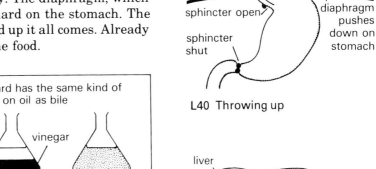

L40 Throwing up

In the duodenum
Three lots of liquid deal with food in the duodenum.

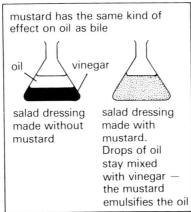

mustard has the same kind of effect on oil as bile

oil — vinegar

salad dressing made without mustard

salad dressing made with mustard. Drops of oil stay mixed with vinegar — the mustard emulsifies the oil

L41

1. **Bile** is made by the liver and stored in the gall bladder. Bile breaks fats into small drops which are easier for enzymes to digest. It's called **emulsifying**. Bile also neutralizes the acid in food from the stomach.

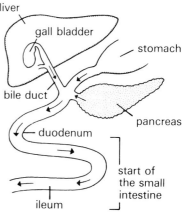

L42 In the duodenum

2. **Pancreatic juice** comes from the pancreas – a gland which is sometimes eaten as sweetbreads. It contains three enzymes which digest carbohydrates, fats and proteins.

3. **Intestinal juice** is made by the intestine walls. It contains several enzymes dealing with proteins, carbohydrates and fats.

By half way along the small intestine, the gut contains a sludge of water, with glucose, amino acids, minerals, vitamins dissolved in it, some simple fats and fibre. Fibre is more or less undigested material, including cellulose, which is semi-solid. It gives the gut something to push against.

Figure L43 summarizes the process so far – in the diagram, solid black is the insoluble protein. It is partly changed into amino acids in the stomach and completely broken up in the small intestine. Where does carbohydrate start to be digested? Do minerals get broken up as they go through the gut into anything smaller?

food at start	in mouth	in stomach	in small intestine	after digestion
protein				amino acids
carbohydrate				glucose
fats				simple fats
minerals				minerals
vitamins				vitamins

L43

Absorption

Digested food has to get through the gut walls and into the body proper. Once in the body, it's carried away by the blood. What is absorbed where?

In the stomach
The only foods absorbed this early in the gut are ones which are dissolved already. Alcohol and glucose are absorbed in the stomach.

In the small intestine
Most digested food is absorbed in the **ileum**. The ileum has a large surface – larger that you would expect, considering the space it takes up. The inside surface is long and thin and folded (Fig. L45). The larger the surface, the more food can get through.

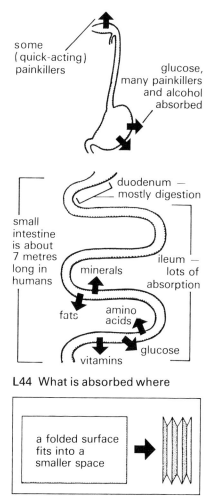

L44 What is absorbed where

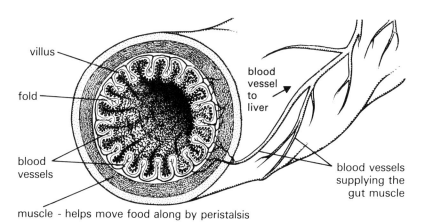

muscle - helps move food along by peristalsis

L45 The inside of the gut is folded

a folded surface fits into a smaller space

L46

The folds have lots of smaller finger-like folds called **villi** all over them. Villi are very fine and delicate. Around 100 grams of their tissue is lost each day. The cells are digested with the rest of the food. New cells are made to replace the lost ones.

You have about 9 square metres of absorbing surface in your gut. How does that compare with the floor area of the room you're in?

Soluble food is pushed against the villi by gut movements like peristalsis. Blood vessels running up inside the villi carry away glucose and amino acids.

Inside a villus (one of the villi) there is a separate tube called a **lacteal.** Simple fats travel through this in a liquid called **lymph,** related to blood.

The soluble foods eventually end up in the liver, where they are sorted.

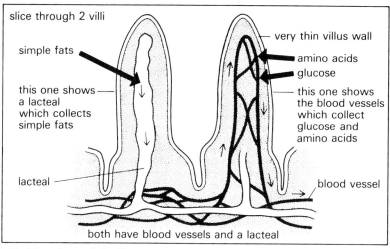

L47 Slice through 2 villi

In the large intestine

It takes time for food to get through the large intestine. One might ask why, when all the useful stuff has been removed. In lots of plant-eaters (look at the next page) this is where cellulose gets digested. Also, undigested food gets concentrated into handy packages.

Water is absorbed in the colon. If the colon doesn't remove enough water, the result is diarrhoea ('the trots' or 'the runs'). Sufferers usually feel thirsty. In bad cases people have died from loss of water. One disease which causes diarrhoea is cholera.

If food spends too long in the large intestine, it can get too dry – constipation strikes. A diet with lots of fibre – cereals and other plant foods – prevents constipation. All being well, faeces can be pushed out of the gut at convenient times. Faeces contain many bacteria.

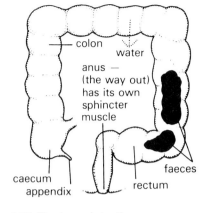

L48 The large intestine

Cholera is a disease caused by bacteria which live in the gut. Loss of water caused by cholera can kill people. It is passed from person to person through bacteria in faeces, which contaminate food or water.

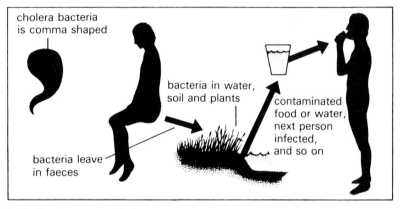

L49 Cholera transmission

Questions

1. Copy this out and fill in the gaps:

   Food is moved along the gut by _____ in which _____ contract behind the food and push it along. On swallowing, the food is pushed like this down the _____ and into the stomach where _____ in the food are killed by acid and food is held for a while. The digestion of _____ begins. Food, called _____ passes into the _____, the first part of the small intestine. Here, _____ from the gall bladder breaks _____ down into tiny droplets. Pancreatic juice from the _____ and intestinal juice from the _____, both contain _____ which continue digestion. In the _____, _____ takes place when digested food enters _____ vessels or lacteals. _____ _____ and water are left in the gut. In the colon, _____ is absorbed into the blood leaving a semi-solid material, called _____, in the rectum. The wastes leave the body through the _____ from time to time.

2. Match up the jobs in column B with a part of the body in column A (see opposite).

Write your answers as full sentences.

A	B
The epiglottis	is the first part of the small intestine.
A villus	is a finger-like projection from the gut wall. It makes absorption easier.
The appendix and caecum	covers the top of the air tube when food is swallowed.
The liver	form a home for bacteria which digest cellulose for herbivores.
The duodenum	makes bile which is stored in the gall bladder. It does lots of other things too.

75

Food and the liver

Digested food is carried away from the small intestine in blood and lymph. It all ends up being sorted by the liver.

The liver is the largest gland in a human. Collect the same mass in books or bean bags and feel what you carry around without noticing. Sorting food is one of the liver's most important jobs. It does lots of other things as well – such as making bile.

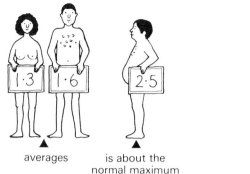

averages   is about the normal maximum

L50 Average mass of liver in kilograms

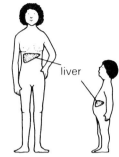

liver

L51 In small fat children, most of that bulging tummy is due to the liver

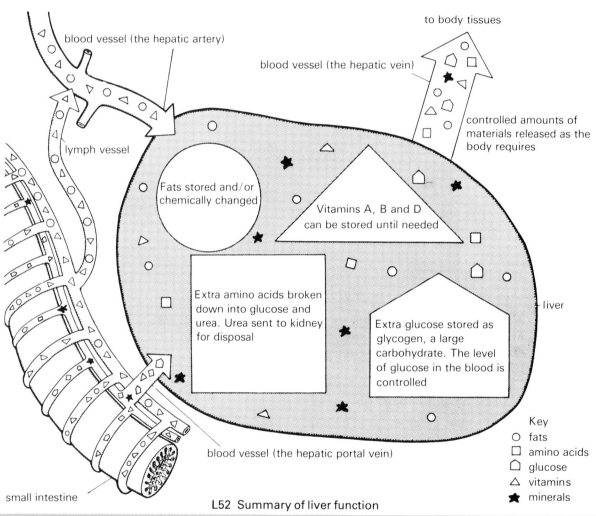

to body tissues

blood vessel (the hepatic artery)

blood vessel (the hepatic vein)

controlled amounts of materials released as the body requires

lymph vessel

Fats stored and/or chemically changed

Vitamins A, B and D can be stored until needed

Extra amino acids broken down into glucose and urea. Urea sent to kidney for disposal

Extra glucose stored as glycogen, a large carbohydrate. The level of glucose in the blood is controlled

liver

blood vessel (the hepatic portal vein)

small intestine

Key
○ fats
□ amino acids
⬠ glucose
△ vitamins
★ minerals

L52 Summary of liver function

Summary
Digestion is the break-down of food, mechanically by teeth and muscles (if necessary) and chemically by enzymes. Large food particles (large carbohydrates, proteins and fats) are broken down into small soluble ones (glucose, amino acids and simple fats). This occurs in the first part of the gut. The gut is a long tube running through the body. Food is moved through the gut by peristalsis. Later in the gut, the digested food is absorbed into the blood and taken, via the liver, to the body tissues.

Photosynthesis

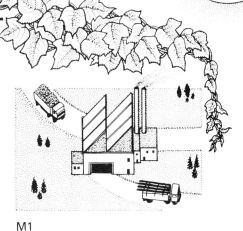

The three main types of food are base on the sugars which green plants make, using a process called **photosynthesis**.

Imagine a factory. In the factory are machines which change raw materials into something useful. The machines, of course, need a power source.

M1

The plant is like a factory – the machines are **chloroplasts**, containing **chlorophyll** (the important bit). They make **glucose** (and oxygen) using **carbon dioxide** and **water** as raw materials. The **sun** is the power source that makes it all go.

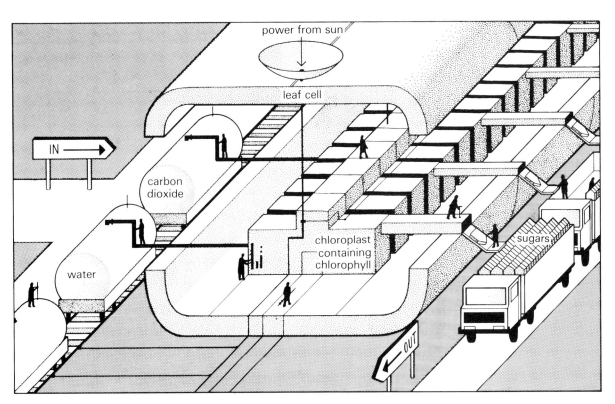

M2 Chlorophyll factory

The word equation for photosynthesis is:

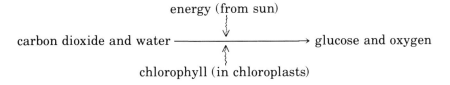

carbon dioxide and water $\xrightarrow[\text{chlorophyll (in chloroplasts)}]{\text{energy (from sun)}}$ glucose and oxygen

On the next few pages you'll find each bit of this equation looked at in more detail.

Chlorophyll – the green stuff

Only green leaves can make sugars – photosynthesize. Colourless ones can't. Some strains of tobacco and barley plants produce seeds which come up as **albino** seedlings.

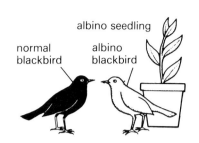

M3 Albino organisms have no colour

If normal and albino seeds are planted together, both will start to grow.

When food supplies in the seeds run out, the albino seedling dies. The green seedling is making its own food and goes on growing (Fig. M4).

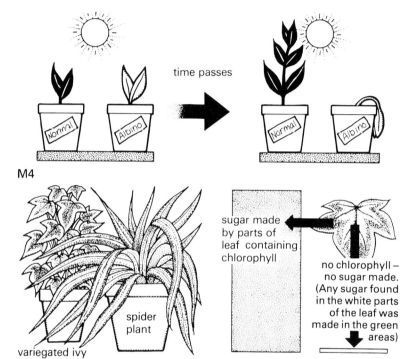

M4

Variegated leaves are part white and part green (Fig. M5).

At the end of a sunny day there is a lot of starch in the green part of a variegated leaf, very little starch in the white part. The green colour shows where chlorophyll is in a leaf.

Plants must have chlorophyll to make sugar, which is then stored as starch.

sugar made by parts of leaf containing chlorophyll

no chlorophyll – no sugar made. (Any sugar found in the white parts of the leaf was made in the green areas)

variegated ivy

spider plant

M5 The results of testing variegated leaves for sugar

Where to look for chlorophyll
Chlorophyll is found in plant cells.

If you look at a slice of plant under a microscope, you often see lots of little boxes.

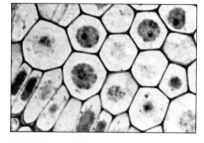

M6 Plant cells under the microscope

Plant cells are a bit like a carton of milk, with a tough case or wall of cellulose around the cell contents.

Chewing makes holes in the cell wall so we can get at the contents and digest them. The cellulose goes more or less straight through the gut as fibre (in human beings).

cell contents

cell wall of indigestible cellulose surrounds cell contents

M7 A plant cell

Inside the cell

Inside the cell, the working parts come in little packages.

These packages are:
Nucleus – controls the cell.

Chloroplasts – full of chlorophyll.

Vacuole – a bag of liquid with salts and sugars dissolved in it.

All these are surrounded by:
Cytoplasm – carries out the instructions of the nucleus.

Cell membrane – controls what goes in and out of the cell.

Cellulose cell wall – gives the cell its shape.

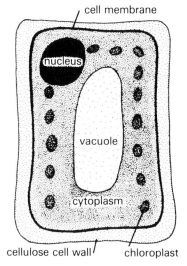

M8 Inside a plant cell

Chlorophyll needs to trap as much light energy as possible, so cells containing it are spread out in thin layers. Why don't leaves have a single layer of cells (Fig. M9)?

M9 Simple layer of cells

A plate of cells isn't very strong, so leaves have branching ribs or veins like the sticks in a fan. These support the leaf blade. They also carry water to the leaf cells and remove glucose solution (Fig. M10). But all these cells tend to lose water faster than the plant can afford. So a layer of cells around the leaf, called the **epidermis**, helps to hold everything together. It also produces a transparent waterproof covering – the **cuticle** (Fig. M11).

But the waterproof cuticle makes it difficult for gases to move in and out. To solve this, there are holes for gas exchange, usually in the lower epidermis. There are air passages under or around the cells which contain chlorophyll. These allow gases to move around inside the leaf (Fig. M12).

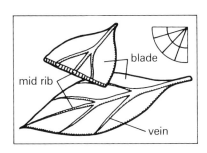

M10 Veins provide strength

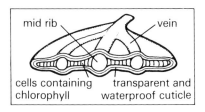

M11 And a cuticle is waterproof

Most plants have large thin as possible leaves, and hold them so that they catch as much sunlight as possible.

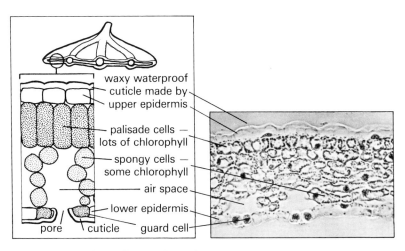

M12 Section of a leaf through a microscope

79

Sunlight

Sunlight contains a lot of **energy**.

Energy is odd stuff – you can't touch it. We know energy is there when something happens. It takes energy to make a noise, to run, to grow.

Energy comes in several forms – like heat or electricity or stored in a chemical. It can be changed from one form to another (Fig. M13).

Energy is measured in **joules**. Joules are very small units. A match has about 2000 joules of chemical energy in it which can be changed into heat and light. A gram of sugar made in a plant has about 16 000 joules trapped in it (Fig. M14).

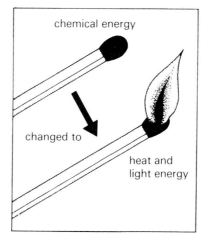

M13

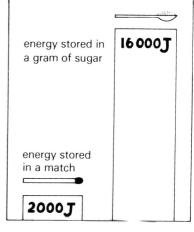

M14 Energy stores

Plants and light energy

Green plants can change light energy into chemical energy. Without light, plants die.

A plant in a dark cupboard develops very differently from another similar one on a windowsill. This happens even if they are both watered and looked after carefully (Fig. M15).

The one in the light will go on growing. After a time the one in the dark will die. Plants must have light energy for photosynthesis and life.

Which of the plants in Fig. M16 is photosynthesizing? One or both? Only the one in daylight. The one at night isn't.

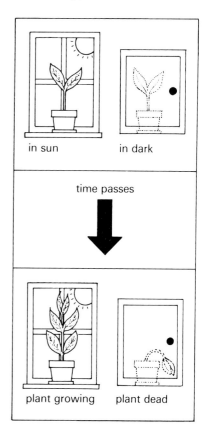

M15 Plants need light energy

M16 Which plant is photosynthesizing?

Will any kind of light do?
Everyday white light is a mixture of different colours (Fig. M17).

Plants grown in red or blue light do well. Plants in green light die.

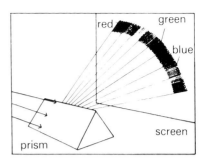

M17 White light is a mixture of colours

This is because the green part of the light bounces off the leaf – which is why the leaf looks green. Red and blue light is absorbed (taken in) and used in photosynthesis (Figs. M18 and M19).

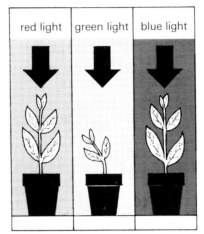

M18 Plants use blue and red light

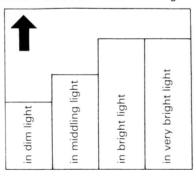

M19

Does the amount of light matter?
Yes. Photosynthesis goes faster – up to a point – as light gets brighter (Fig. M20).

Plants grown in the shade look different from those grown in the sun. Often they are taller or have more leaves. This is to make up for the lack of light (Fig. M21).

Some plants prefer shady places. Liverworts are one kind. They are simple non-flowering plants. Look for them on the banks of streams (Fig. M22).

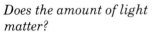

M20 Amount of sugar made in photosynthesis

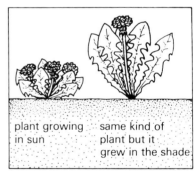

M21

M22 Shade preferring plants

81

Raw materials for photosynthesis

Carbon dioxide

Plants must have carbon dioxide. Without it, they die. We can show this by keeping a plant in a jar with a pot of sodium hydroxide. Sodium hydroxide removes all the carbon dioxide from the air. (Fig. M23).

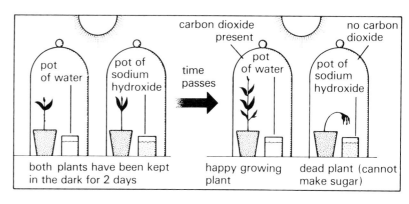

M23 To show plants need carbon dioxide

Glucose is made up of a ring of carbon atoms with hydrogen and oxygen attached. Carbon dioxide can provide the carbon and the oxygen.

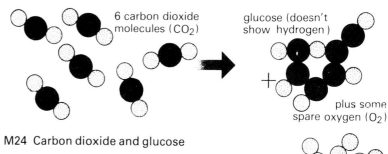

M24 Carbon dioxide and glucose

The more carbon dioxide, the more sugar – up to a point (Fig. M25). Greenhouse crops can be made to grow better if carbon dioxide is added to the air.

Carbon dioxide gets into a leaf through the pores. A nail varnish print of a leaf surface will show the position of the pores.

Each pore leads into the air spaces inside the leaf and so to the **palisade cells.** The kidney-shaped **guard cells** control the size of the pore. The guard cells and the pore together are called a **stoma** (plural – **stomata**).

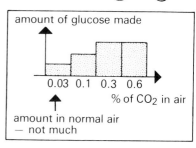

M25 More CO_2, more glucose

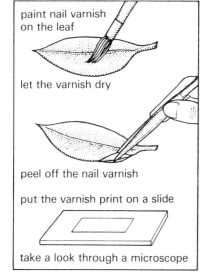

M26 Making a print

To make a nail varnish print:

Take a tough leaf like privet. Paint nail varnish on it (the under-side is best). When the varnish is dry, peel it off. You only need a little bit. Put the varnish on a slide (try to get it flat). Look at it through a microscope.

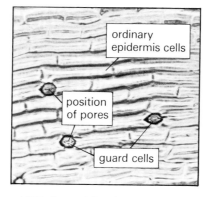

M27 A varnish print

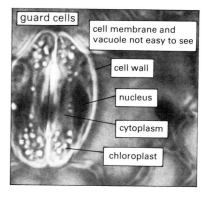

M28 A close-up of a guard cell

How do plants control their pores?

Pores are open during the day (Fig. M29). Plants lose water through the pores and on a hot day may lose so much they wilt. At night, the guard cells close the pores to slow down water loss (Fig. M30).

Most pores are on the underside of the leaf, in the shade. That's where most water is lost.

An experiment to show where plants lose water
Collect some leaves from one plant. Try to make them roughly the same size. Spread Vaseline on the top side of some, the bottom side of the rest. Hang them on a line.

After two hours, look at them again. The ones with Vaseline over their pores won't wilt. The ones with open pores shrivel up.

If the leaves are weighed before and after hanging, you can tell just how much water they lose.

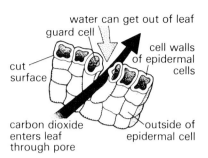

water can get out of leaf
guard cell
cell walls of epidermal cells
cut surface
carbon dioxide enters leaf through pore
outside of epidermal cell

p.s. the cuticle has been left out to reduce muddle

M29 Pore open

weighing things tells you more		
leaves with	at start, mass in g	after 2 hrs, mass in g
Vaseline on top	2.4	1.8
Vaseline on bottom	2.4	2.3

M31 Results of an experiment with Vaselined leaves

guard cell

things can't get in or out

M30 Pore closed by guard cells

Water

Plants need water for many activities, including photosynthesis. Carbohydrates have hydrogen in them. Plants get the hydrogen by splitting up water, using light energy from the sun. With carbon dioxide and hydrogen, the plant makes glucose. This is how the plant stores some of the sun energy. The oxygen left over when the water splits up is given off as a gas.

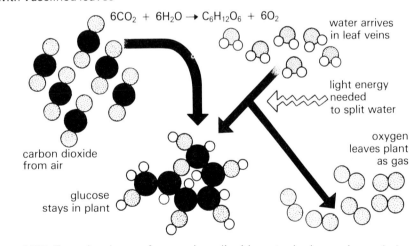

$$6CO_2 + 6H_2O \rightarrow C_6H_{12}O_6 + 6O_2$$

water arrives in leaf veins

light energy needed to split water

oxygen leaves plant as gas

carbon dioxide from air

glucose stays in plant

M32 To make glucose from carbon dioxide, extra hydrogen is needed

Questions

1. You are given an odd looking leaf (maybe tropical) and asked to find out where its pores are. How would you do this? It turns out to have pores on both sides of the leaf in about equal numbers. You are a bit surprised. Suggest at least one reason why a leaf might have stomata on both sides.

2. (a) Draw a large picture of a plant cell (say a palisade cell). Label it. Make sure you show where chlorophyll is found in the cell.
   (b) Name the jobs these cells do: guard cells, epidermal cells, palisade cells.

3. The earliest green plants did not have leaves. Photosynthesis went on in their stems. Later plants developed leaves. What advantages did this change bring? Why are leaves the shape they are?

4. (a) One plant is kept in red light and another in green. Which will photosynthesize? Give a reason for your answer.
   (b) Ivy often grows in a pattern so that no leaf shadows another. Why do you think this is?

The product – what it's all about

M33 Leaf discs cut with a cork borer are easy to handle

Glucose
Most plants promptly turn glucose into starch. It's fiddly to test for glucose in a leaf, but you can look for starch.

Testing a leaf for starch

1. Cut out a piece of leaf with a cork borer. Use a leaf which has been in the light for several hours (Fig. M34).

2. Kill the leaf discs by putting them into boiling water for 30 seconds. This destroys the cell membranes. Now we can get at what's inside the cells (Fig. M35).

3. The colour of chlorophyll may stop us seeing the test result, so dissolve it out with boiling meths. The meths will turn green as the leaf goes white. Do use a hot water bath – **not** a Bunsen burner. (The beaker of boiling water from Fig. M35 is fine.) Meths burns all too easily.

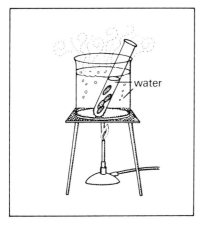

M34 Boil leaf discs in water to kill them

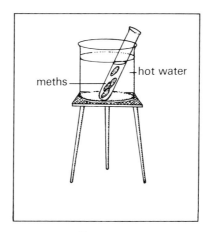

M35 Pour off water and add meths. NB No bunsen!

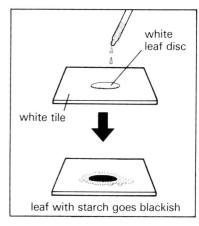

M36 Add a few drops of iodine solution

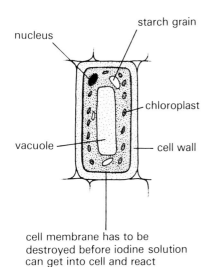

M37

4. Now do a normal starch test. Add a few drops of iodine solution. The leaf should turn blackish because of the starch in it (Fig. M36).

If you don't get the result you expect, try thumping the leaf disc around a bit. The iodine solution may not have got into the cells. Remember, too, there may not be any starch in the leaf because it's all been used up during the night.

Question

Look back over the photosynthesis experiments so far. Make a list of those where you could use the starch tests above to check the results. Choose one and redesign it using the starch test. Give each step and the reason for each step.

Oxygen

Oxygen is a waste product of photosynthesis – luckily for us (see next chapter). During the day it can get out of a leaf through the stomata. At night respiration, which goes on all the time, will mean the plant uses up oxygen (Fig. M38).

not enough light so no photosynthesis so no oxygen produced

M38

The production of oxygen can be used to show that photosynthesis is happening. You can show that water plants produce oxygen if you collect all the gas they give off. It takes a day or two to get enough to test (Fig. M40).

The bubbles of gas are easy to see especially if pondweed is kept in bright light. Up to a point the more light the faster photosynthesis goes and the more oxygen bubbles appear.

The gas from the water plants relights a glowing splint (usually!), so it really is oxygen.

M39 Close-up of pondweed

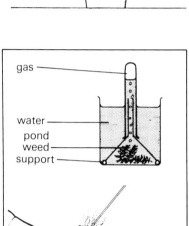

M40 Pondweed experiment

Questions

1. Here are some facts about plants when they photosynthesize. How would you show they are true? You can write less if you draw diagrams.
   (a) They need light.
   (b) They need carbon dioxide too.
   (c) They must contain green chlorophyll.
   (d) They make carbohydrates.
   (e) They also produce oxygen.
2. A leaf was half covered with black paper for several hours on a sunny day (Fig. M41). Sample A was taken from the uncovered side. Sample B was taken from the covered side. The samples were tested for starch in the usual way. Which would you expect to contain starch and why?
3. You decide to grow your own pineapple plant from the top of one you've eaten. You plant it in a pot with damp compost (Fig. M42). You tie up the pot in a plastic bag (a big one with lots of air inside). Then you put it in a warm place near a window. What does the pineapple need to grow? How are you providing these things?

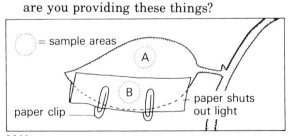

M41

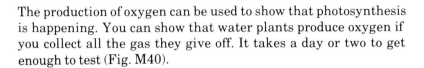

M42

Summary and crossword

Summary

Photosynthesis only happens in green plants in the light. Carbon dioxide and water are turned into glucose and oxygen by chlorophyll. Plants' leaves trap as much light energy as possible.

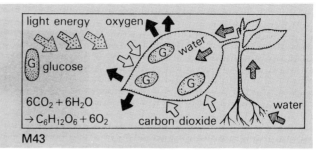

$$6CO_2 + 6H_2O \rightarrow C_6H_{12}O_6 + 6O_2$$

M43

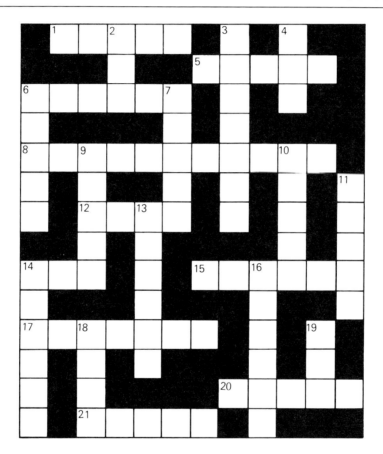

Clues across

1. Flat part of leaf.
5. Long thin part of gut where most food is absorbed.
6. Supports leaf surface and acts as liquid transport tube.
8. The green stuff in plants.
12. Small amounts of fluoride are _____ for your teeth.
14. An energy store which can be embarassing.
15. A large carbohydrate – check it out with iodine.
17. This controls a cell.
20. The part of the tooth above the jaw.
21. A molar or an incisor is a _____.

Clues down

2. This includes carbon dioxide and oxygen.
3. Absorbed in the stomach. Cheers!
4. A long tube running through the body.
6. Bread mould.
7. Carries digested food around the body.
9. Energy for photosynthesis.
10. The largest gland in your body.
11. Used to dissolve chlorophyll out of leaves.
13. Left over at the end of photosynthesis, luckily for us.
14. Bread mould is one.
16. Guts _____ proteins when they've been digested.
18. Renin will cause milk to do this.
19. A large milk-producing herbivore.

Strange feeders – carnivorous plants

Carnivorous plants play the food game in an unusual way. They trap and digest insects (mostly).

They are green plants. They photosynthesize and make their own sugars. So why do they need to feed on insects? The answer lies in the soil – they live in bogs and swamps.

Boggy areas are often short of **nitrogen** which plants need to make protein. Carnivorous plants trap insects in various ways and make enzymes to digest them. There are surprising numbers of them around the world.

Pitcher traps (Fig. M44)
Pitcher plants are excellent insect catchers. Insects are attracted by the nectar. Once they start on the downwards trail, they slip on waxy scales (rather like walking on a pebbly slope or an icy road). Downward-pointing hairs make it harder to get out.

The insects drown in the digestive fluid. Again, the soft parts are broken up by enzymes and are absorbed (especially the amino acids) by the leaf. The hard parts are left.

Sticky traps (Fig. M45)
Sundew leaves have long hairs covered with sticky drops of liquid. If an insect lands it is trapped by the sticky hairs. The leaf curls up and suffocates it.

Glands in the leaf produce enzymes which digest the soft parts of the insect. These are absorbed by the leaf – especially the amino acids. The hard parts are left.

Snap traps (Figs M46 and M47) Well, nearly – the **Venus' fly-trap** takes a few seconds to close.

There are trigger hairs on the inside blade of the leaf. If an insect touches them twice in 15 seconds, the trap is sprung. The double touch means the leaf doesn't close when rain hits it.

The long spines interlock and stop the insect getting out. Digestive enzymes break down the usable (soft) bits of the insect in about three days. Then the trap reopens.

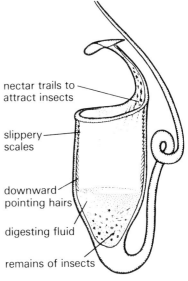

M44 Looking inside a pitcher

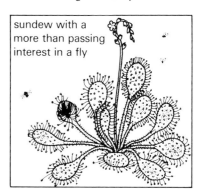

M45 Sundew with a more than passing interest in a fly

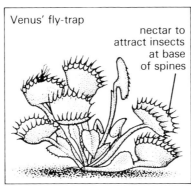

M46 Venus' fly-trap

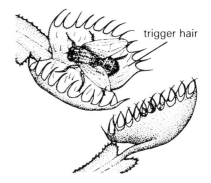

M47 The trap at work

Questions
You might look back at food types, digestion, enzymes and photosynthesis before doing the questions.

1. In your own words explain how three kinds of carnivorous plants trap insects. Write from the insect's point of view.

2. 'Green plants can make their own food'. How true is this of carnivorous plants? Give reasons for your opinion. Write from the plant's point of view defending your position as a true plant, even if you do eat meat in a way.

3. Fertilizers usually kill carnivorous plants. Can you think why?

Symbiosis

Symbiosis means 'living together'. Two different kinds of organism co-operate so that both gain from the arrangement. Often feeding is important. All sorts of combinations are possible.

Animal/animal

Nile crocodiles often have leeches living in their mouths and sucking their blood. Egyptian plovers feed on leeches. The crocodiles let the plovers go in and out of their mouths, and don't try to eat them. The birds get food and the crocodiles get rid of the leeches.

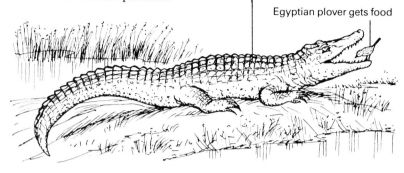

Nile crocodile gets a clean-up

Egyptian plover gets food

M48 Animal/animal symbiosis

Plant/animal

A number of animals without backbones (**invertebrates**) have green plants living symbiotically inside them.

Hydra is an animal related to jellyfish and sea anemones. It is often green, because it has single-celled green plants – **algae** – living inside its own cells.

The alga gets some protection and transport. Hydra gets extra oxygen and food materials.

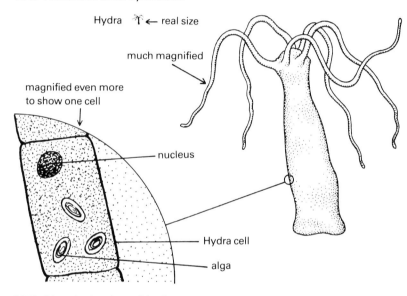

Hydra ← real size

much magnified

magnified even more to show one cell

nucleus

Hydra cell

alga

M49 Plant/animal symbiosis

Bacteria/animal

Bacteria which digest cellulose live in the cow's rumen. They provide extra glucose for their host (the cow). The bacteria gain a damp, food-filled, protected place to live. Many bacteria live like this.

Some bacteria in the human gut provide us with one of the B vitamins.

See also page 38.

human being gets Vitamin B

bacteria get food water and warmth

M50 Animal/bacteria

Plant/plant

Lichens are common – if you live in an area with clean air. They are a good example of symbiosis.

Lichens come in various shapes. They are all a combination of a fungus and an alga (Fig. M52).

A fungus like Mucor must have dead plants or animals to live on. The fungus in a lichen gets its food from the green alga living inside it. The alga gets protection against drying up.

M51 Lichen on a tree

Lichens can be tough. One kind, called 'reindeer moss', is found under the snow in the far north. Other kinds live on hot, dry mountainsides.

The fungus provides the attachment to the tree or stones and the outside of the lichen. The algae live a protected life but light can easily reach them through the transparent fungi cells.

Lichens cannot cope with air pollution. Sulphur dioxide kills them. They absorb it from polluted air through their surfaces.

Scaly lichens (Fig. M53) survive better than feathery ones (Fig. M51). They have much less surface area for sulphur dioxide to get in through. What types of lichen can grow in your area?

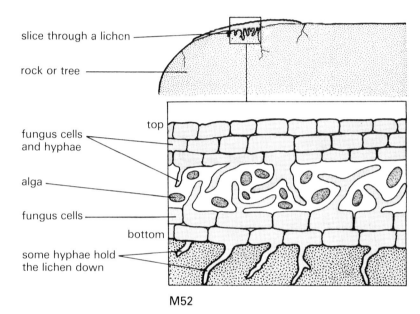

slice through a lichen

rock or tree

top

fungus cells and hyphae

alga

fungus cells

bottom

some hyphae hold the lichen down

M52

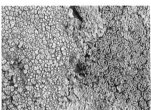

M53 Both scaly lichens shown here are firmly attached to the surface they are growing on

Questions

1. What is meant by symbiosis? Give one example.

2. Fungi are not green and cannot make their own food. Explain how the fungus **Mucor** and the fungus in a lichen solve their food problems.

3. Orchids have tiny seeds with almost no stored food. They can only germinate when a particular fungus is also in the soil. First the fungus produces enzymes which digest the decaying leaves in the soil. The orchid and the fungus grow using this food supply. When the orchid, a green plant, is larger, it provides food for the fungus, which grows among its roots. What food would you expect the plant to supply, and how was it made? What is this kind of partnership called?

4. Carry out a lichen mapping expedition in your area. How polluted is it? You will have to do some research in the library to help you make the maps.

Respiration

N1

If you did, and had the same body mass as the person in the diagram (65 kg), you'd need about 11 000 kilojoules (11 megajoules) of energy. Energy is measured in SI units called joules (J). 1 J is very small, so measurements are often in kilojoules (1 kJ = 1000 joules) or megajoules (1 MJ = 1000 kJ).

The energy you need depends upon your age, body mass, sex and how active you are.

Nearly every process in a living organism needs energy. Respiration is the process which provides it. How much energy is needed?

In 24 hours, you might expect to spend time as shown in Fig. N1.

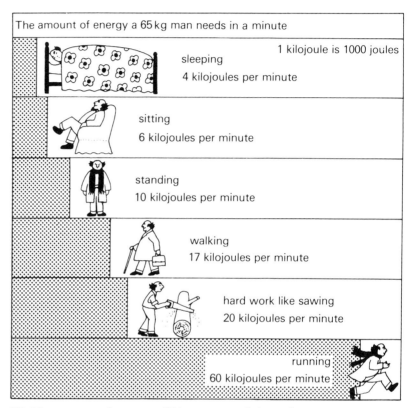

N2 The amount of energy a 65 kg man needs in a minute

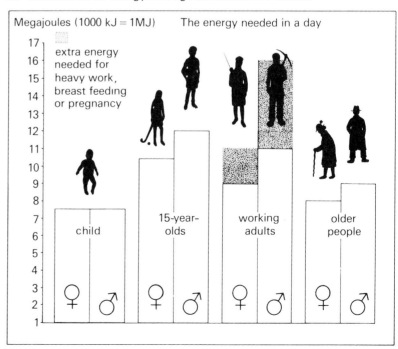

N3 The energy needed in a day by different people

Questions

1. Look at Fig. N2.
   (a) Which activity uses up twice as much energy as standing?
   (b) If you were a 65 kg man, how much energy would you use if you (i) ran for 5 minutes, (ii) walked for 5 minutes, (iii) sat for 12 minutes, (iv) slept for one hour?

2. Look at Fig. N3.
   How many megajoules of energy are needed in a day by (i) a child, (ii) an old lady, (iii) a man doing light work, (iv) a pregnant woman?

Many of the joules needed in a day are provided in a meal like the one shown in Fig. N4.

Question

If you gave a child the meal shown in Fig. N4, how much more energy would he or she need to get through the rest of the day?

Amount	Food	Energy
250 g	tomato soup	702.5 kilojoules
200 g	chicken	1544.2 kilojoules
250 g	potato chips	2472.5 kilojoules
150 g	peas	410 kilojoules
150 g	ice cream	1207.5 kilojoules
	Total	6336.7 kilojoules (or 6.3 megajoules)

N4 Energy in a meal

The food is digested in the gut and sorted by the liver to provide the fuel which cells use – **glucose**. A living organism is a bit like a machine. Both a car and a dog take in fuel (petrol or glucose) and oxygen. These are turned into heat, waste gases and energy. The car and the dog use the energy to move. Puppies use the energy to grow as well.

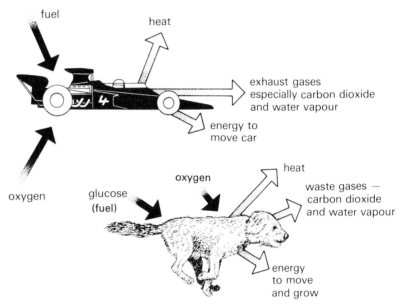

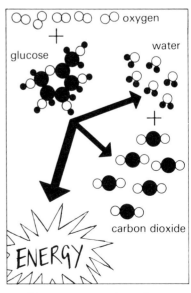

N5 Cars and dogs both need fuel and oxygen to move

When glucose is broken down, the energy stored is set free and used by body cells for growth, repair and movement. Some energy changes into heat.

The word equation for respiration goes like this:

glucose burns in **oxygen** to produce **carbon dioxide** and **water** as well as **energy**

You may see it written as:

$C_6H_{12}O_6 + 6O_2 \rightarrow 6CO_2 + 6H_2O + energy$
(glucose)

This type of respiration, which uses oxygen in breaking up glucose, is called **aerobic** respiration. On the next two pages are some experiments to show when it's happening and when it isn't. They show it happens in plants as well as animals.

N6 The molecules of respiration

The evidence for aerobic respiration

Aerobic respiration uses up oxygen.

Respiration takes place in every living cell – but we can use whole organisms to show that it happens.

Glucose is used up, so the dry mass (the mass of everything except water) drops. This experiment shows that live beans lose dry mass in 24 hours. Dead (boiled) beans don't.

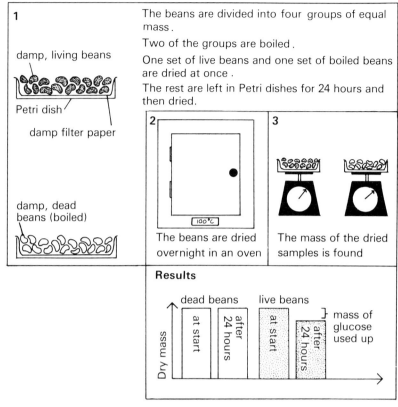

N7 To show that dry mass is lost

Energy is produced – some of it as heat. This experiment shows that live beans produce heat. Dead beans don't.

Some energy is used in movement.

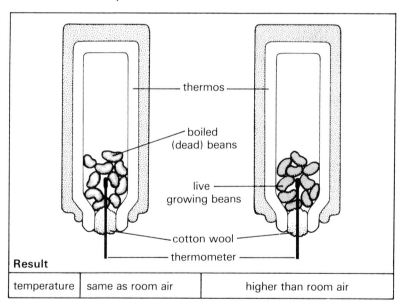

N8 To show that heat is produced during respiration

Questions

1. Explain why live and dead beans were used in Fig. N7. Why were some beans dried at once and others left for 24 hours? The live beans lost weight. Why?

2. Look at the experiment in Fig. N8. What could be done to improve this experiment?

Gases and respiration

Only a fifth of the gases in air can be used in respiration. The one fifth is oxygen, of course.

Oxygen is used up in aerobic respiration – it is removed from the air. In a closed container which contains living organisms the amount of air gets smaller as oxygen is used up (so long as any carbon dioxide produced is removed) (Fig. N10).

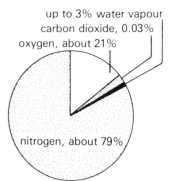

up to 3% water vapour
carbon dioxide, 0.03%
oxygen, about 21%

nitrogen, about 79%

exact percentages vary with the dampness of the air

N9 The gases in air

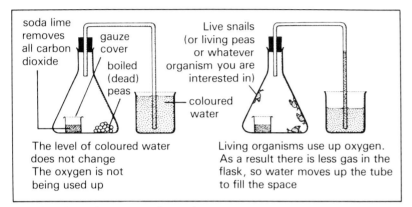

soda lime removes all carbon dioxide

gauze cover

boiled (dead) peas

Live snails (or living peas or whatever organism you are interested in)

coloured water

The level of coloured water does not change
The oxygen is not being used up

Living organisms use up oxygen. As a result there is less gas in the flask, so water moves up the tube to fill the space

N10 To show that oxygen is used up

Lime water is a useful test for respiration. We can take all the carbon dioxide out of air. After the air has passed through a flask of living organisms, it turns lime water milky. The organisms are giving off carbon dioxide.

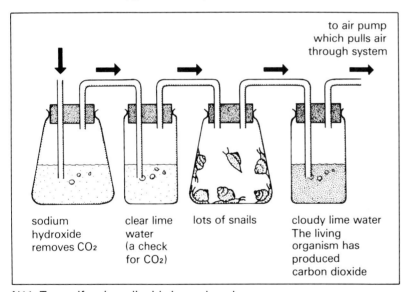

to air pump which pulls air through system

sodium hydroxide removes CO₂

clear lime water (a check for CO₂)

lots of snails

cloudy lime water
The living organism has produced carbon dioxide

N11 To see if carbon dioxide is produced

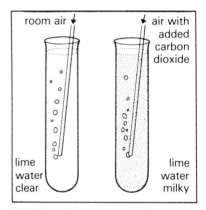

room air

air with added carbon dioxide

lime water clear

lime water milky

N12 Use lime water to show the presence of carbon dioxide

Carbon dioxide is produced. The test for carbon dioxide uses lime water. This goes milky when carbon dioxide is present. There is a little carbon dioxide in air normally, but not enough to change lime water.

Extra carbon dioxide in the air of a crowded room makes people feel groggy and long for fresh air. We have carbon dioxide testers in our bodies. They give an indirect warning that oxygen is getting low.

Questions
1. Look at Fig. N10
   (a) How is carbon dioxide removed from the flasks?
   (b) How is the uptake of oxygen measured?
   (c) What would the effect of having lots more snails in the flask be?

2. Look at Fig. N11. The experiment uses live organisms. What should we also do to check that it is the snails' respiration which makes carbon dioxide and not, say, something their shells are producing? Draw the apparatus you would use.

Carbon cycle

Carbon is rare on Earth – perhaps 0.02% of the crust by weight and 0.05% of the air by volume. Tied up in various chemical forms, carbon makes up ¼ (25%) of living organisms. (Fig. N13).

N13

What little carbon there is is passed around and used again and again.

Carbon dioxide is 'fixed' by green plants in photosynthesis. It is trapped as glucose and can be change into other chemicals that plants need (Fig. N14).

Animals get their carbon by eating plants or other animals. Decomposers get theirs from dead animals and plants.

Chalk, coal and oil all contain carbon from the bodies of organisms long dead.

Plants, animals and decomposers all respire and lose carbon as carbon dioxide to the atmosphere (Fig. N15).

When people burn coal and oil, carbon returns to the atmosphere.

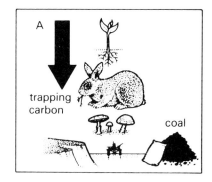

N14 Trapping carbon

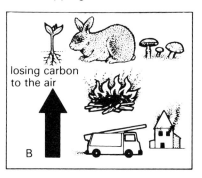

N15 Losing carbon to the air

Putting all this together produces the **carbon cycle**. (Figs N16 and N17).

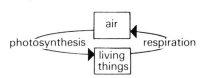

N17 The basic carbon cycle

The basic relationship between respiration and photosynthesis is well balanced. What about areas where we are interfering?

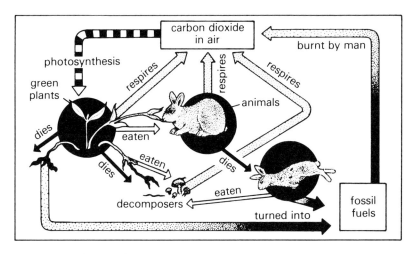

N16 The carbon cycle

Burning fossil fuels

The large-scale burning of fossil fuels by man is very recent – has it changed anything? When fossil fuels are burnt, two things are added to the atmosphere: **carbon dioxide** and **dust**.
Carbon dioxide disolved in rainwater produces a dilute acid which is often called **acid rain**. A lot of acid rain can kill trees and other organisms. Carbon dioxide and dust can also make the atmosphere heat up.

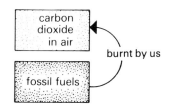

N18

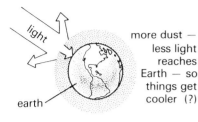

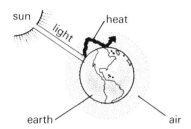

N19 More dust, a cooler Earth?

Dust
Some light arriving at the edge of the Earth's atmosphere is reflected (bounced) away. Light which hits the Earth helps warm it up. More dust might mean more reflection, less light hitting the Earth, and so a cooler place to live in – maybe.

Carbon dioxide
Extra carbon dioxide may produce a 'greenhouse' effect and warm up the Earth. Here's how it works. Light goes through air (and glass) and hits the Earth. Some is changed to heat and bounces back. Heat won't go through air which is full of carbon dioxide (or through glass) very well. It stays near the Earth and the temperature rises (Fig. N20).

This might make the Earth warm up – just like the inside of a car on a sunny day. The whole inside of the car can get so hot that a dog or a baby can die of heat stroke.

Which wins?
Carbon dioxide levels have risen.

So have dust levels, and so has world average temperature.

But it's not simple. We've only been counting for a few years. If we look back further in time, the world's average temperature has varied a good deal (Fig. N21).

It is possible that the temperature changes of recent years are part of the Earth's normal temperature changes.

So why worry?
Cooling might mean an Ice Age; warming might mean floods as the ice caps melt. The evidence above doesn't say whether a large change caused by man is happening. Changes like this usually take thousands of years. The human race might not be able to tell what is happening for many years. By that time it might be too late to do anything to put things right.

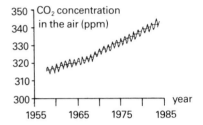

N20 Graph showing change in carbon dioxide levels (measured at the end of the summer in Hawaii)

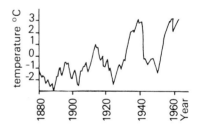

N21 Average temperature in January in New York

Questions

1. Make up an experiment which you could do in the laboratory which would show that a burning match or small candle gives out carbon dioxide.

2. Fig. N20 shows the carbon dioxide levels in air, measured in Hawaii between 1957 and 1984. Did the carbon dioxide level increase, decrease or remain the same? In 1985 the level of CO_2 was just under 0.035%. Has the pattern in Fig. N20 continued? Why does the level go up and down in a regular wave pattern?

3. Why aren't we suffocated by the carbon dioxide we breathe out?

4. Explain what the carbon cycle is. Write sentences or draw a diagram in which you use each of the following words at least once. Underline each word the first time you use it. You can use them in any order.
   photosynthesis respiration
   carbon dioxide glucose
   energy decomposers
   coal man

Anaerobic respiration

Anaerobic respiration is respiration **without oxygen.**
In some cases it is also known as **fermentation.** A few
bacteria always respire like this. They are killed by oxygen.
Yeast is a single-celled fungus that can respire with or
without oxygen.

N22 Magnified yeast cells

In bread recipes, yeast respires aerobically and produces water
and carbon dioxide. The carbon dioxide bubbles make the bread
rise.

Without oxygen, yeast respires anaerobically. It still produces
carbon dioxide, as the test on the right shows.

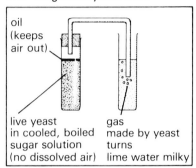

live yeast
in cooled, boiled
sugar solution
(no dissolved air)

gas
made by yeast
turns
lime water milky

Without oxygen, yeast cannot break down glucose completely, to
produce only carbon dioxide and water. Alcohol is produced as
well. Seeds can respire without oxygen for a while. Both they and
yeast stop when the amount of alcohol they produce poisons them.

N23 Anaerobic yeast

Alcohol still contains energy and makes a good fuel. Anaerobic
respiration doesn't release as much energy as aerobic respiration.

Animal muscle cells sometimes don't get enough oxygen to
respire aerobically. They can manage without oxygen for a short
while – say while running a race. They don't make alcohol – they
produce **lactic acid.** Too much lactic acid hurts – you get cramp.
When the activity stops, extra oxygen is needed to get rid of the
lactic acid in the muscles.

Cells vary in their ability to manage without oxygen. Brain cells
cannot survive as long as muscle cells. They die within a few
minutes if their oxygen supply is cut off.

N24 Alcohol is a fuel and will
burn to give heat and light

Summary
Respiration is the process by which living
things break down glucose to release energy.
Aerobic respiration happens when oxygen is
available and it releases more energy than
anaerobic respiration (no oxygen around). By
photosynthesis and respiration, carbon moves
backwards and forwards between the
atmosphere and living things – this
continuous (we hope) exchange is known as
the carbon cycle.

Questions

1. (a) Write out the word equation for aerobic
respiration.
(b) Which of the following is probably
respiring aerobically?
(i) muscles in a sleeping cat
(ii) muscles in a race horse near the end
of a long race
(iii) yeast making beer in a home
brewing kit
(iv) a preserved earthworm
(v) the cells of a grass leaf at any time
during the day
(vi) your muscles as you do this bit of
work.

2. Describe in your own words, experiments
which show that:
(a) dry mass is lost in respiration
(b) oxygen may be used up in respiration
(c) a named type of energy is released by
respiration
(d) carbon dioxide is produced by
respiration

3. The French used to use the foam from the
top of their beer to make bread rise. Why did
this work?

Breathing-1

Living organisms have a gas moving problem. For aerobic respiration, cells must have oxygen and they make carbon dioxide which they have to get rid of. On the next few pages are various ways of solving this problem – by **breathing**.

Breathing involves
1. a **respiratory surface** for gases to move through – in and out of the organism.
2. a **way of moving the gases** to and from the respiratory surface.

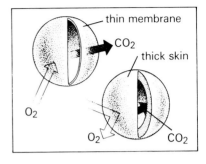

O1 Thin surfaces

How to spot a respiratory surface
Respiratory surfaces are **thin** so gases can diffuse through them fast.

Respiratory surfaces are **damp** because gases need to dissolve in water to diffuse fast.

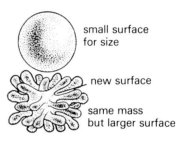

O2 Large surfaces

Respiratory surfaces are **large** compared to the rest of the material an organism is made of.

The more surface – the more gas can get through at a time.

Moving gases
Over a small distance, diffusion is good enough (Fig. O3).

Otherwise, organisms need some way of **pumping gases** to and from the respiratory surface (Fig. O4).

They also need something to **carry gases** around inside the body. This is often blood – which does many other jobs as well.

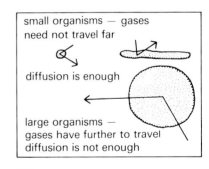

O3

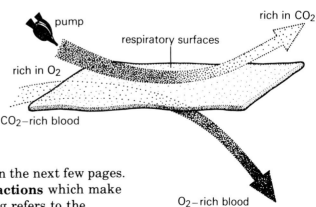

O4 Larger organisms need pumps

Watch out for these ideas about breathing on the next few pages. (PS: Respiration refers to the **chemical reactions** which make energy available to the organism. Breathing refers to the movement of gases in and out of the lungs. Beware of mixing up breathing and respiration.)

Breathing and small organisms

Single cells are tiny and have a large surface area for their volume. Many (like Amoeba) manage on their own in water or very damp places. Others, like the muscle cell, live as part of a larger organism which keeps them damp.

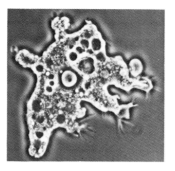

Amoeba, a single-celled animal
O_2 diffuses into cell

CO_2 diffuses into water
gas exchange all over cell

O5 Amoeba – a single celled animal

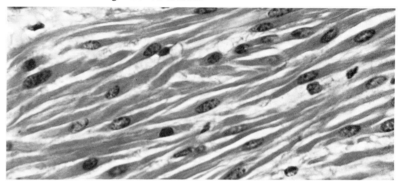

O6 Some muscle cells

Some **single celled plants** can manage in slightly drier places. Their cell walls keep water in but slow down gas exchange. They don't need energy for moving and can manage with slow gas exchange.

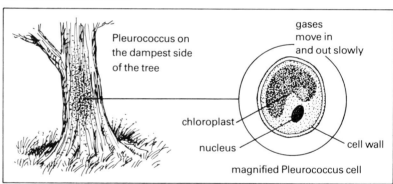

Pleurococcus on the dampest side of the tree

gases move in and out slowly

chloroplast
nucleus
cell wall
magnified Pleurococcus cell

O7 Pleurococcus – a single celled plant

Larger plants don't need energy for moving. Slowish gas exchange is enough for most of the plant. Their leaves are thin and they have extra air channels inside the leaf to increase the surface for gas exchange.

Some larger animals manage by being very thin. Gases don't have far to diffuse across such thin bodies. Look for a **planarian** (a flatworm) in a pond.

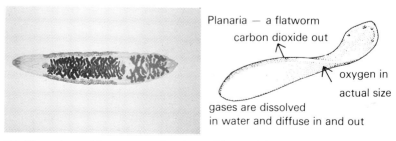

Planaria — a flatworm
carbon dioxide out
oxygen in
actual size
gases are dissolved in water and diffuse in and out

O8 Planaria – a bigger organism but still very thin

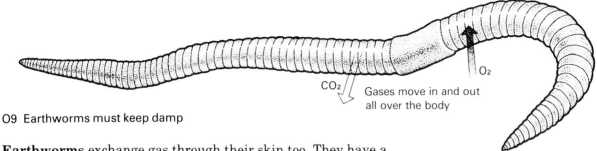

O9 Earthworms must keep damp

Earthworms exchange gas through their skin too. They have a simple blood system to carry gases around their bodies. However, they are really rather large to rely on their skins, and as a result they are slow movers. They also must stay in damp soil to keep their skins wet.

It's safest to avoid the word 'breathe' when talking about green plants. In the light, they photosynthesize (and respire as well). Carbon dioxide goes in and oxygen comes out – the opposite of what happens in an organism which is only respiring. If you're not sure, talk about 'gas exchange'.

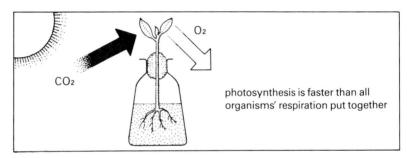

O10 Gas exchange in sunlight

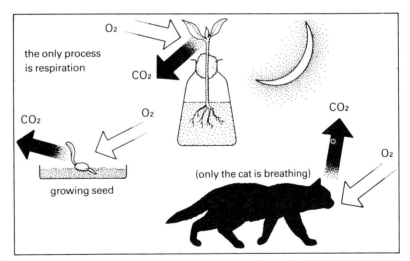

O11 Gas exchange without light

Questions

1. In your own words explain briefly
   (a) why you can't rely on diffusion alone to get gases in and out of your body.
   (b) why a dog needs lungs but Amoeba doesn't.
   (c) why a cat needs lungs but a gooseberry bush (of the same mass) doesn't.

2. So why do nurses' remove flowers from patients' rooms at night?

3. You are a small organism with ambitions to grow large. You go shopping for a respiratory surface. What are the qualities you look for and why?

Breathing and middle-sized organisms

In water

Some fish are large and most them move a lot. They need a lot of oxygen. They have **gills** to absorb the oxygen dissolved in water. **Gills** are bunches of blood vessels in a thin membrane bag. Many larval (very young) fish and tadpoles have gills which trail free in the water (Fig. O12).

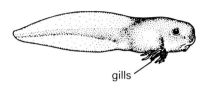

O12 Tadpole

Free gills are likely to get damaged, especially if they are large. Adult fish have a gill cover (**operculum**) for protection (Fig. O13).

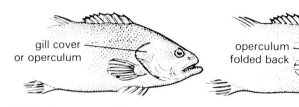

O13 Gill covers and gills

The gills are arranged in 4 layers on each side, supported by gill arches (Fig. O14).

The gills are in the form of filaments covered in masses of folds. This gives them a large surface area.

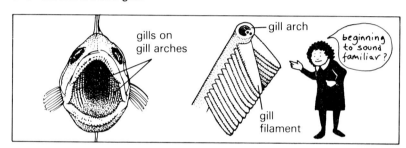

O14 Gill arches

The more active a fish is, the more efficient its gills need to be. The gills must be very good at absorbing oxygen from water.

Water goes in through the mouth and out past the gills (Fig. O15). A fast mover like a mackerel just swims along with its mouth open – plenty of water flows across the gills.

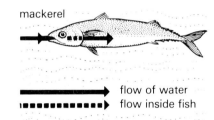

O15 Water flow

Slower fish need a pump to push water across the gills fast enough. The floor of the mouth drops and pulls in water (Fig. O16a).

The mouth shuts and the floor of the mouth moves up. Water is pushed back between the gills and out (Fig. O16b).

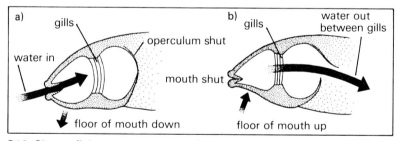

O16 Slower fish pump water over their gills

Also the operculum flap can move in and out. This helps suck water between the gills. There is a steady flow of oxygen-rich water past the blood vessels in the gills.

A fish like a plaice spends a lot of time lying still on the bottom without breathing.

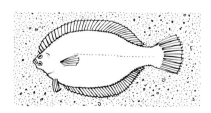

O17 Plaice on bottom

100

On land

Insects in water may have gills. Gills tend to dry out easily so insects on land developed a piped air system – the **tracheae**.

Along the side of an insect are a row of holes – **spiracles** (Fig. O18). Spiracles have hairs around them to filter dust.

These lead into tubes (**tracheae**) which branch and get finer (Fig. O18a)

Large tracheae have spiral rings of **chitin** to hold them open. The smaller tubes do not. Their walls get thinner and thinner (Fig. O18b).

The finest tubes (**tracheoles**) end up inside cells. Gases diffuse in and out through these tubes (Fig. O18c).

In small insects like fruit flies or slow larger ones, like caterpillars, gases move in and out by diffusion alone (Fig. O19).

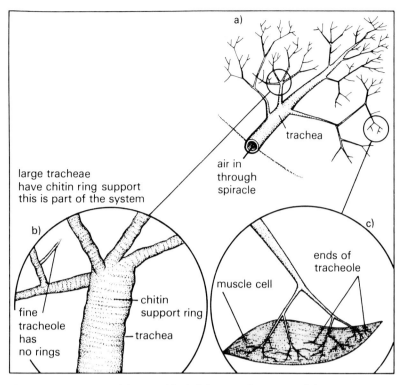

O18 The tracheae: (a) magnified, (b) magnified more, (c) magnified most

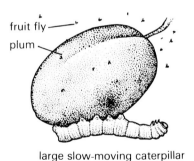

O19 Diffusion is enough for some insects

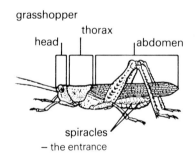

O20 More energetic ones need a piped air system

Large active insects like grasshoppers and bees have movements of the abdomen which pump air in and out of the large tubes.

Tracheae work very well – in fact water insects with gills also have tracheae. Some have breathing tubes leading into tracheae (Fig. O21).

However, gas exchange in tracheae relies on diffusion. Diffusion only works over small distances, so insects cannot become very large. Animals of any size need another way of breathing. They have lungs.

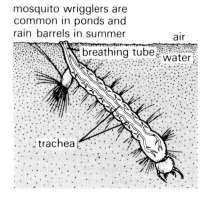

O21 Some underwater insects have tracheae

101

Breathing and larger organisms - the lungs

Large active animals like mammals need a really good gas exchange system – the **lungs**.

The respiratory surface is folded away inside a mammal and is very large indeed.

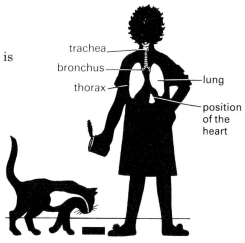

O22 The position of lungs

Air has quite a journey to reach the respiratory surface. Air entering through the nose travels down the wide trachea, which must be kept open. Complete rings of support material would make the neck stiff, so the job is done by semi-circular bits of **cartilage** which allow the neck to bend. (Fig. O24).

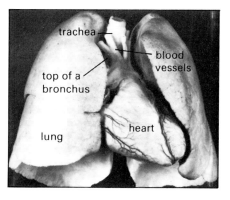

O23 Real lungs

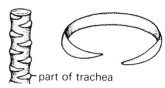

O24 The tracheae is kept open by semi-circular supports (not complete rings of cartilage)

Cartilage appears in other bits of the body – the bendy bit of your nose, part of the ribs. Look at the breast bone of a chicken – the front part is cartilage. It's easiest to see in a young bird. Cartilage is often an early stage in bone growing.

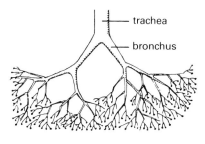

O25 Tubes branch and branch until they end in alveoli

The trachea branches to form two bronchi, one to each lung. Bronchitis is a disease in which the bronchi get inflamed. The bronchi branch and eventually end in the folded respiratory surface, tiny bags of air called **alveoli** (Fig. O26). You have at least 300 million of them, all with thin damp walls. Together they make up most of the spongy lungs – and weigh a bit over a kilogram. The lungs reach right up to your collarbone.

The alveoli have very thin walls and are wound about by capillaries which also have very thin walls. Oxygen and carbon dioxide can diffuse from blood to air and back with ease.

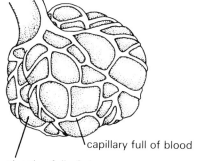

O26 An alveolus – we have between 300 and 700 million of them

Air leaving the lungs is rather different from what it was like when it came in. On the way out it has less oxygen, more carbon dioxide. What happens to the oxygen? Where does the extra carbon dioxide come from? The answer is: from body tissues through the blood.

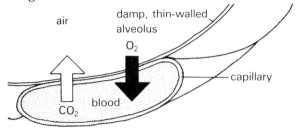

O27 A close-up of a capillary and alveolus

O28 Or to put it another way

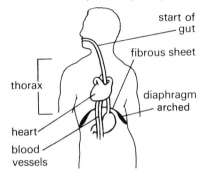

O29 The position of the diaphragm

Blood arrives in the lungs low in oxygen but rich in carbon dioxide from respiring cells. In the capillaries, blood is flowing very close to the air in an alveolus. Carbon dioxide diffuses from the blood into the lungs and oxygen diffuses the other way.

Question

Look at the table below. It shows the results of measuring the amount of dissolved gas in blood entering and leaving the lungs. Which sample, A or B, was blood leaving the lungs and why?

Vol. of gas in 100 cm^3 of blood	Sample A (in cm^3)	Sample B (in cm^3)
nitrogen	0.9	0.9
oxygen	19.0	10.6
carbon dioxide	50.0	58.0

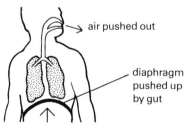

O30 Breathing in using the diaphragm

O31 Breathing out using the diaphragm

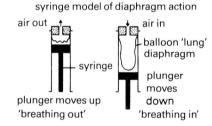

O32 Syringe model of diaphragm action

Lungs have no muscles and cannot pump air themselves. They rely on the steady work done by the diaphragm and the muscles between the ribs. You notice the movements most when they aren't even. Laughing and crying involve a deep breath in followed by several short sharp breaths out.

The **diaphragm** causes over half the air movements when you rest. It divides the body cavity in two parts. Only the gut and some large blood vessels and nerves go through it. You can feel your diaphragm if you push your fingers under your ribs.

It makes the upper part of the body – the **thorax** – into an airtight box. The only way in and out of the lungs is through the trachea.

When the diaphragm goes flat you breathe in (Fig. O30). Air is pulled into the lungs as it is into the syringe model in Fig. O32b. When the diaphragm arches up, it pushes air out. It pushes your guts around at the same time (Fig. O31).

Watch an animal breathe and you'll see the abdomen go in and out with the movements of the diaphragm. You'll also see the rib cage move.

103

The diaphragm works with the muscles and bones of the chest to move air in and out of the lungs.

The wall of the thorax is not stiff like the walls of the syringe. The ribs form a cage around the lungs.

One set of muscles pulls the rib cage up and out. Another set pulls the ribs down and in. They act rather like a pair of bellows.

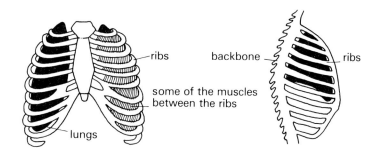

O33 Rib cage from the front and from the side

The various muscles produce a high pressure in the thorax to push air out and a low pressure to draw air in. The pressure changes are not great. They are cancelled out by water pressure only 25 cm below the surface.

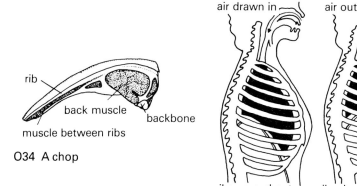

O34 A chop

O35 Ribs and diaphragm work together

The speed at which the system works varies. Your rest speed is probably around 10–15 breaths a minute. Compare yourself with a gerbil or a mouse. Large animals breathe more slowly than small ones. Breathing rate goes up as you run.

Whatever you're doing there is a fair amount of movement of the lungs inside the thorax. To prevent them rubbing, there is a double **pleural membrane** around the lungs. There is a film of liquid between the membranes. The lungs can slip up and down a bit but they still have to move with the thorax walls.

If these pleural membranes get inflamed or there is too much **pleural liquid** between them, breathing can become very painful. This happens in the disease called pleurisy.

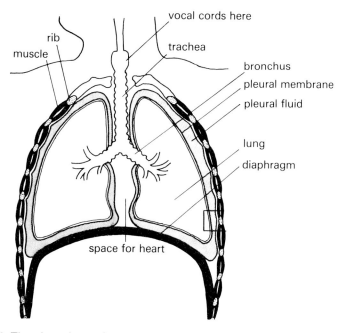

O36 The pleural membranes

Lung cleaning mechanisms

Respiratory surfaces are very delicate. Lungs inside the body are protected from knocks but cold and dirt can still damage them.

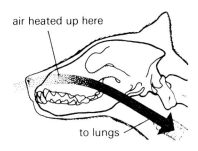

O37 Heating air

Cold
Air is warmed when an animal breathes air through its nostrils. This skull (Fig. O37) shows the position of the **turbinal bones.**

In living animals, they are covered with a net of blood vessels. When an animal breathes in, the air passes between the turbinal bones. It travels near the warm blood and heats up.

On a very cold day, you get a tight feeling when you breathe in. This warns you that air isn't warming up quite enough.

Dirt
Anything besides air which gets into the lungs can clog up and damage delicate tissues. There are two dirt filters.

One filter is in the nose, on the turbinal bones. The other lines the larger tubes in the lung.

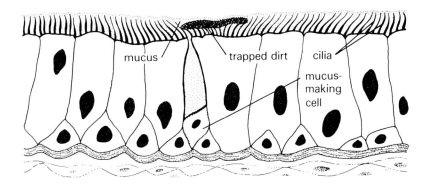

O38 Cilia and mucus trap dirt

Both consist of **mucus** – a sticky gooey material (snot, basically) plus minute hairs called **cilia.** Dirt sticks to the mucus. The cilia move the dirty mucus out of the way.

Cilia act like thousands of oars set in the body walls. Anything on them is passed along – either to the back of the nose or up the trachea. In both cases, the trapped dirt is usually swallowed unnoticed. (Bacteria are killed by stomach acids.)

If the system has extra work to do – say when you have a cold or something has gone down the wrong way – you cough or sneeze.

It's a good idea to cough freely, as coughing clears air tubes. If cilia are missing or don't work, coughing may be the only way to clear the lungs.

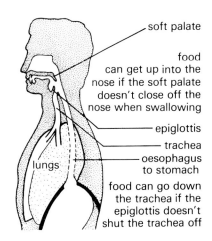

O39 Flaps to protect the lungs

Questions

1. In your own words explain briefly
   (a) why its best to breathe through your nose and not through your mouth.
   (b) why dirt can harm your lungs.
   (c) what mucus does.

2. The largest beetle is only the size of a mouse. Give one reason why they can't grow any larger.

Smoking

Tobacco smoke paralyses the cilia, so dirt and mucus don't get swept up out of the lungs. Instead they collect and have to be coughed up – hence smokers' cough.

Tobacco smoke triggers other damaging changes in the lung – so they can't work so well. Short term effects are breathlessness and finding rushing around less easy. You need oxygen to be active. Long term effects may be diseases like bronchitis, lung cancer or heart disease. The heart tends to be overworked as it tries to make up for the lack of oxygen in the blood.

Smokers aren't the only people to suffer from lung diseases. People with jobs which involve breathing in a lot of dust – like slate workers – often have lung problems. Anyone living in a big city area with high air pollution has a greater chance of cancer of the respiratory organs (lungs, trachea, bronchi) than someone living in an area with clean air.

The map (Fig. O41) doesn't mean that if you live in Birmingham you are bound to get cancer – it suggests your risk is greater than some one who lives at X. Air pollution may overload lung-cleaning mechanisms and trigger a disease.

Smokers have their own private air pollution on top of what everyone breathes – an extra overload. The only cheering thing is that damaged lung-cleaning mechanisms, given time, can repair themselves (Fig. O42).

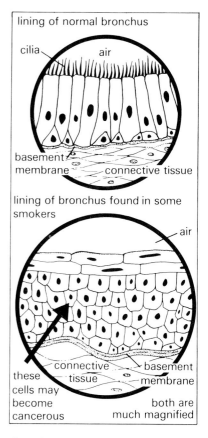

O40 Smoking can change lung cells

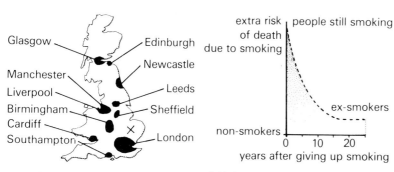

O41 Shaded areas are where more people than average die from cancer of the respiratory organs

O42 It's worth giving up smoking

More information from:
The Health Education Council,
78 New Oxford Street,
London WC1

Questions

1. Make a collage of the adverts for cigarettes, tobacco etc. from any two magazines. Count up the people you know who smoke and who don't smoke. Write down your results.

   Ask any two people you know who smoke why they smoke. Write down what they say. Ask any two people you know who don't smoke why they don't. Write down what they say.

2. Find one newspaper article about the risks of smoking. Cut it out if you can and underline the most important bits.
   Put the whole lot in a folder.
   Add one other thing (picture, photo tape recording, booklet, anything) which adds something new to what you've collected.
   Bring the whole lot along to class.

Summary and questions

Summary
Breathing involves a respiratory surface for the exchange of gases between an organism and its environment. In larger animals, this surface may be developed into tracheae, gills or lungs. In addition a pump or pumps may keep the gases moving to and from the surface, especially in large and active animals.

Questions

1. Copy out and fill in the blanks.
   Breathing involves a _____ surface which must be _____ and _____ and large so that oxygen can get _____ an organism fast enough. The gas _____ _____ leaves an organism through this surface. Sometimes there is a pump to help the gas movements especially in _____ and active animals. In man, the two _____ make up the respiratory surface. There are _____ main breathing movements. One is caused by the muscles of the _____ and the other by the muscles between the _____.
   Oxygen is carried to the organs of the body from the respiratory surface by _____.

2. Mix and match. Write out full sentences beginning with a word in column A and ending in a phrase from column B.

A	B
(a) A trachea	cover their respiratory surfaces with a gill cover.
(b) Gills	are the respiratory organs of an insect.
(c) Lungs	is the tube to the lungs in a mammal.
(d) Alveoli	are the respiratory organs of a fish or tadpole.
(e) Tracheae	are the entrance to an insect's respiratory organs.
(f) Spiracles	are the respiratory organs of a mammal or bird.
(g) Fish	are the place where gases are actually exchanged between air and blood in a mammal.

3. The graph shows the changes in volume of air moving in and out of a person's lungs during an experiment.

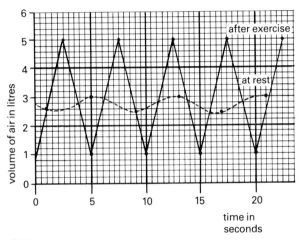

O43

   (a) How many breaths a minute does the person take at rest? And after exercise?
   (b) At rest, what is the volume of air in the lungs at the end of a breath in? and a breath out? So how much air is actually moving in and out of the lungs in each breath?
   (c) Answer the same questions for the breaths taken after exercise.
   (d) Summarize the effects of taking exercise on the patterns of breathing in this person.

4. (a) Draw a graph using this information:

% CO_2 breathed in	0·04	0.80	2.0	3.0	5.0	6.0
Breaths per minute	14	14	15	15	19	27

   (b) What is the effect on increasing carbon dioxide levels on breathing rate?
   (c) Why do you think this happens?

107

Why move?

It's obvious why things move – or is it? Make your own list to check below. (Hint: **moving** is any change in position; **locomotion** is a change in place.)

Here are some of the reasons:

1. Organisms move to collect the raw materials they need to live – such as sunlight and food.

2. They move to get out of problem situations – such as being eaten, or poor weather, or climate changes.

3. They move to avoid overcrowding.

4. And they move for sex.

P1 A lion moves in to catch its prey

Question

Look at the examples of movement below. In each case say what is moving and why.

a)

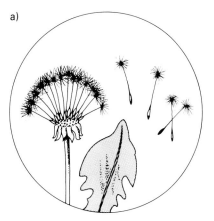

b)

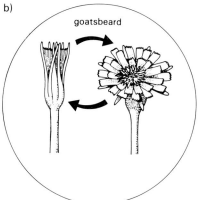

goatsbeard

c)

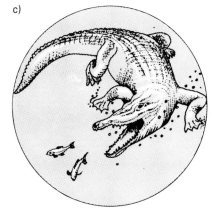

d)

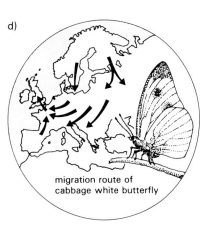

migration route of cabbage white butterfly

e)

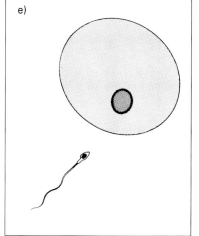

f)

P2

Some organisms 'hitch' lifts to save energy – examples include pollen, some seeds, and gliders.

Many organisms are self-propelled – using lots of energy in the process.

Movement can involve the whole of an organism, or just a part.

Organisms need mechanisms
(a) for movement
(b) for working out where they are going and how far they have got – **sensing changes** – and
(c) for making sure everything works together when it is supposed to – **co-ordination.**

They need an energy supply too.

All this includes green plants, which manage to combine some of their moving with growing.

P3 Flying squirrels are really gliders

a)

b)

mudskipper eyes are good in and out of water

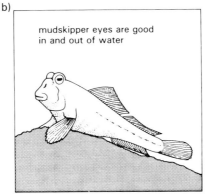

c)

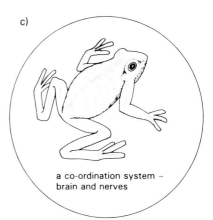

a co-ordination system – brain and nerves

P4 Mechanisms for (a) movement, (b) sensing changes, (c) co-ordinating movement

A bit about wind

Gentle winds are often useful to organisms. Grasses and trees such as oak and elm rely on wind to carry pollen from flower to flower. Many small animals and seeds are dispersed (spread out) by wind.

Strong winds cause problems. Hot desert winds can dry out organisms – another reason why some cacti are fuzzy. Strong mountain winds blow away small weak organisms. There are few mountain insects, and they often have no wings. Crawling among sheltered plants and rocks is safer than flying. The way an organism can and does move is greatly affected by the environment.

P5 Wingless earwig from Kilimanjaro

109

Dispersal - the hitch-hikers

Organisms need space, for growth and for collecting raw materials such as water. Once they have grown roots, plants are stuck in one spot – it is their seeds that travel. This spreading out is known as **dispersal**. Any part of a plant which is dispersed is called a **propagule**. Animals must disperse, too. They can usually move themselves, perhaps in different ways at different stages in their lives. Some, like seeds, rely on help. How do they manage?

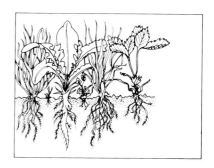

P6 Plants compete for space, light and water

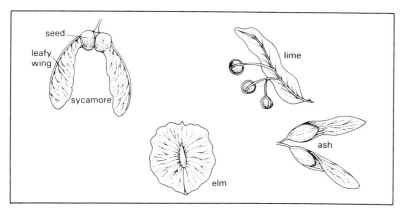

P7 Wings

The most popular way to hitch a lift is by **wind.**

Small seeds float away, and so do fungal spores and bacteria. All these propagules are light. Heavier ones may have **wings** or **parachutes.**

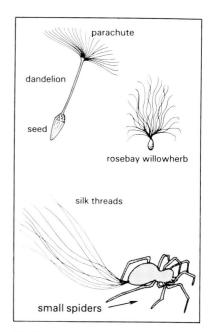

P8 Parachutes

Both parachutes and wings catch the wind and hold the seed in the air longer. Some small animals use the same trick. Money spiders 'balloon' from place to place on silk threads, and aphids ride wind currents from plant to plant.

Some plants help themselves. Poppy heads dry out and sway in the wind. The seeds fall out through small holes which open when the weather is dry.

More excitingly – some plants catapult their seeds away from them. Geraniums do this. The fruit dries and twists suddenly, flinging the seeds out. The wind helps, too.

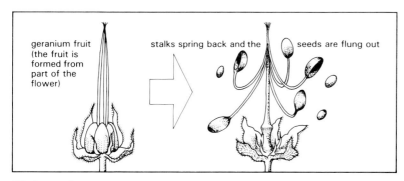

P9 Catapults

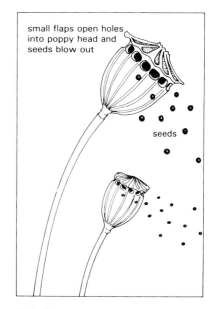

P10 Poppy pepper-pots

Seeds can be carried by **animals**, often when the fruit is eaten. The seed may be dropped – like an apple whose core you throw into a hedge – or it may be eaten as well. Then the seed travels through the gut and out the other end – along with instant manure. Some 'stones' have to be partly digested before the seeds inside can begin to grow out.

Animals which store seeds for food and forget them also help in dispersal. Squirrels are an example.

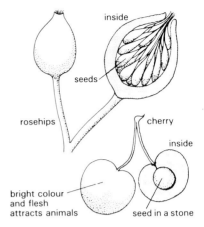

P11 Goodies

And of course there are seeds with hooks – the ones that really do hitch lifts on an animal's fur, a bird's legs and your trousers.

Some small insects use the same trick. There are mites which hitch lifts on locusts' wings and many other examples.

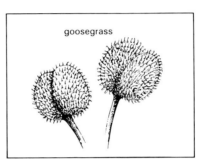
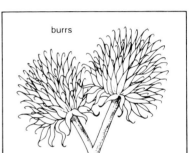

P12 Goosegrass, burrs – and hooks

Lastly, some things are dispersed by **water**.

Life started in water. Seaweeds and other water plants rely on water currents to disperse them. So do many small water animals.

Island plants often travel to other islands by water. Coconuts have a hairy husk which helps them float. They are not damaged by salt water – they travel all over the world. They may also carry small animals like ants with them.

P13 Water travel

Question

Write out the whole paragraph below, filling in the spaces.
Moving from place to place is also called _____.
Movement also includes changes in position – for example, plant leaves turning in order to catch as much _____ as possible.

Other reasons for moving include finding a mate, avoiding _____, finding _____ and escaping from _____. Most organisms use up _____ in moving, but some are carried from place to place by wind, _____ or _____. This is often true in the dispersal of _____, but it is also the way some small animals travel.

111

Single cells and movement

Single cells, on their own or as part of a larger organism, have two (or three) ways of moving – unless they just drift.

Cytoplasmic movements
These keep the contents of plant cells moving. In some cells, the cytoplasm can be seen streaming around the edges. This helps mix up materials in the cell. Some people think threads of cytoplasm connect cells, and things like sugars can be passed from cell to cell in this way.

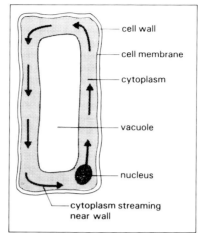

P15 Cytoplasmic streaming

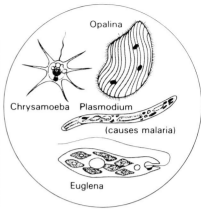

P14 Some single celled organisms. PS: You'd need a microscope to see all these cells

Cytoplasmic streaming can move cells from place to place. White blood cells and animals like Amoeba travel this way. They live in liquids (water, blood and so on) but usually move on a surface.

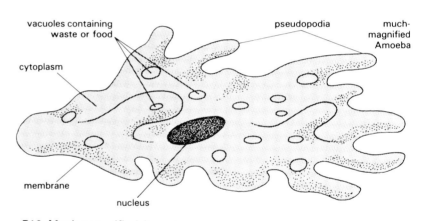

P16 Much-magnified Amoeba

The large projections are called **pseudopodia**. They are important in moving and in trapping food. Pseudopodia are temporary – always being formed and then disappearing. They are produced by cytoplasmic streaming.

These cells seem to change their cytoplasm from being jelly-like to being quite runny. The runny and jelly parts move against each other to move the cell. This uses up energy. It is not certain exactly how Amoeba and white blood cells move.

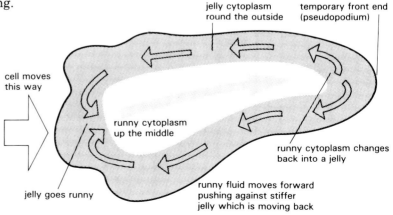

P17 Cytoplasmic streaming in Amoeba

112

Flagella and cilia – the moving threads

These are thread-like and they beat against the liquid around them, pushing or pulling the cell along. They allow cells to move freely in liquids like water and blood. They differ in size and numbers.

Flagella come in ones and twos, and are long compared to their cell.

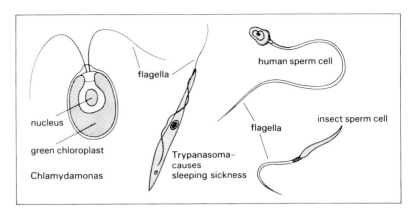

P18 Organisms with flagella (magnified)

Cilia are smaller and are found in large groups. They beat in rhythm, and in action look like a field of grass rippling in the wind.

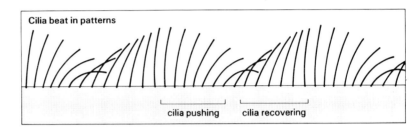

P19 Cilia beat in patterns (enormously magnified)

Single celled organisms like Paramecium have cilia for moving and food collecting. Larger organisms find other uses for cilia. The cells lining the air passage in your lungs use cilia to help remove particles of dirt.

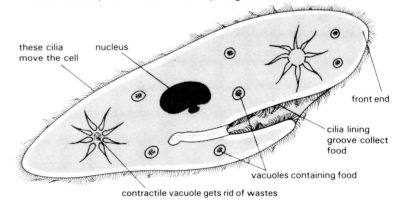

P20 A paramecium from a pond (much magnified)

Questions

1. Name
   (a) one cell you're sure is a plant, and say why (don't use the plant cell diagram for cytoplasmic movement)
   (b) two single cell organisms (not parts of organisms) moved by flagella
   (c) one organism in which cytoplasmic movement is important. How does cytoplasmic streaming work (as far as we know)?
   (d) two organisms which move by cilia. Explain how cilia work – diagrams may help. What can they be used for besides locomotion?

2. Draw and add two labels (as well as the name) to
   (a) a seed dispersed by wind
   (b) a seed dispersed by animals
   (c) a self-propelled seed
   Explain why these kinds of dispersal are so important to green plants. Write at least four sentences.
   (d) an animal dispersed by wind

Muscles and soft-bodied animals

Larger animals rely on muscles for movement. Muscles use up energy when they **contract** – become short and fat – and pull against something. For soft-bodied animals that something is water.

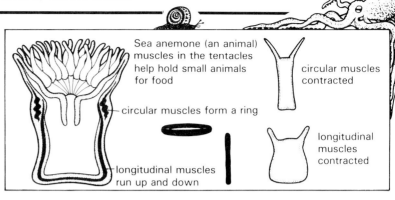

Sea anemone (an animal) muscles in the tentacles help hold small animals for food

circular muscles contracted

circular muscles form a ring

longitudinal muscles contracted

longitudinal muscles run up and down

P21

In most movements two sets of muscles are needed, one to do and one to undo. They act in turn. When one set is contracted, the other **relaxes** – allows itself to be pulled out long and thin again. Such alternating muscles are called **antagonistic muscles**. Pairs of antagonistic muscles move animals like the earthworm. In this case the water they push against is inside the animal.

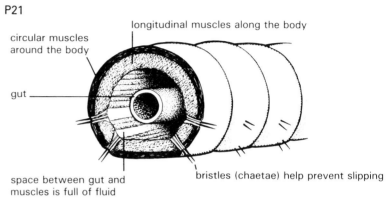

circular muscles around the body

longitudinal muscles along the body

gut

space between gut and muscles is full of fluid

bristles (chaetae) help prevent slipping

P22 Muscles in an earthworm (this just shows three segments)

The circular and longitudinal muscles take it in turns to contract and make a pattern of waves down the worm's body.

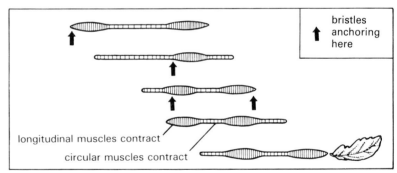

bristles anchoring here

longitudinal muscles contract

circular muscles contract

The bristles anchor different parts of the worm as needed.

P23 Top view of worm moving

Questions

1. Leeches are soft-bodied animals which can move by looping (see right). They have circular and longitudinal muscles which act antagonistically in their body wall. Which are contracted in A and which in C?

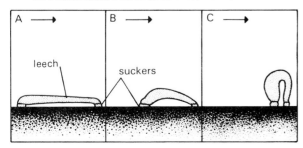

A

leech

B

suckers

C

P24

2. Explain what is meant by the following – and give an example in each case:
   (a) dispersal
   (b) propagule
   (c) antagonistic muscles
   (d) cytoplasmic streaming
   (e) pseudopodium

3. Draw and label
   (a) Amoeba
   (b) Paramecium
   (c) a section through an earthworm
   What is the big difference (in your opinion) between the movement of the earthworm and movement in Amoeba and Paramecium?

Muscles and bones

Vertebrates – animals with bones – have something solid for muscles to pull on. Here are a pair of antagonistic muscles in the human arm. The **biceps** flexes the lower arm – pulls it up – when it contracts. The **triceps** extends or straightens the arm. Try it.

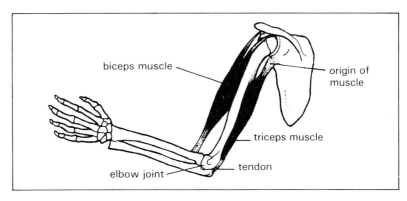

P25 Muscles and bones

Like many muscles, the triceps and biceps are attached to bone by **tendons.**

Muscles (meat) are red. They have a good blood supply – they do a lot of work. Tendons are white, tough and non-stretchy. Live bone is pinkish – there's a lot going on inside (including making red blood cells).

There are two main kinds of muscle cell.

Striated muscle has long muscle cells with many nuclei. It looks stripey under a microscope. It's the muscle you can choose to use – or not.

Smooth muscle has no stripes and one nucleus in each cell. This kind of muscle is found in the walls of guts, blood vessels and the uterus – you don't consciously control it.

Both kinds of muscle use lots of energy and have a good blood supply. They are also carefully controlled – even if you're not aware of it. It hurts when things go wrong. Tetanus happens when all the muscles of the body contract together. It is caused by a toxin (poison) made by a bacterium. It's not only painful – both sets of breathing muscles cancel each other, so you can't breathe. Other systems also fail and you die. Could anti-tetanus jabs be a good idea?

Muscles and bones act as a lever system to move loads.

All is well as long as bones don't bend, joints don't seize up, and your muscles can provide enough pull.

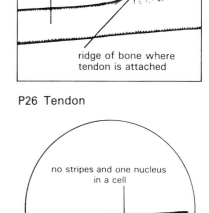

P26 Tendon

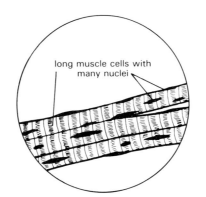

P27 Smooth muscle

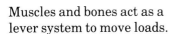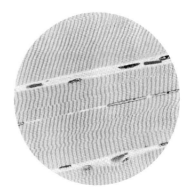

P28 Striated muscle

115

Bones and joints

Bone is strong and light. **Strength** comes from the material and from the way it is arranged. Bone is made of calcium salts held together by fibres of collagen (a protein). **Lightness** comes from using as little solid bone as possible.

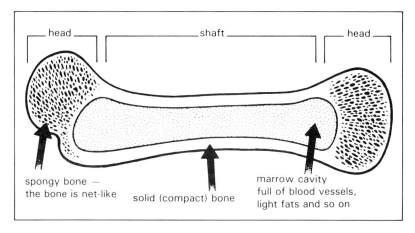

P29 Section through a long bone

Short bones may be a thin shell of solid bone around spongy bone. Saw a vertebra in half and see.

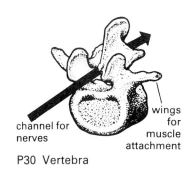

P30 Vertebra

Even solid bone isn't solid. Running through it are blood vessels surrounded by bone-making cells. Bones need constant repair. If bone cells die, as they do as people get older, bones become brittle.

Bones grow, often from cartilage-like pre-bones. **Cartilage** proper is found in the ear and end of the nose. It is quite flexible (it has no calcium salts). In bones, cartilage is gradually replaced by bone – starting in the middle of the shaft.

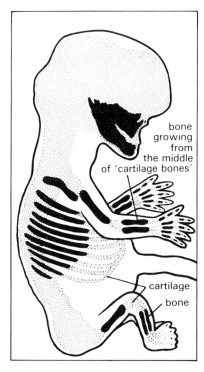

P31 9-week human fetus

Bone doesn't stretch. For a marrow cavity to grow, bone must grow on the outside while material is removed from the inside.

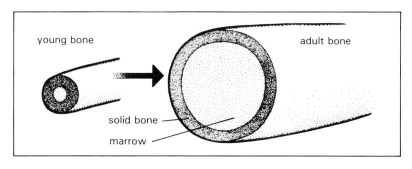

P32 Bone growth

116

Joints happen where bones meet. They are often made to allow movement. The basic synovial or moveable joint looks like Fig. P33.

Cartilage provides a smooth surface with a bit of give.
Synovial membrane lines the joint. It makes synovial fluid.
Synovial fluid fills the small space between the bone heads. It acts as a lubricant and reduces friction.
Capsule helps hold the joint together. There are also ligaments (not shown) doing this job.

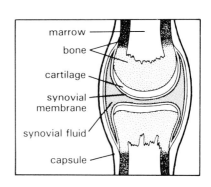

P33 Section through a joint

Joints move in various ways. The simplest movement is gliding, where one bone slides across another. Gliding joints are found between some of the bones of the hands and feet. In other joints, movement may be more complicated. Four other types of joint are shown in Fig. P34.

Cartilagenous joints
These allow a limited amount of movement. They are not synovial joints.

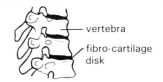

Example: between the vertebrae, where disks act as shock absorbers.

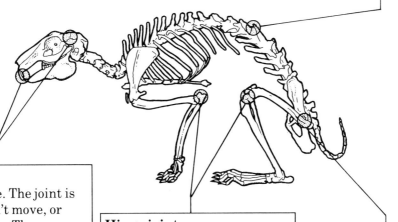

Fixed joints
Bone meets bone. The joint is strong but doesn't move, or only gives a little. These aren't synovial joints.

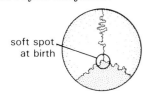

(Skull bones are not quite fixed at birth, to allow easier delivery.)
Examples: bones of skull, teeth in jaw.

Hinge joints
Bones fit neatly together and act like a door hinge. The joint moves backwards and forwards but not sideways.

Examples: joints between finger bones, knee joint.

Ball and socket joints
The joint allows a lot of movement – this type is most likely to dislocate.

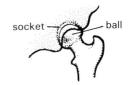

Examples: hip and shoulder joints.

P34 Types of joint

The human skeleton

The skeleton is a collection of bones which supports soft organs like the guts; protects delicate ones like lungs, brain and kidneys; and provides something for muscles to pull on.

X-rays show up bone structure. They can go through soft tissues but not through the calcium salts in bones.

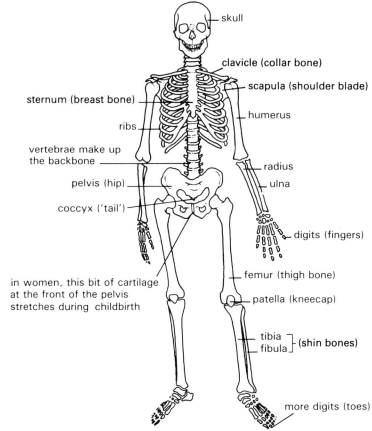

skull

clavicle (collar bone)

scapula (shoulder blade)

sternum (breast bone)

humerus

ribs

vertebrae make up the backbone

radius

ulna

pelvis (hip)

coccyx ('tail')

digits (fingers)

in women, this bit of cartilage at the front of the pelvis stretches during childbirth

femur (thigh bone)

patella (kneecap)

tibia
fibula } (shin bones)

more digits (toes)

P35 Male skeleton

The bones of the skeleton can be divided into two groups: the **axial** skeleton, based on the backbone, and the **appendages**.

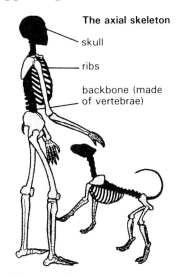

The axial skeleton

skull

ribs

backbone (made of vertebrae)

and the appendages

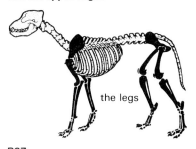

the legs

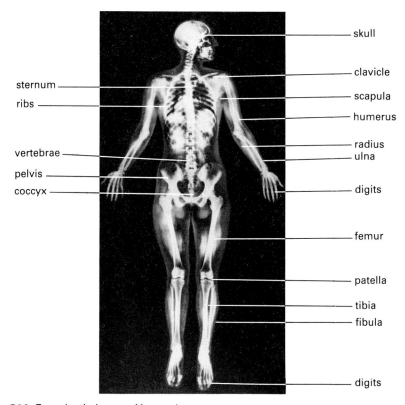

skull

clavicle

scapula

humerus

sternum

ribs

radius
ulna

vertebrae

pelvis

coccyx

digits

femur

patella

tibia

fibula

digits

P36 Female skeleton – X-rayed

Summary and questions

Summary

All living things move – that is, change their position in some way. Dispersal involves moving to new places to prevent overcrowding. Many organisms move themselves; others (especially the seed plants) take advantage of wind, water and animal movements. Active movement comes in many forms. Single cells move either as the result of the beating of hair like flagella or cilia, or by cytoplasmic movement. Many-celled animals use muscles which contract and pull against something – body fluids in the case of worms. Paired muscles contract and relax in turn to produce complete movements and are known as antagonistic muscles.

In vertebrates, the body is supported and protected by bones (plus cartilage). They are arranged as a skeleton, made up of an axial skeleton plus appendages. Bones are strong and light. Muscles move the body by pulling on the bones, which act as levers. Joints – where bones move against each other – are designed for strength and reducing friction. There are three main kinds of joint: fixed, cartilagenous and synovial joints. Synovial joints include gliding joints, ball and socket joints and hinge joints. Each of these allows a different kind of movement.

Questions

1. Consider the following muscles and bones:

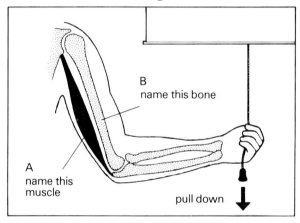

B name this bone

A name this muscle

pull down

P38

    (a) Name muscle A.
    (b) Name bone B.

2. Explain the difference between each of these pairs:
    (a) the biceps and triceps
    (b) solid (compact) bone and spongy bone
    (c) bone and cartilage
    (d) the axial skeleton and appendages
    (e) smooth and striated muscles

3. (a) Draw a hinge joint. Give two examples of this kind of joint.
    (b) Draw a ball and socket joint. Give two examples of this kind of joint.
    (c) Draw a diagram to show how a muscle is attached to a bone.

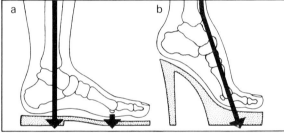

a   b

P39

4. The diagrams show which bones take the body mass when different kinds of shoe are worn. It is often said that very high heels cause foot troubles – do the diagrams support this idea? Explain your answer.

5. Explain why each of these is true:
    (a) Synovial fluid is important for easy movement.
    (b) Bones like vertebrae have large projections sticking out.
    (c) There is a lot of space inside bones.
    (d) The skull bones of new born babies haven't completely fused (stuck together). They can still slide a bit.
    (e) Diseases like arthritis and osteoarthritis are very painful.
    (f) X-rays show up bones.

Walking and running

Legs keep the body off the ground.

Short splayed legs (attached on the sides) mean slow moving.

Legs placed under the body mean speed. It helps if they're long.

Once off the ground and on four legs an animal becomes rather like a bridge.

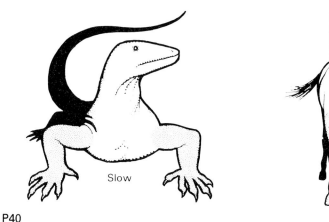

P40

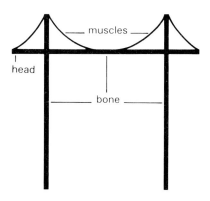

P41 Four legged animals when raised off the ground are like bridges

Many small runners and jumpers have bendy backbones. The flexible spine means extra spring for extra speed. Rabbits and greyhounds are like this.

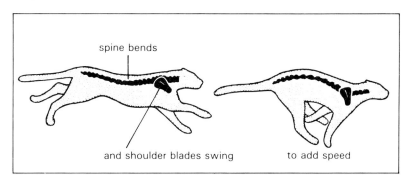

P42 Flexible spines mean speed

Larger and heavier animals like horses have a stiffer backbone – luckily for us. Their speed comes from long legs.

Some speeds for short distances
cheetah – 50 mph +
greyhound – 40 mph
racehorse – 40 mph
black mamba – 7 mph
(that's fast for a snake)

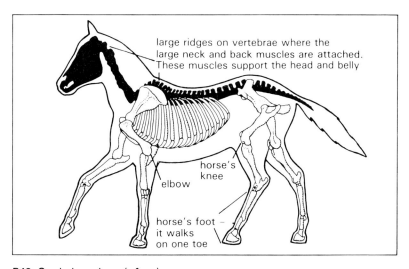

P43 So do long legs (often)

However, the larger you get, the easier it is to break your legs as you run – why?

One problem is that bones are bones – whatever size they are, the material is the same. A large animal like the elephant has enormously thick leg bones, and needs them.

A rabbit the size of an elephant would collapse – its bones would be crushed by its own weight. Body mass increases faster than leg size. The body mass of a large animal is more than its bones and muscles can support, unless it has extra thick bones like the elephant. (That's why *really* large animals – whales – live in the sea, where the water supports them.) An elephant's legs are strong enough for running but aren't springy enough for jumping. It's quite safe to keep elephants in zoos with only a ditch between them and the visitors.

rabbit blown up to same size as elephant

P44 Large animals have to have large bones

Human beings are among the few animals to walk upright for much of their lives. It's meant changes to muscles and bones, especially in the foot and back. Some changes are not complete, which is why people have hip and back trouble as they get older – and feet ache if they are badly treated. Changes in the pelvis mean birth is more difficult for humans than for other animals. Babies have to turn a corner to get out, instead of having a straightforward slide helped by gravity.

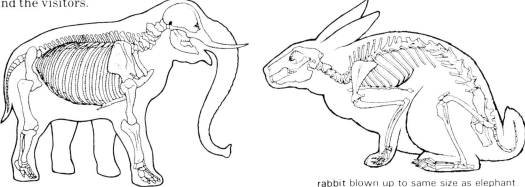

extra curve near the bottom of the backbone in an adult

curve changes

arched foot (apes and monkeys have flat feet)

baby's spinal column (backbone) curves very like that of any other fourfooted animal

P45 Changes in spine curvature with age

121

Flying

You've always wanted to fly? Well, you'll have to make some changes.

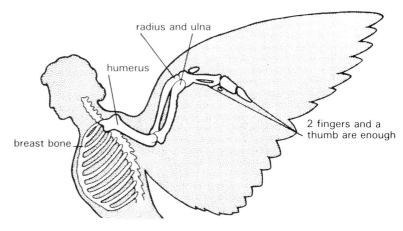

P46 First transformation

1. You'll need a **large surface** to push against the air. Bats use skin, birds have feathers. Either way your arm bones will have to change.

2. You'll need **muscles** to move your flying surface. Birds have a large keel instead of a flat breast bone for attaching their flight (breast) muscles. You'll need a keel sticking out over a metre in front of you. At least a third of your weight will be flight muscles.

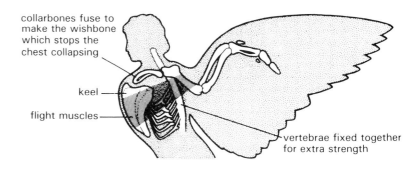

P47 Second transformation

3. You'll have to **lose weight.** Birds have many hollow bones.

4. Ways of saving weight might include giving up half your sex organs, sweat glands and jaw. Birds do it. You could also get smaller. **Air spaces** are useful in breathing. Air sacs in them can open off the lungs and help gas exchange. A large heart helps. Flight muscles need a lot of fuel

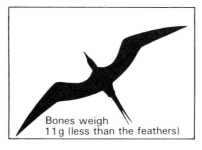

P48 Frigate birds are over 2 metres wingtip to wingtip and weigh the same as a chicken

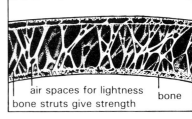

P49 Slice through the long bone of a bird

5. To avoid a nose-dive, reduce the size of your head. Some of your brain will have to go. The rule is: develop the bits you need for flying and shrink the rest.

6. You'll be warmer with feathers all over. Balancing is easier with tail feathers. Claws are better for landing than flat feet, and you'll need strong walking muscles, attached to your feet by long tendons.

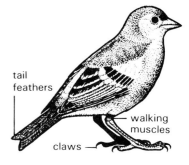

P50 No comment

Question

Draw your own third, fourth and so on transformations. What do you end up with?

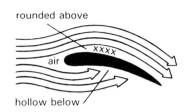

Flying

Learning to use the equipment takes practice. Flying involves keeping up and going forward. **Keeping up** is easy. The shape of the wing near the body does it – like an aeroplane wing (Fig. P51).

Air going **over** the wing speeds up. The result is low pressure (at xxxx) which pulls the wing up. This is called lift.

rounded above

xxxx

air

hollow below

P51 Section through a wing

Going forward. The wing-tips flick back and down much faster than the rest of the wing, and push the bird along.

tip flick

end of power (pushing) stroke

recovery stroke

start of power stroke (wing comes back and down)

P52 Flying

Flying speeds

Wing shapes and feather patterns vary with flying speed (Figs P53 and P54). Why do vultures go in for slow soaring and swifts for rapid dives?

narrow swept-back wings (less drag)

P53 100 mph – swifts

wide pinion feathers keep a bird steady at slow speeds

big broad wings

P54 Slow soaring – vultures

Feather type

There are pinion feathers, down feathers and several types in between. They are all made from much-changed skin cells.

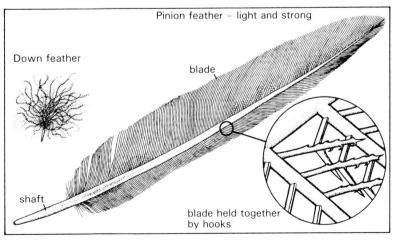

Pinion feather – light and strong

Down feather

blade

shaft

blade held together by hooks

P55 Feathers

Swimming

Fish push water backwards – mainly with their tails – and end up moving forwards themselves.

The backbone acts as a chain of levers which can move from side to side. (In swimming mammals like whales, the backbone moves up and down.) The final powerful flick of the tail is the end result of a wave of muscle contractions moving down the body.

The muscles are arranged in blocks or segments and fit neatly together. Fast fish are more muscular than slow ones and make better eating.

Fast fish are also more streamlined. Water slows moving objects by swirling around them and by sticking to them (friction). The result is called drag. Ways of reducing drag vary with speed but a smooth outline helps – and smooth scales.

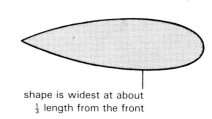

a streamlined shape

shape is widest at about ⅓ length from the front

P56 A streamlined shape

    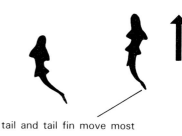

tail and tail fin move most

P57 Swimming movements

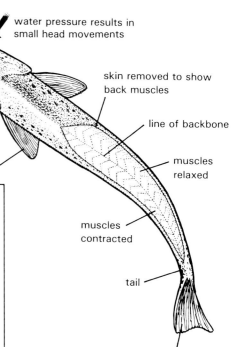

water pressure results in small head movements

skin removed to show back muscles

line of backbone

muscles relaxed

fins supported by cartilage

muscles contracted

tail

tail fin

P58 Fish showing the patterns of the back muscles

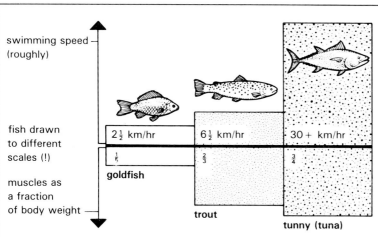

swimming speed (roughly)

fish drawn to different scales (!)

muscles as a fraction of body weight

2½ km/hr	6½ km/hr	30 + km/hr
$\frac{1}{5}$	$\frac{2}{3}$	$\frac{3}{4}$
goldfish	trout	tunny (tuna)

P59 More muscle means greater speed

Control is the job of the fins, apart from the tail fins. The main brakes are the **pectoral fins**, with help from the **pelvic fins** in rapid halts. The pectoral fins alone might have an effect like stopping a bike suddenly using only the front brakes.

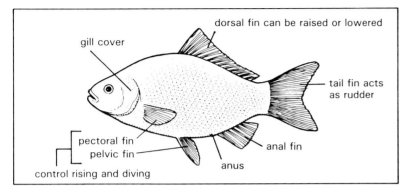

P60 Fins from the side

Keeping up. Muscle, bone and cartilage are heavier than water. Sharks, all cartilage and flesh, have to swim all the time or they sink. Bony fish (most of the ones you eat) have a float inside them – a **swim bladder** full of air (mostly oxygen) which opens off the gut.

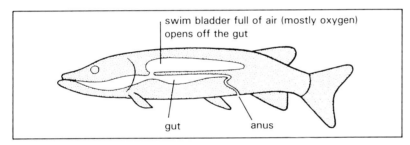

P62 Swim bladder (fish in section)

Fish can control the amount of air in the swim bladder so that they balance exactly.

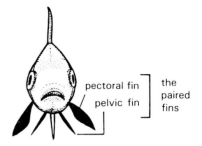

P61 Fins from the front

Rolling movements are also controlled by the paired fins – with help from the **anal** and **dorsal** fins, adjustable up-and-down fins. They act rather like a boat's keel, and also prevent side-to-side swings or yawing.

Fins can change their job and do the pushing in some fish. They can also be used for protection.

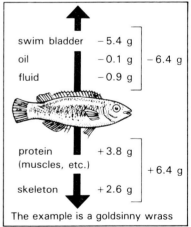

P63 The swim bladder is part of the reason a fish stays up

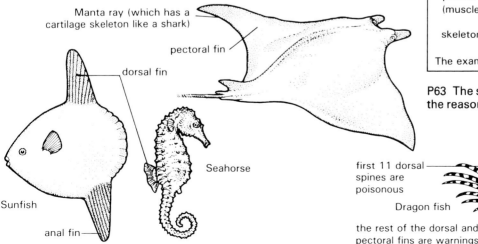

P64 Fin styles

Green plants and support

Plant cells have walls around them made of cellulose fibres, which don't stretch in mature cells.

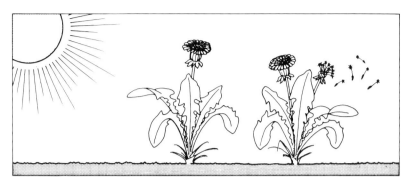

P65

Plants need to hold up leaves, flowers and fruits, so support matters.
They have a system based on the cell.

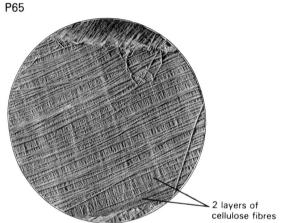

2 layers of cellulose fibres

P66 Much-magnified view of the surface of a plant cell

Because it has a cellulose cell wall, a plant cell can be held rigid by pressure from inside, rather like a car tyre. An animal cell would burst. Instead of air, water does the pushing. The pressure per square centimetre is about 2½ times the pressure in a tyre. It's called **turgor** pressure. A cell full of water is said to be **turgid**.

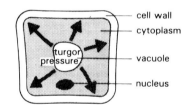

cell wall
cytoplasm
vacuole
nucleus
turgor pressure

Without enough water to keep up the pressure, a plant wilts.

this plant's cells are **not** turgid!

P67

Some cells have extra strengthening materials laid down in various patterns, such as rings or spirals, or in cell corners. Some of the patterns are more complicated.

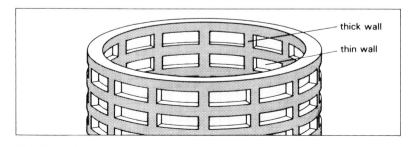

thick wall
thin wall

P68 Part of a tube-shaped cell

Strengthened cells often do two jobs – they give support, and they transport materials like water. They are grouped in **vascular bundles** in stems, roots and leaves. It's like the steel in reinforced concrete – great strength for as little weight as possible.

Heavier plants need more support. Vascular bundles join up and develop into wood – which does not rely on full turgor pressure (its cells don't have to be full of water).

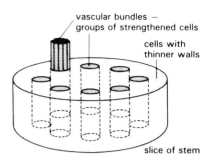

P69 Slice of stem

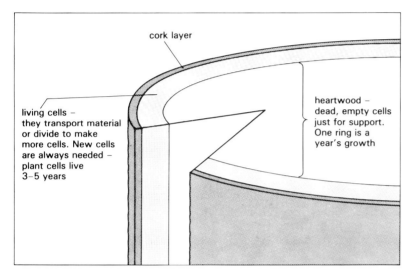

P70 The layers of a tree trunk

In tropical rain forests most nutrients are near the surface of the soil. The tree roots, therefore, are also fairly shallow. Really tall trees may need extra support. They have huge buttress roots which may grow four metres out. You may find small buttresses holding up alder trees in a swamp area.

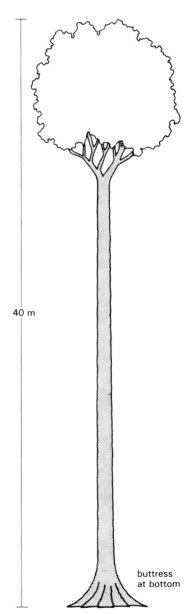

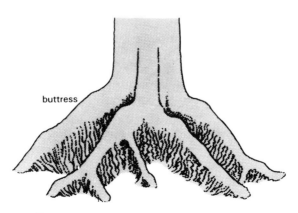

P71 Buttress roots

127

Green plants and movement

Most plants, at least as adults, are firmly fixed in place. Only parts of them move. There are two ways that they do it.

1. Growth movements
These can be movements away from things or towards them.

Shoots grow towards light.

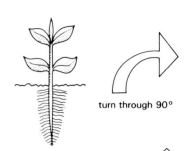
turn through 90°

Shoots grow away from gravity, roots towards it.

P72 Movement towards light

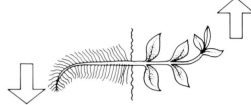

P73 Movement and gravity

Directional growth (**tropic movement**) involves tips of roots or shoots. Cells in the sides of the tip grow at different rates to cause tropic movements. These movements are controlled by chemicals called hormones. More on page 158.

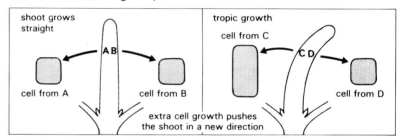

P74 Movement as the result of growth

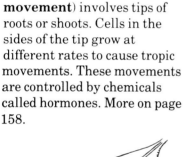

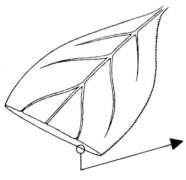

P75 Reversible movements by stomata

2. Reversible movements
These are due to temporary changes in cells. Water can be pumped in and out of cells. This is how guard cells open and close pores in leaves.

Movements like this are important in plants where the flowers or leaves open and close during a day. They work the same way in the leaf-collapsing sensitive mimosa.

Some cells in the mimosa act as hinges. When they lose water and collapse, the leaf flops. Pumping water back into the cells takes longer (and it needs energy).

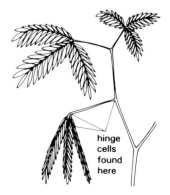
hinge cells found here

P76

Exoskeletons – or living in armour

There are many (more than a million) types of animals with soft insides and hard outsides, or **exoskeletons**. Exoskeletons are built of **chitin**, which is layered like plywood. They have three main advantages:

(a) they are very strong
(b) they protect soft tissues
(c) they stop the animal drying out on land

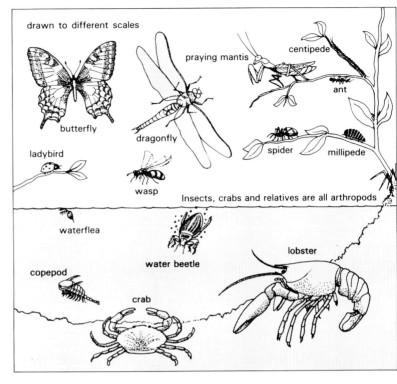

P77 Animals with exoskeletons

Joints are different in structure but act rather like hinge joints. A crab's claw has several, so it can move in different directions. (See Fig. P78.)

Exoskeletons don't stretch. In order to grow, an animal has to shed a layer of chitin and grow while the next layer is hardening. It's a dangerous time and needs a lot of energy. Another problem is that large exoskeletons must be thick and heavy, if they aren't to buckle. Only well-fed crabs and lobsters supported by water get very large.

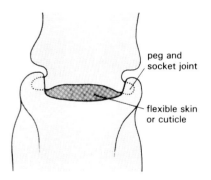

P78 A crab's joint

Muscles pull on the exoskeleton in antagonistic pairs – though the layout is a little different from that in vertebrates.

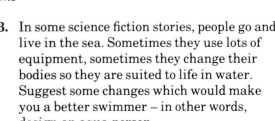

P79 Comparing joints

Questions

1. From the movement point of view, would you rather be an animal with an exoskeleton, or a plant? Why?

2. Why aren't there wasps the size of elephants (as in the monster movies)?

3. In some science fiction stories, people go and live in the sea. Sometimes they use lots of equipment, sometimes they change their bodies so they are suited to life in water. Suggest some changes which would make you a better swimmer – in other words, design an aqua-person.

Summary and questions

Summary
Organisms with backbones walk, run, fly and swim. They all have the same basic skeleton, but the shape and size of their bones depends upon their way of life. Large animals have large bones for strength, flyers have light hollow bones and so on. They all use muscles to move bone (or cartilage) 'levers' so that they push against something – the ground, air or water. Some animals are streamlined and muscled for speed, but many others do very well at slower speeds.

Arthropods have exoskeletons of chitin around their soft tissues. Muscle attachments and joints are different from those of endoskeletons (inside skeletons, of bone or cartilage) but they produce similar movements. Chitin is light and strong in small animals. The amount needed for larger animals rapidly becomes very heavy. Plant support is based on the reinforced cellulose cell wall – this allows water pressure to hold small plants up. Further reinforced cells – wood – hold up larger plants. Plant movements are either tropic (growth) movements, or small reversible changes due to water being moved in and out of cells.

Questions

1. Explain the difference between
   (a) an endoskeleton and an exoskeleton
   (b) antagonistic muscles in an insect's leg and antagonistic muscles in a man's leg
   (c) a peg and socket joint, and a ball and socket joint
   (d) turgid and flaccid

2. Why can't
   (a) a mouse be the size of an elephant?
   (b) an elephant jump?
   (c) swifts fly slowly?
   (d) goldfish swim fast?

3. Explain the difference between
   (a) pectoral and pelvic fins
   (b) anal and dorsal fins
   (c) paired fins and other fins
   (d) the spine movements of a whale and a trout
   (e) pinion and down feathers
   (f) the blade and shaft of a feather
   (g) the appendages of a fish and a bird

4. Say whether (and why) you would expect
   (a) manta rays to have swim bladders
   (b) dragon fish to be fast swimmers
   (c) frigate birds to fly slowly easily
   (d) a rhinoceros to run but not jump
   (e) a flounder (living on the sea bottom) to be streamlined
   (f) feathers to have hollow shafts

5. Explain the following:
   (a) Antagonistic muscles are important in the movement of fish.
   (b) Both fish and birds need to be streamlined if they are to move fast.
   (c) The tail fin is not important for forward movement in fish like sea horses and manta rays.
   (d) A bird has an enlarged breastbone called a keel.
   (e) Birds have many hollow bones.
   (f) Animals that move fast often make good food.

6. In your own words explain how
   (a) a bird keeps up
   (b) a bird moves forward in the air
   (c) a fish moves up and down in the water

7. (a) What parts of a plant need to be held in the air and why?
   (b) How do the cells on each side of a shoot bending towards light differ?
   (c) Why don't the insides of an arthropod ooze out at the joints?
   (d) Why is the extra supporting material in some cell walls arranged in rings or honeycombs instead of solid sheets?

8. Reinforced concrete has iron rods inside it which give it strength. It was invented by a gardener called Joseph Monier. It is quite likely that he got the idea from the plants he worked with. Explain how that might be.

Control

It's no good being able to move if you don't know where you're going, or control your movements.

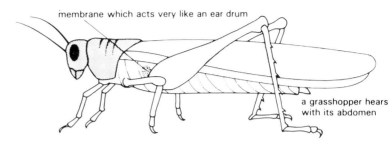

Q1 Organisms have receptors

The next section is about controlling movement. Cells in general are sensitive to changes around them. Large organisms need the following things:

(a) Special organs sensitive to changes – for example, receivers to tell the difference between light and dark or to pick up noises. Such organs are called **receptors**.
(b) Organs to sort the information and make decisions about what to do. The brain and spinal cord do this in more advanced animals. Insects have bundles of nerves rather than a true brain.
(c) A way of sending messages – whether it's information to the brain or orders to the muscles. The job is done by nerves and chemicals called hormones.

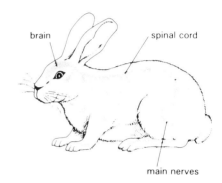

Q2 And organs to sort information

The next few pages are about **receptors.** They look rather different, but they all have
(a) a nerve link to the brain
(b) a good blood supply (even if it's not shown on the diagram)
(c) sensitive cells

Receptors are often in an animal's head (near the brain), pointing in the direction the animal is moving in, and well protected. Animals without brains, such as insects, may have sense organs in unusual places – 'ears' in the legs or wings, for example.

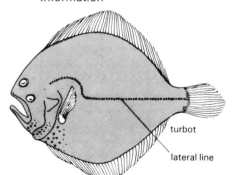

Q3 Lateral lines detect pressure changes

Something which triggers a receptor is known as a **stimulus** (plural: stimuli).

Stimulus	Receptor
light	eyes
sound	ears
pressure	pressure receptors in skin, and lateral line in fish
gravity	sacculus and utriculus in ears (more later)
head movements	semi-circular canals in ears
chemicals in air	nose
chemicals in food	tongue

This list doesn't cover everything.
We have receptors for heat and cold in our skin. (Rattlesnakes can detect infra-red (warmth) and catch mice in the dark.) Our muscles have stretch receptors to check how far they move. There are nerve endings which signal pain when they are stimulated.

131

Skin is a sense organ

Receptors in the skin are nerve endings, wrapped in various ways.

This skin is from the fingers, so no hair is shown. The layer below the epidermis is the **dermis** and below that (just under the pressure receptors) is a layer of fat cells. Blood vessels have been left out.

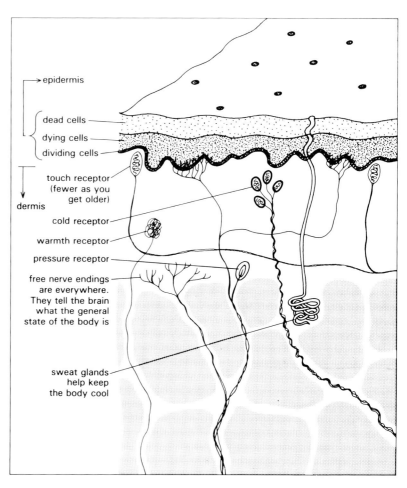

Q4 A section through skin

Choose an ideal injection site

The more receptors in an area of skin, the more sensitive it is. Find the area with the fewest.

One person lightly touches another (who has their eyes shut) with one or two points of the straw. They guess whether it is one or two points. Look at the sample results (Fig. Q5). Which was the most sensitive area? If I were to try this test I would change the number of times one point was tried. Why?

Question

Look up skin in the index. Use the extra references to draw a large diagram of a section through skin based on the one above but with blood and hair and so on added in.

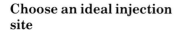

	Sample results			
	Area tested	point separation	right	wrong
bent straw with ends cut to points	upper arm	one point	4	6
		2 mm	1	9
		5 mm	2	8
		7 mm	4	6
		1 cm	3	7
	back of hand	one point	5	5
		2 mm	0	10
		5 mm	5	5
		7 mm	4	6
		1 cm	8	2
vary this distance	ball of thumb	one point	8	2
		2 mm	6	4
		5 mm	8	2
		7 mm	10	0
		1 cm	10	0

Q5 Choosing injection sites

The outside of the eye

Light receptors are delicate things. Eyes are well protected in bony containers with fatty padding and eyelids, plus tears to wash away grit and kill bacteria.

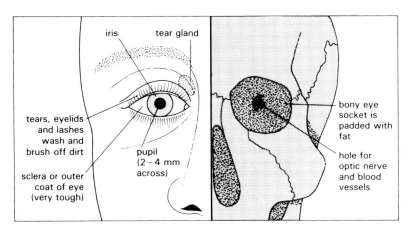

Q6 Eyes are well protected

The eye muscles, attached to the eye and eye socket, swing the eyeball around in its socket. They also keep the eye moving very slightly all the time. The eye is like a TV camera rather than a stills camera. Usually it moves so that light from things you are interested in falls on the middle of the light-sensitive cells inside the eye. The **iris** controls the amount of light entering the eye.

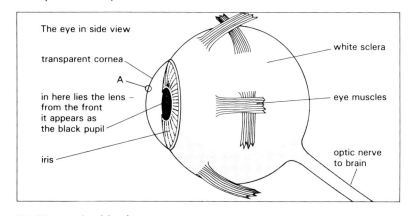

Q7 The eye in side view

The iris contains muscles which control pupil size.

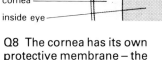

Q8 The cornea has its own protective membrane – the conjunctiva

Pupil contracted	**Pupils dilated**
Can be as little as 1 mm (-) across	Can be 8 mm (——) across

 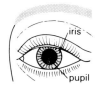

in bright light (helps to protect light-sensitive cells – but sun can still blind you), or with some drugs, e.g. barbiturates and opiates.	in dim light, with strong emotions (fear/sex), or with some drugs, e.g. cocaine.

Q9 The iris controls light entering the eye

colours and spots on the iris are individual, like fingerprints

circular muscles contract and pupil gets smaller (constricts)

radial muscles contract and pupil gets larger (dilates)

pupil

Q10 A close-up of the muscles of the iris

Inside the eye

The light-sensitive cells are the most important structures inside the eye. There are millions of them in mammalian eyes, arranged in a layer called the **retina**. The cells come in two kinds – rods and cones.

Rods
You have about 120 million rod cells. They work best in dim light and cannot detect colour. They are mainly found at the edges of the eye. Night animals have extra rods.

Cones
You have about 7 million cones. They give you colour vision but are not sensitive to dim light. Many are clustered in the middle of the back of your eye. Animals with colourful mates or food are likely to have extra cones.

Other parts of the eye are devoted to making sure a sharp image falls on the retina, to protecting it, and to taking messages from the receptor cells to the brain.

X (Fig. Q12) is the blind spot. It has no sensitive cells – only nerve fibres to the brain. In the centre of the eye is the fovea – the most sensitive part, where most cone cells are.

The **choroid** contains blood vessels which supply the inner eye with food and oxygen. It is dark in colour to absorb light and stop light rays reflecting around inside the eye. The blood vessels leave the eye at the same place as the optic nerve.

The two **humors** fill the eyeball and help keep it in shape. Glaucoma is caused by having too much fluid in the eye. It hurts and can cause blindness if untreated.

Judging distances and looking for danger
Some animals have their eyes on the sides of their heads. As a result they see different things with each eye, and they can see a great deal of the area around them. This is useful to animals which are hunted.

Hunting animals and ones which jump from tree to tree are more likely to have their eyes on the front of the head. This allows them to judge distance. To look at the same object, the eyes have to turn in. The closer the object, the more turning is needed. You'll see this if you look at the tip of your nose. Your brain uses the amount of turning to work out distance. The slightly different views seen by each eye also give a 3-D view of the world.

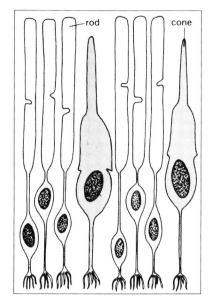

Q11 Light sensitive cells

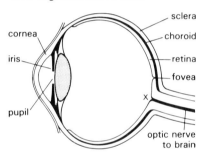

Q12 Section through the eye

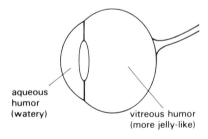

Q13 The two humors

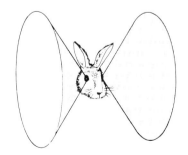

Q14 Rabbits see quite different things with each eye. How much do the fields of vision of your eyes overlap?

Accommodation, or focusing, is important because light from any point you look at is spreading out. Light rays from the point must be bent if you are to see it clearly.

Most of this is done by the cornea, while fine focusing is done by the lens. Light from a distant object needs less bending to focus it. A thinner lens can do the job.

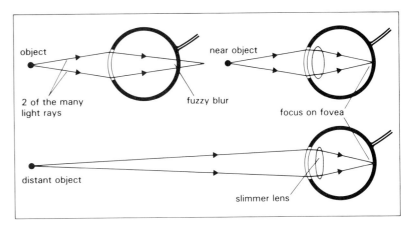

Q15 Focusing involves changing the shape of the lens

When you are young, your lenses are fairly soft and can change shape easily. The shape of the lens depends upon the muscles which hold it in position. It goes stiff with age and the muscles may also become weaker. Because of this, older people may not be able to focus on near objects easily. They need glasses for reading.

The ciliary muscles and accommodation
Near objects
The muscles of the ciliary body contract and pull on the sclera – not the lens. The sclera gives a little and this lessens the pull on the fibres. The lens becomes rounder and can bend light more.

Far objects
The ciliary muscles relax. The scleroid pulls at the fibres. The fibres pull the lens thinner. Light is bent less.

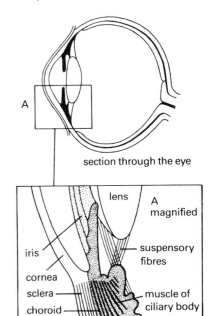

section through the eye

A magnified

Q16 The lens changes shape because of the action of ciliary muscles

Problems may occur if the eyeball is not a perfect sphere.

Long sight – short eyeball
Light from near objects falls behind the retina.
A converging lens helps – it starts bending the light before it reaches the eye.

Short sight – long eyeball
Light from distant objects focuses in front of the retina.
A diverging lens helps – spreads light further out so that it focuses on the retina.

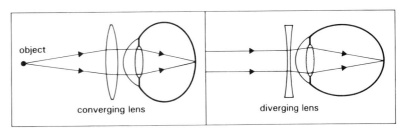

Q17

The ear and sound

Sound is vibration. For us to hear anything, the ear has to change vibrations in air into electrical impulses, signals to the brain. Vibrations in air have to be collected, amplified and finally changed into electrical signals.

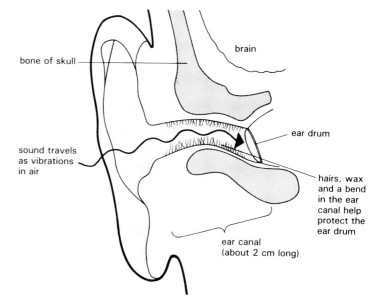

Q18 The human outer ear in section

The outer ear

The outer ear may have a flap which may move to direct sound vibrations to the ear drum. When the sound wave hits the ear drum the stretched skin of the ear drum moves.

Q19 Some animals have no outer ear – just an exposed ear drum

The middle ear

On the inside of the ear drum is a tiny bone, the first in a chain of three which stretch across the air filled bony cave of the middle ear. When the ear drum moves, so do these bones, which act as levers and amplify the movement.

Q20 The middle ear in section

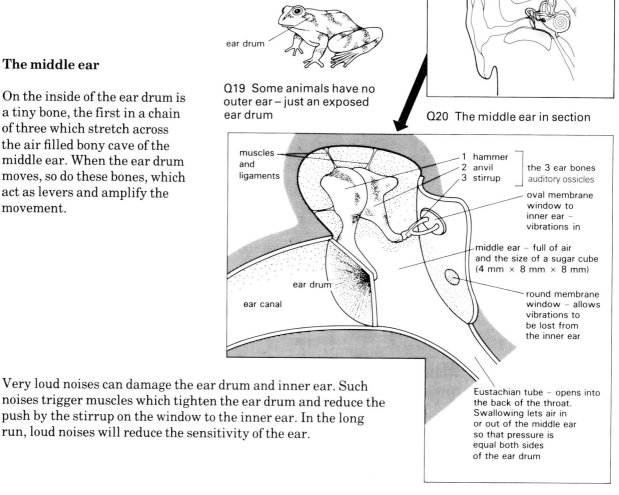

Very loud noises can damage the ear drum and inner ear. Such noises trigger muscles which tighten the ear drum and reduce the push by the stirrup on the window to the inner ear. In the long run, loud noises will reduce the sensitivity of the ear.

Q21 Section through the middle ear to show the ear bones

The inner ear

The last bone in the chain moves a membrane 'window' into the inner ear. The window is part of the wall of the cochlea. The **cochlea** (which means 'snail') is a membrane bag full of fluid, floating in cushioning fluid. It really is snail-shaped – 5 mm high and 9 mm across at the base. As the stirrup moves, the fluid in the cochlea moves. Eventually the movement is lost through another 'window'. On the way the vibration travels through the snail shaped cochlea.

Inside the cochlea are two layers of membrane joined by sensitive cells. The membranes run around the coil of the 'snail'.

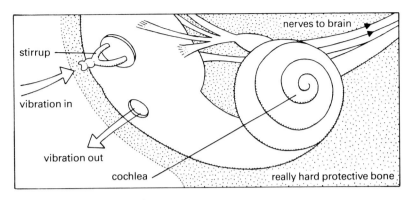

Q22 The 'sound' part of the inner ear

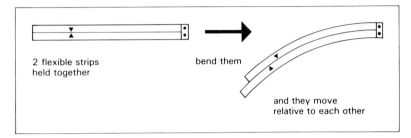

Q23 If two membranes bend, they move against each other

If the membranes bend, they move relative to each other and the hairs are pulled. This triggers the sensitive cells to send a message to the brain.

Membranes near the bottom of the cochlea's coil bounce and bend to the fast vibrations of high noises. Those at the top of the coil move to slow vibrations – low noises.

Young humans can hear frequencies of 20 (low) to 20 000 (high) cycles per second. Many animals can hear much higher noises. They use them for everything from calling mother (baby mice) to working out where they are and where food is (bats).

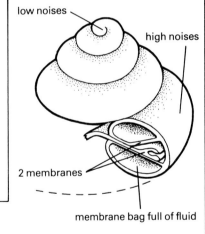

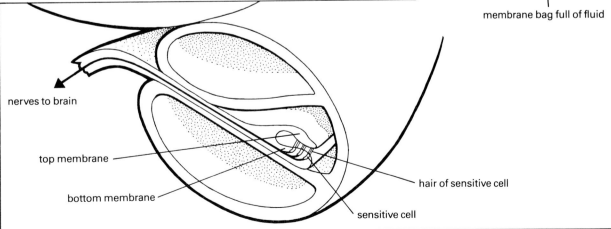

Q24 Inner ear enlarged to show sensitive cells

Chemicals-tasting and smelling

The senses of taste and smell are both involved with chemicals. Chemicals in food are detected mostly in the mouth. Chemicals in the air are picked up by noses – though insects as usual don't follow the rules.

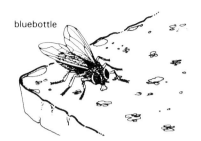

bluebottle

Q25 Bluebottles (blow flies) have chemical receptors in the mouth **and** legs

Smell

Smells vary a lot. It is not clear exactly how the receptors work, but smell is an important part of taste. Try eating mashed apple and mashed onion while holding your nose. It's not easy to tell the difference. Smell matters in sorting good food from bad, in avoiding poisons, and in sex. Some animals find their mates by smell, and for many smell triggers sexual behaviour. (It's important for humans, too.)

Inside, the nose is damp. The chemicals in the air dissolve in a film of liquid on top of the receptor cells. Chemicals which dissolve in fat also trigger the receptor cells. Very small amounts of air-borne chemicals can be picked up.

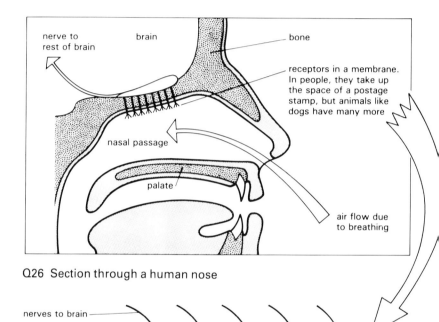

nerve to rest of brain

brain

bone

receptors in a membrane. In people, they take up the space of a postage stamp, but animals like dogs have many more

nasal passage

palate

air flow due to breathing

Q26 Section through a human nose

nerves to brain

nucleus

receptor cell

other supporting cells make up the membrane

fine hairs waving in a water film

Q27 Receptor cells from the nose, enlarged

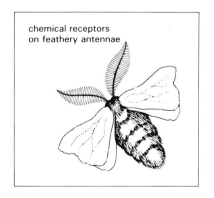

chemical receptors on feathery antennae

Q28 Male silkworm moths can find a female 2 km away by scent alone. Human chemical receptors are not keen by the standards of many animals

Taste

You taste less than you think. Only four basic kinds of flavour really affect the tongue – sour, bitter, sweet and salty.

Not all the tongue is sensitive to chemicals, and some areas are sensitive to particular tastes.

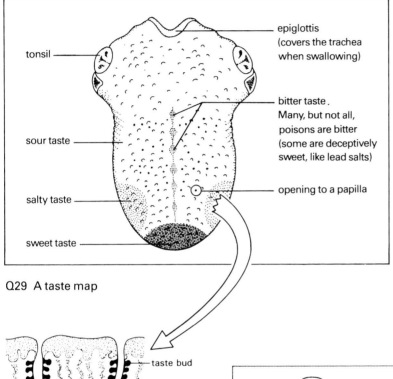

tonsil

epiglottis
(covers the trachea
when swallowing)

bitter taste.
Many, but not all,
poisons are bitter
(some are deceptively
sweet, like lead salts)

sour taste

salty taste

opening to a papilla

sweet taste

Q29 A taste map

Taste map of the tongue
Work out a way of checking your own tongue. This pattern can vary a lot – your tongue may be different.

The receptors are called **taste buds** and are found on the sides of small bumps called **papillae.**

Taste buds are sensitive to chemicals dissolved in water – solid salt has no taste. Taste buds can 'change taste' – perhaps because the cells in them do not live long. New and perhaps different cells are always being added to taste buds as replacements.

taste bud

papilla

Q30 Section through a papilla

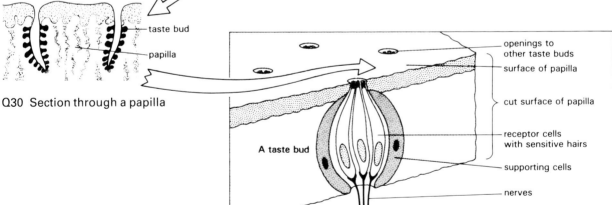

openings to
other taste buds

surface of papilla

cut surface of papilla

A taste bud

receptor cells
with sensitive hairs

supporting cells

nerves

Q31 A taste bud in a papilla

Taste buds don't have to be inside. The sturgeon has taste buds on the underside of its snout. They are used to sense food on the bottom of the river.

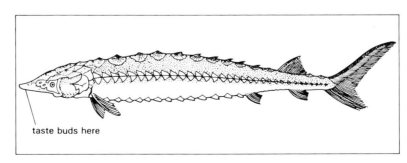

taste buds here

Q32 Sturgeon

Gravity and movement

Gravity

A buried seed has no light to guide it. **Geotropism** – growth in response to gravity – results in shoots growing up and roots growing down.

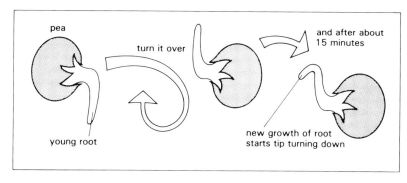

Q33 Plant roots grow 'down'

The response is quite fast. It seems that in plant cells there are particles heavy enough to sink to the bottom of the cell, whichever side that is. This shows the cell which way is down. However, cells can be fooled.

If plants are grown on a turntable, shoots grow towards the centre, roots away from it. From the plant's point of view the middle of the turntable is 'up' and the edge is 'down'.

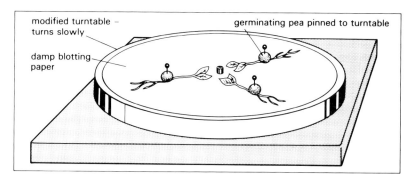

Q34 An experiment involving artificial gravity

Not all stimuli produce tropic reactions

Touch causes mimosa leaves to flop. Venus' fly-traps close on flies. The stimulus is touch, again, but one tap is not enough. The sensitive hairs of the leaf need to be stimulated several times in a short time, quite lightly – just like a fly blundering around on the leaf.

The leaves of plants like chrysanthemums react to the pattern of light and darkness (that is, how long the days are). This triggers the plant to flower at the right season. Covering the growing tips makes no difference – it's the leaves that detect the light periods.

Plants may not have special sense organs but they do have many cells sensitive to stimuli.

They may only be able to respond to stimuli very simply. With light, for example, they may only react to its direction, or to the fact it's there. Many animals do this too, if they only have light-sensitive cells instead of proper eyes.

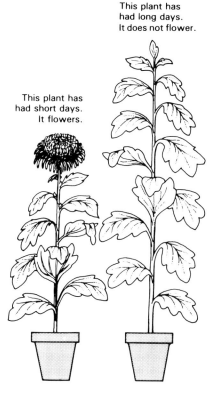

This plant has had long days. It does not flower.

This plant has had short days. It flowers.

Q35 Chrysanthemum growth and day length

The inner ear isn't just used for hearing. It also helps you to keep your balance. When it is confused you become dizzy.

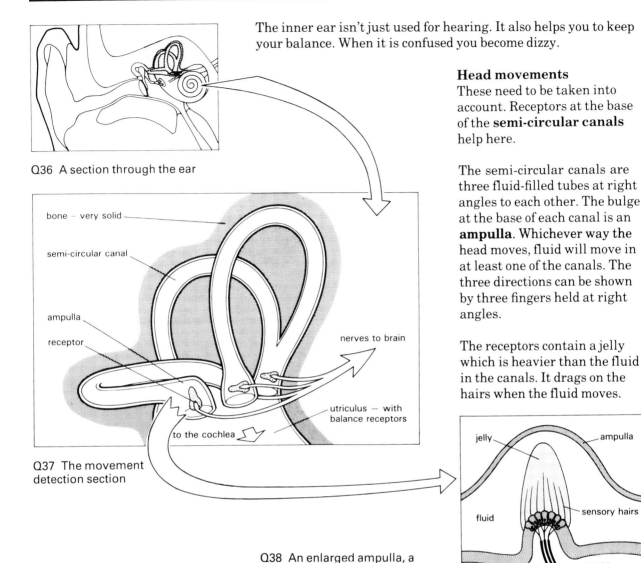

Q36 A section through the ear

Q37 The movement detection section

bone – very solid

semi-circular canal

ampulla

receptor

nerves to brain

utriculus — with balance receptors

to the cochlea

Head movements

These need to be taken into account. Receptors at the base of the **semi-circular canals** help here.

The semi-circular canals are three fluid-filled tubes at right angles to each other. The bulge at the base of each canal is an **ampulla**. Whichever way the head moves, fluid will move in at least one of the canals. The three directions can be shown by three fingers held at right angles.

The receptors contain a jelly which is heavier than the fluid in the canals. It drags on the hairs when the fluid moves.

jelly

ampulla

fluid

sensory hairs

nerves

Q38 An enlarged ampulla, a movement detector.

Which way is down?

The brain answers this question using information from the **utriculus**. Receptors are sensory cells with hairs embedded in a jelly. In the jelly are chalk grains. The chalk grains may be touching the hairs. The amount of touch triggers impulses which tell the brain which way up you are.

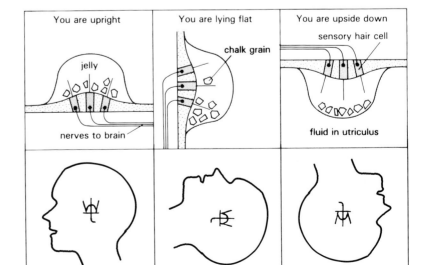

You are upright

jelly

nerves to brain

You are lying flat

chalk grain

You are upside down

sensory hair cell

fluid in utriculus

NB. Only one receptor is shown for simplicity. You have lots

Q39

Plants and stimuli

Do plants have special sense organs? What kinds of stimuli can they react to?

Light
A leafy shoot grows towards the light. A young plant grows faster without any light.

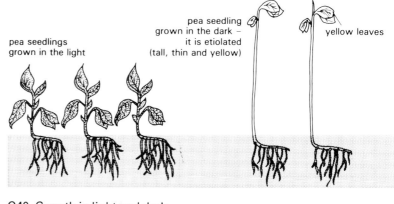

Q40 Growth in light and dark

Cells at the growing tip respond to light. A plant in a light-proof collar will bend, if the tip is in the light. A plant with a light-proof cap won't bend.

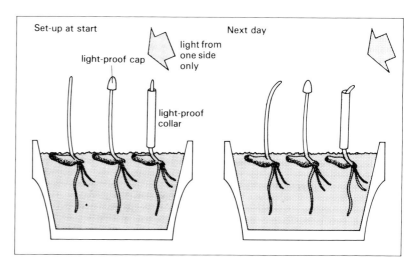

Q41 A light growth experiment – does the tip matter in light responses?

The experiment (Fig. Q41) shows that the cells at the tip are affected by the light, but cells a little further back are the ones that react.

It probably works like this: a growth substance is made at the tip. This travels down the shaded side of the plant to the growing region, where it causes cells to grow and bend the plant.

Growth reactions or tropisms (this one is **phototropism**) can be towards the stimulus or away from it. Growth towards the stimulus is said to be **positive.** Shoots show positive phototropism. Growth away is called **negative.** Roots show negative phototropism.

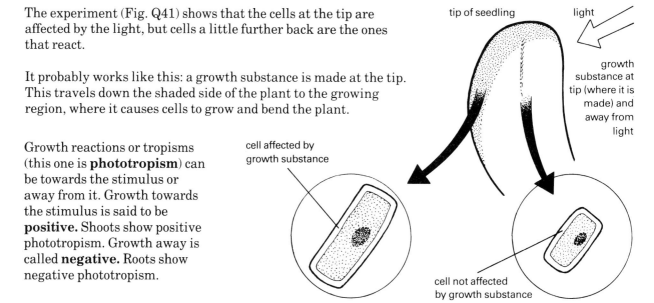

Q42 Growth substance controls cell size

Summary and questions

Summary
In order to survive, organisms must know something about changes in the world around them. They have receptors – groups of cells sensitive to changes. Stimulus is a word for any change which affects a particular receptor.

Receptors include eyes, ears, tongues, noses and skin in animals. In plants, cells at growing tips respond to stimuli with tropic reactions. Other cells are also sensitive.

Questions

1. You have fried bacon for breakfast. Copy and fill in this table which describes the event. The first part is done for you.

Event	Stimulus	Receptor
seeing the bacon	light	eye
feeling the bacon as you take it out of its wrapping		
hearing the bacon cooking		
smelling the bacon		
feeling the hot bacon once it's cooked		
eating the bacon		

2. When you have a bad cold, you sometimes get a dripping nose. The drip includes a lot of liquid from your tear glands – the liquid runs down into the back of your nose. Alexander Fleming grew bacteria on agar jelly as part of his research. He noticed that where these nose drips landed, the bacteria died. What does this suggest about the way tears protect your eyes?

3. (a) Explain why shoots grow up even in the dark. Use the following words in your answer: geotropism, phototropism, positive, negative.
   (b) Explain why flowering in plants like chrysanthemum and tobacco is not a tropic reaction. Use the words: sensitive, tip.
   (c) How could you show that plant roots are positively hydrotropic – that is, they grow towards water? Make sure the root is not reacting to light or gravity in your experiment.

4. In the text there were no large completely labelled diagrams of the eye or the ear – because they take up a lot of room and are a bit much all at once. However, you now have all the information needed to draw these diagrams, and you should have them in your notes.

   Use a whole page for each diagram of a slice through the eye or the ear.

   On the eye you should label:
   lens, ciliary muscles, retina, blind spot, **pupil, iris, choroid, sclera, retina, fovea,** optic nerve, cornea, eyelid, eyelash, eye muscles, aqueous humour, vitreous humour.

   On the ear you should label:
   inner ear, middle ear, outer ear, earlobe, ear canal, ear drum, hammer, anvil, stirrup, oval window, round window, Eustachian tube, utriculus, semicircular canals, cochlea, nerves to brain, fluid, bone.

   It may help to do a rough sketch first to make sure everything fits in. Use one colour for bones, another for liquids, and so on to reduce confusion.

5. Pick an animal other than a human or a pet, and explain how it uses its senses to
   (a) choose a suitable place to live (not too hot or cold, safe from predators and so on)
   (b) find food
   (c) communicate with others of its own kind – for example when choosing a mate

6. Explain
   (a) why **three** semi-circular canals are needed
   (b) why you think that the inner ear has such hard bones to protect it
   (c) how the ear protects itself from damage by loud noises
   (d) the job of the Eustachian tube

143

Nervous systems in action

Information from receptors is converted into a response by the nervous system. Nervous systems can be very simple. Jellyfish have a network of nerve cells which stimulate muscles to contract (Fig. R1).

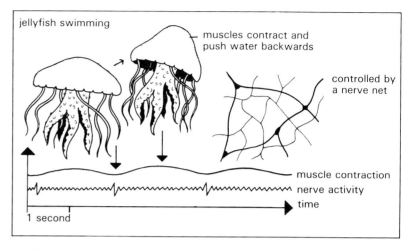

R1 Simple nervous control

Vertebrates have more complex systems. The brain sorts information and controls responses. There is help from the spinal cord, and groups of nerve cells.

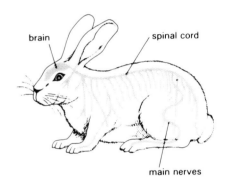

R2 A mammal's nervous system

Nerve cells

Nerve cells are cells which are specialized in conducting electrical impulses.

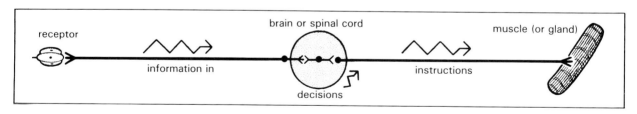

R3 Nerve cells carry information to and from the brain

Some are long enough to stretch from brain to toe tips and are very fragile. The fibres of cells like these are usually found in bundles in a protective coat. These bundles are the nerves. The individual nerve cells are called neurons.

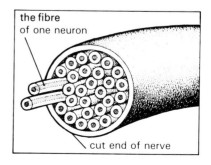

R4 Neurons are packaged for safety

A neuron consists of a cell body with its nucleus, a long fibre and some kind of connector to other cells. The type of connector depends upon the job the cell does though they all work in much the same way. The diagram (Fig. R5) shows a cell which carries instructions from the brain to muscles and so the connector is flattened for communicating with muscle cells.

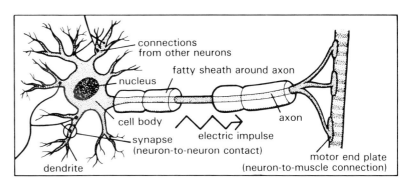

R5 An enlarged motor neuron

Axons and **dendrons** are the long fibre of a neuron. They can be very long. Dendrons carry electrical impulses towards the cell body. Axons carry impulses away from the cell body.

Many animals have axons and dendrons insulated with fat. Electrical impulses move faster along axons and dendrons which are insulated. If an animal loses its insulation, something very like a short circuit happens, and control of the muscles is lost. This something happens as the result of disease.

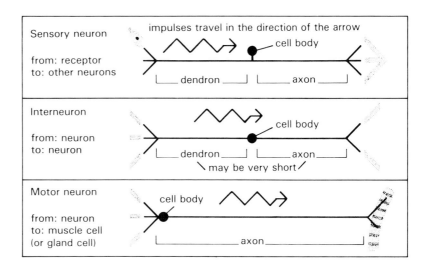

R6 A neuron's structure depends upon its job

Synapses

Connections between a neuron and other cells may come as a surprise. There is always a tiny gap between the neuron and its neighbour. At the gap the electrical message is converted into a chemical form. The chemical rapidly diffuses across the minute gap and causes a new electrical impulse on the other side. The impulse may travel on in (if the new cell is a neuron) or trigger a muscle to contract.

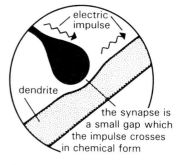

R7 A synapse

145

Reflexes

Most of the time your muscles work for you, you are completely unaware of their activities. They are controlled by simple reflexes, automatic events involving few nerve cells and lots of feedback. Stretch reflexes help keep your body in the position you have chosen. Fig. R8a shows an arm held level (supporting this book perhaps). In (b) the arm starts to droop. The muscle starts to stretch and a sensory receptor in the muscle picks this up. The electrical impulse travels along the sensory neuron and stimulates the motor neuron. The motor neuron (Fig. R8c) transmits impulses which cause the muscle to contract. It goes on contracting until the stimulus stops because the sensory neuron stops sending 'stretch' signals. That happens of course when the arm is level.

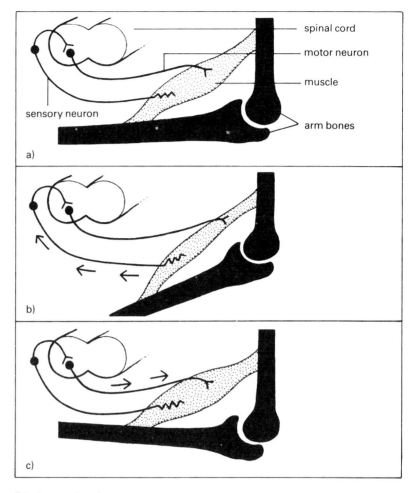

R8 A stretch reflex

Some reflexes are in response to external stimuli. The eye blink (how close can things get to your eyes before you have to blink?) and the knee jerk are examples. Fig. R9 shows the knee jerk in more detail.

1. The tendon below the knee is tapped. This stretches the tendon and the muscles in the thigh. Receptors in the muscles are stimulated and send a signal to the central nervous system (CNS).

2. The impulse crosses the spinal cord as an interneuron is triggered.

3. The interneuron triggers a motor neuron which stimulates a muscle – and the knee jerks. (Interneurons also have connections to the brain – so you know the knee is jerking, but you can't stop it.)

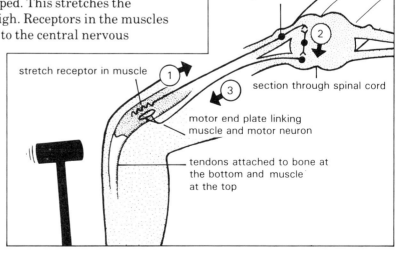

R9 A knee jerk reflex

Behaviour

All the things a whole organism does make up its behaviour. Behaviour is aimed at obtaining food, avoiding damage and breeding.

Instinct and learning

Instinctive behaviour is programmed – inherited with other instructions for building and running the body.

Learning involves changing behaviour. It can be hard to sort it out from instinctive behaviour.

The digger wasp chooses its prey by **instinct** – anything with the right size, shape and smell is food.

R10 Digger wasps combine instinctive and learned behaviour

Its nest is a hole. It **learns** where the nest is by learning the pattern of rocks and plants around it.

The same applies in higher animals

Any small moving spot counts as food to the frog, and triggers trapping actions – as long as it's close enough.

R11 An example of instinctive behaviour

A deaf bird will sing some kind of song. To sing is instinctive.

Young birds can learn tunes from birds around them – within limits. Song **pattern** is learned.

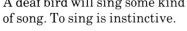

R12 Learning often builds on instinct

Communicating

Signals between animals are important. They are used for finding mates, teaching the young, avoiding fights and recognizing friends.

Signals can involve scent, sound or sight. They are especially important for **social behaviour**. A group of animals can do more than one animal can. Social behaviour is how they co-operate. Signals help to co-ordinate the group, whether for defence or attack.

musk ox group defence

wolves attack – only effective against single animals

R13 Social behaviour shown by attackers and attacked

The central nervous system

Very simple behaviour can happen without a central nervous system (CNS). Reflexes do not really involve the CNS, but all more complex activities need large groups of nerve cells to control them.

The CNS is a tube made up of a network of neurons and other cells. Bulges grow and fold at one end to form a brain. The CNS is connected to the rest of the body by nerves.

The brain is basically the same in all vertebrates (animals with backbones). It has three bulging areas:
1. forebrain
2. midbrain
3. hindbrain

In animals like the frog each part is roughly equal in the adult. Each of the lobes has its own job, and receives information from particular sense organs.

The importance of the different lobes is related to size. In humans the cerebrum is huge. It has folds to provide extra surface for neuron cell bodies. These give the brain its grey colour.

The brain has two halves and the two halves do not do things equally well.

The left side of the brain controls the right side of the body, and the right the left.

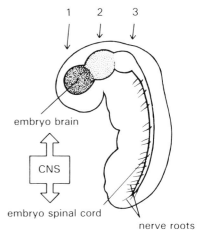

R14 The embryo brain

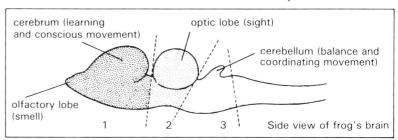

R15 Side view of a frog's brain

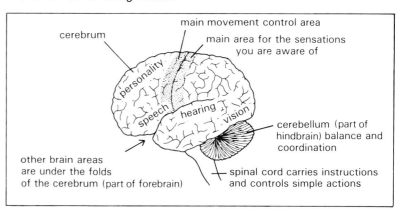

R16 Parts of the human brain

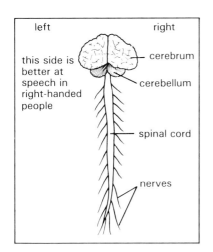

R17 The CNS from the back

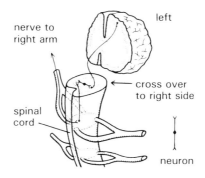

R18 The right side of the brain controls the left side of the body

We can also study the small electrical currents that flow through the brain all the time. Electrodes taped to the skull can pick them up. People vary a lot, but the patterns on the right (an electro-encephalogram or EEG) from a normal brain are fairly typical. EEGs are useful in detecting epilepsy.

The currents are the result of many chemical changes in brain cells. Mental illnesses, like many other illnesses, may partly be caused by some of the chemical reactions getting out of balance.

The mammalian brain is well protected and so complex that many scientists prefer to work with simpler animals. They hope that information from them can be used one day to help explain more complex brains.

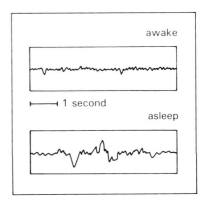

R19 EEG patterns in a normal human brain

The autonomic nervous system

Mammals also have nerves involved in controlling body activities rather than body movement. Neurons of the **autonomic nervous system** go to heart, lungs, liver, glands and gut. One set of nerves speeds up useful body processes like the heartbeat when there is an emergency – danger about. Another set slows things down, returning the body to normal when the danger is past. These nerves come from the hind brain and spinal cord.

Many drugs affect the autonomic nervous system. Nicotine (in cigarettes), caffeine (in coffee, tea and cola) and amphetemines are stimulants – like danger. Alcohol, barbiturates, tranquilizers and opiates (heroin & co.) push the system in the opposite direction. They are depressants, and addictive into the bargain.

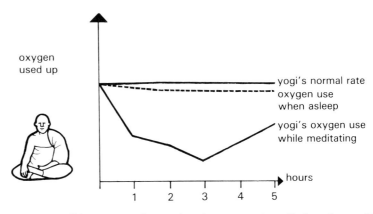

R20 It is possible to control consciously some automatic functions with training

Question

Earthworms have a simple nervous system. Their 'brain' is a large group of nerve cells near the head. There are smaller groups of nerve cells called ganglia in the other segments of the body. Study the table on the right. What is the importance of the brain in controlling the worms' behaviour?

Activity	Whole animal	Without 'brain'
mating	normal	same as normal
reaction to light	moves away from bright light	moves towards bright light
simple learning, e.g. moving towards food	normal	same as normal
overall activity	normal	increases

Animal hormones

Some body activities are not easy to control with nervous impulses. Growth, for example, takes a lot of time and involves many cells in a complicated pattern of changes. Chemical messages between cells keep the body acting as a whole. The chemicals which form the messages are called **hormones**. They are mainly made by groups of cells called **ductless** or **endocrine glands**. Hormones are carried away from ductless glands and around the body in the blood. Each hormone affects particular tissues and organs in its own way.

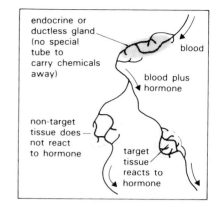

R21 Endocrine glands

The leader of the endocrine glands is the **pituitary**. It makes hormones which control the other ductless glands, and is affected by chemical messages from other parts of the body.

The pituitary is a bulge in the base of the brain. It is connected to the brain by both blood vessels and nerves. It provides a link between hormone control and nervous control.

Here are four more examples of hormones. Note how important it is to have the right amount of a hormone.

1. Insulin

This is made in the pancreas. It allows the body to use sugar efficiently. It increases glucose storage in the liver and allows other cells to take in glucose. It is especially important after a meal when the glucose level in the blood rises. Too little insulin and glucose reaches high levels in the blood. The kidney gets rid of the extra glucose and the body can run out of glucose. This is one form of diabetes.

R22 Human brain (sliced to show the pituitary, which would otherwise be hidden by the bulging cerebrum)

pituitary gland (pea-sized in people)

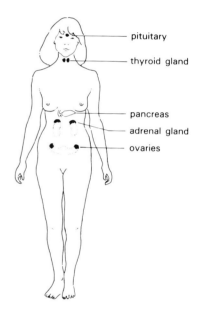

R23 The position of the endocrine glands

2. Thyroxin

This is made in the thyroid gland. In humans it controls the rate of energy production and reactions in cells generally. Too much thyroxin and you are over-active; too little and you are sluggish. In animals such as frogs, thyroxin controls the changes of metamorphosis.
Iodine is an important part of a thyroxin molecule.

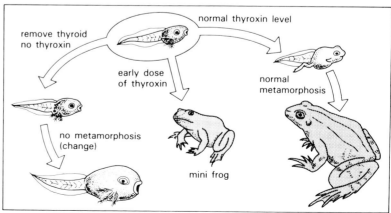

R24 Thyroxin and frog development

3. Adrenalin

This is made in the adrenal glands. Along with part of the autonomic nervous system, adrenalin prepares the body for action.

Adrenalin promotes:
wider air passages (lets more air in)
extra glucose in the blood (for energy)
faster heartbeat
more blood to brain and muscles
the dilation of pupils (lets more light into the eye)
less blood to gut
hair standing on end (makes an animal look bigger)

R25 An irrate cat

4. Sex hormones

These are made by the ovary (oestrogens) or testes (androgens). They are involved in the growth of secondary sexual characteristics, such as wider hips and larger breasts (women) or beards, broader shoulders and deeper voices (men). Taking these hormones away can have a dramatic effect.

Female sex hormones not only affect overall development, they also control the monthly menstrual cycle.

Menstruation is controlled by four different hormones. They are made by the pituitary gland in the brain and the follicle cells in the ovary. Control is complicated, so it isn't surprising that when girls start to have periods they are often irregular. Women differ in the length and timing of their periods, and they may stop altogether in someone suffering great stress.

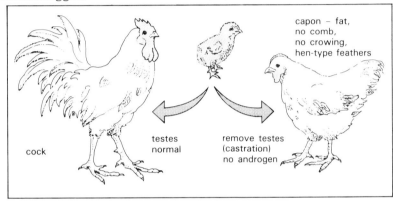

R26 Male sex hormones and poultry

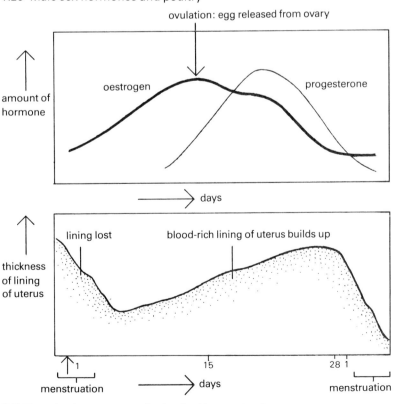

N.B. Two other hormones are also involved in menstruation

R27 The menstrual cycle and hormones. Which of the two hormones triggers ovulation? Give a reason for your answer.

151

Plant hormones

Plant hormones between them control:

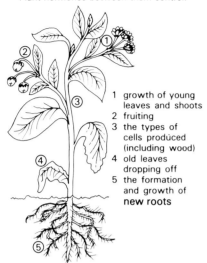

1 growth of young leaves and shoots
2 fruiting
3 the types of cells produced (including wood)
4 old leaves dropping off
5 the formation and growth of **new roots**

R28

This works with auxins from many types of plants. There must be a chemical controlling the growth. It can't be a nerve, they don't work if they are cut. The dark side of the seedling produces lots of auxin, the light side not so much. The auxin diffuses into the agar and then into the new plant. Where there is a lot of auxin, the cells grow faster.

Auxins affect different parts of the plant differently.

Like animal hormones, plant hormones travel distances.

Question

1. (a) Describe the experiments shown in Figs R 29 and R31 in your own words.
   (b) How many seedlings would you use in each case and why?
   (c) Draw the table you would use to record your results for both experiments.
   (d) Give one practical problem you might have with each experiment and suggest solutions.

Plants too have hormones – chemicals which control activities. The first to be discovered were the **auxins**, which are important in tropic movements.

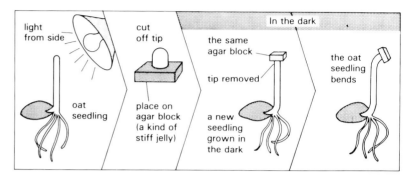

R29 Experiment to show the presence of auxin in growing tips

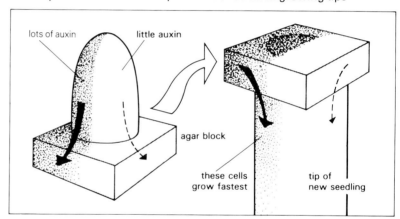

R30 Explaining Fig. R29.

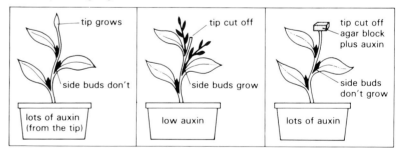

R31 Auxins make tips but not side buds grow.

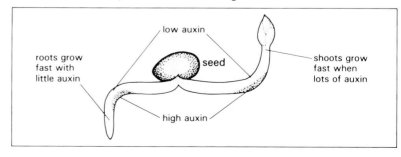

R32 Auxin affects roots and shoots differently

152

Summary and questions

Summary

The workings of an animal's body are coordinated by means of nerves and hormones. There are three main types of nerve cells (neurons): sensory neurons, interneurons and motor neurons. A reflex action involves three neurons, but more complex actions involve many cells and the control of a brain. The brain plus the spinal cord make up the central nervous system. Hormones are chemicals made by endocrine glands. They pass straight into the blood, which carries them to the tissues they affect. The pituitary is a gland in the brain which helps to co-ordinate nervous and hormonal control.

Chemical communication is important in plants. Many of their growth processes are under hormonal control.

	The endocrine system	The nervous system
consists of	ductless glands	a network of neurons
The messages are	chemicals – hormones	electrical pulses
They are transported	in blood	along axons and dendrons
Speed of action is	slow (minutes) except adrenalin	fast (less than a second)
Effects are triggered by	changes inside and outside the body	
and last	quite a long time	a short time
Typical jobs (though these overlap) are	growing, regulating salt and sugar concentrations in the body	walking, flying, picking things up, controlling breathing rate

Questions

1. Which do you think is more important – the endocrine or the nervous system – when
   (a) a cat catches a mouse
   (b) a kitten grows into a cat

2. Write out the passage below and fill in the blanks.
   A nerve cell or _____ consists of a _____ _____ and a long extension called the _____. Around the extension is a sheath made of _____ which is to _____ it. This is needed because nerve impulses are _____. There are three types of nerve cells called _____ _____, _____ _____ and _____. Connections between nerve cells are called _____ and they involve a gap which the impulse must jump _____. In mammals, the central nervous system or _____ _____ _____ consists of a _____ and a _____ _____. Not all animals have a central nervous system – for example a _____ does not.

3. Answer the following questions, giving a reason in each case:
   (a) Can people choose to control their heart rate – normally under the controls of the autonomic nervous systems?
   (b) Do organisms have to have brains?
   (c) Can a brain with a smooth cerebrum do as many things as a brain with a folded cerebrum?

4. Match the structures in A with the jobs they do in B. Write out full sentences.

A	B
The cerebrum	protects the brain.
The cerebellum	is important in learning, thought and controlled movements.
The spinal cord	is important in balance and co-ordination.
The skull	carrys instructions and is important in reflex actions.

5. (a) The constriction of the pupil when a bright light is shone into the eye is an example of a reflex. Explain how it might happen.
   (b) Explain why it is so difficult to study how the human brain works.
   (c) Explain why so much of the sensory area of the brain is for the hands and so little for the arms.

6. Make up an advertisement to sell one of the ductless glands to an organism without an endocrine system.

7. Explain in your own words
   (a) endocrine glands
   (b) hormones
   (c) auxins
   (d) castration
   (e) diabetes

Transport

A passenger list of materials that must move round an organism includes:
- food
- oxygen
- wastes
- hormones

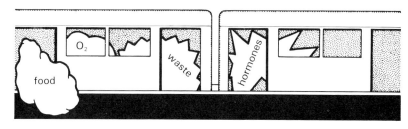

S1 The passengers in a transport system

Small organisms don't have much of a problem – nowhere is far from the outside world.

cytoplasmic movement (streaming)

Amoeba
magnified

diffusion
O_2 CO_2

S2 Small organisms can rely on diffusion

This is not true in larger organisms. Guts and lungs are surfaces where materials can get in and out of an organism by diffusion. They are folded to get a large area into a small space. Most cells are still a long way from those surfaces.

The answer is a blood transport system.

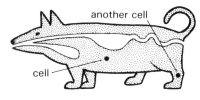

another cell

cell

S3 Cells in larger organisms need help

liquid to carry things

tubes

Eureka!

a pump

Land plants need a transport system too. Leaves must be up in the light to make food. Roots must be in the soil to collect water and minerals. So a transport system of tube cells is needed.

In all cases, materials travel dissolved in water.

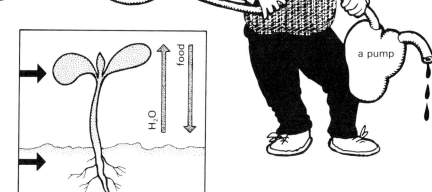

food

H_2O

S4 Land plants transport materials around their bodies too

Diffusion and osmosis are important in moving water. Both happen in non-living and living systems in the right conditions. They are physical processes.

Diffusion you've met before. Particles move at random and end up spread out evenly. A membrane barrier makes no difference as long as it has holes in it big enough for the particles to go through.

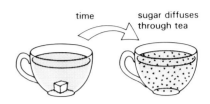

S5 Diffusion

Osmosis happens when a barrier is **semi-permeable** – that is, it lets some (small) things through but not others (larger particles). It's like a sieve.

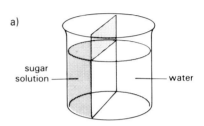

Imagine a beaker divided into two by a semi-permeable membrane. Sugar solution is put in one side, water in the other. The holes are big enough for H_2O molecules, not for sugar molecules (Fig. S6a).

Fig. S6b shows the holes, and the water and sugar particles. To begin with there are more water particles on one side than the other.

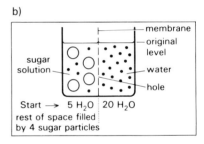

Time passes
Particles move randomly. Some of the water molecules go through the membrane in both directions (Fig. S6c).

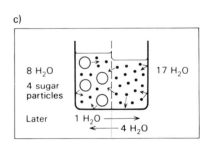

More time passes
Eventually there are about the same number of water molecules on each side of the membrane. The sugar molecules have to stay on the left (Fig. S6d).

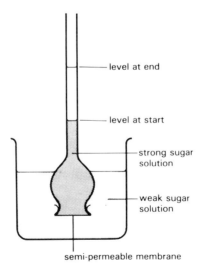

S7 A common demonstration of osmosis

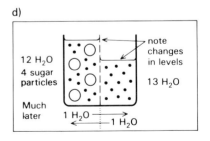

S6 An osmosis experiment. (b) to (d) show the experiment in (a) in section.

The overall effect? Osmosis is the movement of water through a semi-permeable membrane from a dilute solution (or water) to a more concentrated (stronger) one. (It doesn't have to be a sugar solution.)

Osmosis acts against forces like gravity.

As you'll see, it is **very** important to living organisms, their transport systems and their cells.

Transport in plants - water and minerals

The pathway

Small quantities of minerals are taken up by the roots and remain in the plant. They are carried in water which is taken up in enormous amounts. Much of the water absorbed is lost.

The water in soil, plant and air is connected.

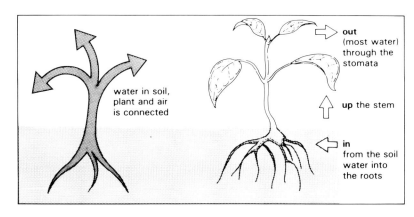

S8 Transport paths

In

Water comes in through **root hairs**. They provide a large surface area, though they are tiny, because a single plant can have millions of them.

Each root hair is a single cell. The cell sap in them is more concentrated than the soil solution. Water enters a root hair by osmosis (and so makes it more dilute) (Fig. S9).

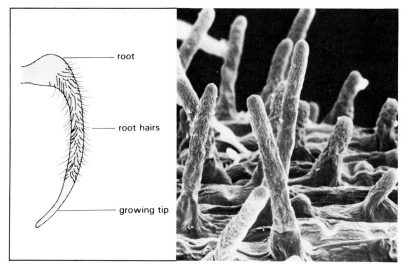

S9 Water enters through root hairs

As a result, the root hair cell's sap is now more dilute than the next cell inwards. Water moves into this next cell by osmosis and so on until the transport tubes are reached. Osmosis provides some of the push needed to move the water upwards, but not much.

Unlike water, minerals don't make their own way into the root hairs. Plants have to pump them in – and use up energy in the process. The energy comes from respiration (Fig. S11).

Up

Water and minerals travel up the stem in **xylem** vessels – hollow tubes. Xylem cells die when they are mature.

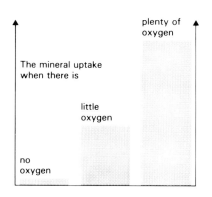

S11 Some evidence for the importance of respiration in mineral uptake

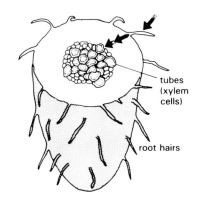

S10 Water moves across the root to the xylem cells

To see the xylem vessels, keep a plant in water coloured with vegetable dye. After a while, cut through the stem. The xylem vessels are the groups of dyed cells.

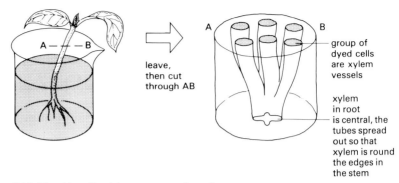

S12 Tracking liquid movement in xylem

Xylem tubes run up the middle of the root but spread out to form small bundles in the stem. This way they provide more support for the plant, which is their other job. Xylem vessels are very narrow and to some extent water moves up them by **capillarity**.

Water is attracted to the walls of a vessel. In a very narrow (capillary) vessel, the attraction is stronger than the weight of the water. The water moves up the tube. This is capillarity.

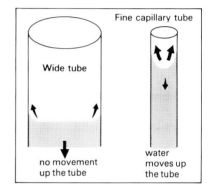

S13 Capillary action

And out
Water evaporates through pores (stomata) in the leaf. The result is low pressure at the top of the plant, which pulls up more water. This is the most important force which moves water in the xylem vessels. Roots are not essential for water movement.

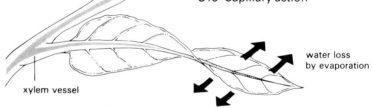

S14 Leaves loose water by transpiration

The rate of water loss (**transpiration**) varies with many things. It can be measured with a potometer. As the plant takes in water, the bubble moves up the glass tube. Its speed depends on the rate of transpiration from the plant's leaves.

Transpiration increases in wind, bright light, dry conditions.

Transpiration drops in still air, the dark, humid (damp) conditions.

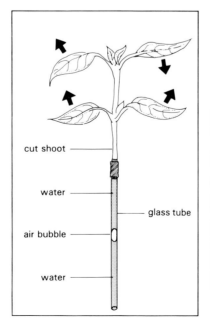

S15 A simple potometer

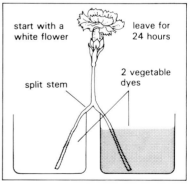

S16 Something to do. Provided all goes well, you will end up with a very strangely coloured flower.

Transport in plants - food materials

Leaves make sugars. They are transported to flowers, fruit, growing leaves (which need more energy than they can trap) and roots.

Are the same tubes used to transport food materials as water? The answer is NO.

Ringing a tree kills it by starving the roots. The ringing removes phloem cells which transport the sugars.

These are living tube cells, and together with xylem they form the **vascular tissue** of a plant.

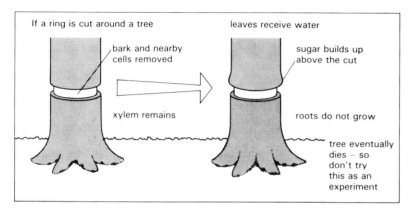

S18 Ringing experiment

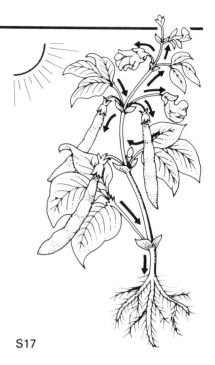

S17

Sap from phloem cells contains a lot of sugar, and also amino acids (the sub-units of proteins). Sap in phloem moves up to 100 cm an hour. This is about half the average speed of water in xylem. Unlike xylem cells, phloem cells must be alive for sap movement. Cytoplasmic streaming may help to move food, but it would not be fast enough by itself. Exactly how materials move in phloem is not yet understood.

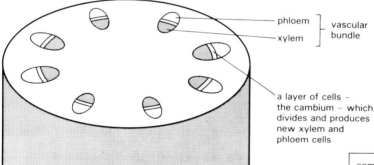

S19 Section of stem showing vascular bundles

Question

Fig. S20 shows a phloem cell and a xylem cell. From what you have read about their functions – the jobs they do – say which you think is which and give a reason for your answer.

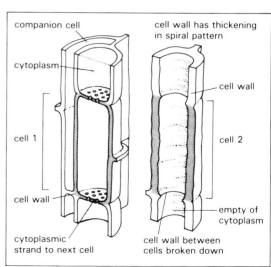

S20

Summary and questions

Summary
Organisms of any size must transport food, oxygen, wastes and hormones around their bodies. This involves a transport system. In plants, this consists of tube cells: xylem and phloem. Water and minerals travel from the roots in xylem cells. Food materials, produced by photosynthesis, are moved in phloem cells from the leaves to the rest of the plant. Phloem cells are living. How materials move in them is not fully understood. Xylem cells are non-living. Liquids are mainly pulled through them by transpiration – the evaporation of water from the leaves. Water enters through root hairs by osmosis. Osmosis is the movement of water through a semi-permeable membrane from a weak solution to a more concentrated one.

Questions

1. Copy this out, filling in the blanks.
   In plants, water enters through _____ _____ by the process of _____. It travels up the stem to the _____ in tubes called _____. It carries with it _____ _____ which also enter through the roots. The water is pulled up by _____ or the _____ of water from leaf surfaces. Food materials such as _____ and amino acids travel in living cells, the _____ which with the _____ form _____ bundles. It is not really understood what moves the nutrient solution, but it does go to such places as _____, _____ and _____.

2. Explain
   (a) why a cell in the muscle of a dog's leg must be near a transport system
   (b) how you could show that water travels in xylem
   (c) the three ways water is moved in xylem (say which is the most important)
   (d) why ringing eventually kills a tree

3. Explain the difference between
   (a) osmosis and diffusion
   (b) xylem and phloem
   (c) roots and root hairs
   (d) transpiration and ordinary evaporation
   (e) the way water gets into a plant and the way minerals get in

4. What is a potometer?
   Suggest three conditions in which transpiration could be increased.
   Suggest three conditions in which transpiration could be reduced.
   How could you show that any two of your suggestions were correct?

5. It is possible to use aphids to investigate the contents of phloem as shown below. Once the aphid 'tap' is prepared, sap can be collected for some time.

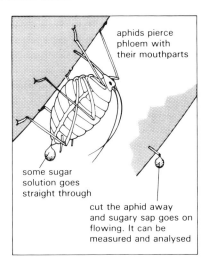

aphids pierce phloem with their mouthparts

some sugar solution goes straight through

cut the aphid away and sugary sap goes on flowing. It can be measured and analysed

S21

(a) What do you think the effect of lots of feeding aphids is on a plant's growth?
(b) Here are the results of a study of the effect of feeding aphids on the growth of lime leaves. Present the information as a graph. Does it support your answer to 5 (a)?

Number of aphids	4	7	10	16	20	21	24	25
Growth of lime leaves in grams per dm^2 of leaf	.85	.7	.6	.6	.5	.35	.25	.3

(c) An animal like a cicada which takes food from xylem vessels grows more slowly than an animal like an aphid which feeds from phloem vessels. Why?

Transport in animals - the blood system

The body fluids in animals transport many things to and from cells – oxygen, food, hormones, heat and wastes. In animals large enough to need one, the blood system contains about a third of the body fluids.

The blood system consists of
blood
+
a pump – the heart
+
vessels

arteries – carry blood from the heart
veins – carry blood to the heart
capillaries – connect arteries and veins

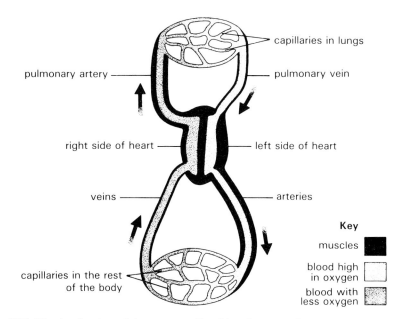

S22 The basic plan of the mammalian blood system (unfolded)

The vessels
The arteries are important in distributing blood. During exercise, the arteries to the legs widen and those to the gut constrict (get narrower). This is possible because they have many muscle cells in their walls. These can relax to allow blood through and by peristaltic pumping (like gut muscles) help keep blood moving.

S23 An artery

If the artery walls stiffen, the heart has to work harder. It's the same if the arteries get narrower. This may happen if fatty materials build up on the inner walls of blood vessels. Cholesterol is just one of these fatty materials.

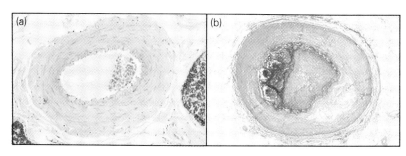

S24 (a) Healthy artery, (b) artery blocked by fats

Arterioles are the smallest branches of arteries. They control the flow of blood into capillaries, thanks to the smooth muscle cells in their walls. These muscles are controlled by neurons of the autonomic nervous system.

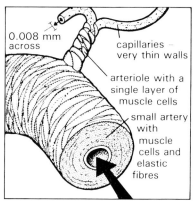

S25 Arteries, arterioles and capillaries

Capillaries are the smallest blood vessels. They wind between body cells. If an artery is a motorway, a capillary is a bicycle path. Their walls are one cell thick, and they leak water and dissolved materials. There are many more capillaries than can be filled at any one time. Only those in areas where blood is most needed contain blood.

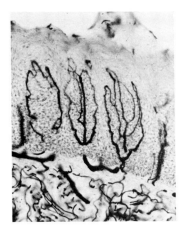

S26 Capillaries in the tongue

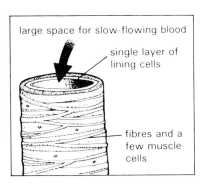

S27 Veins

Veins have thinner walls. Veins don't need thick walls because the blood pressure in them is low. They also need to be 'squeezable'. Veins often run through muscles which move bones. As these muscles contract during body movement, they squeeze the veins and push the blood back to the heart. There are valves inside the vein which stop blood flowing the wrong way. The valves are like pockets.

To see the valves:
Tie a tight bandage around someone's arm. (Don't leave it on long.) Stroke blood back towards the hand to make the valves bulge. (Warning: never do this on your own. Bandages can get stuck.)

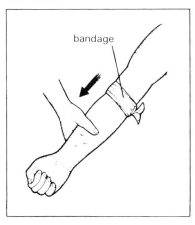

S28 Finding valves

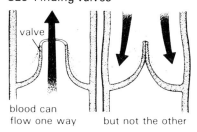

S29 Section through a vein to show the valves open and closed

Varicose veins

Normally blood returns from the feet to the main veins leading to the heart in veins running up the middle of the leg muscles. Small leg movements are enough to keep the blood moving. There are some small veins near the surface of the leg and usually blood runs from them to the main veins. Valves help.

If you stand still for long periods of time, a problem may build up. Without muscle movements to keep it moving, blood tends to flow back into the surface veins and stretch them. The valves don't shut properly, which makes things worse. Varicose veins are these overstretched and painful surface veins.

Watch out for varicose veins in later life if you are female (about a fifty-fifty chance) or end up in a job with a lot of standing (teaching, hairdressing and so on).

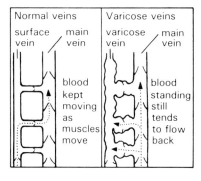

S30 Varicose veins in section

The heart

The heart is a pump – and a very good one at that.

The simplest pump is a length of blood vessel with extra muscle.

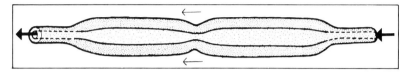

S31 A simple pump

Two such 'hearts' are found in a three-week-old human embryo. To pump more blood, parts of the tube become enlarged. As blood pressure rises, walls become thicker. Valves are needed to stop blood going backwards.

A single pump – the fish heart

Fish have one pump which pushes blood to the gills. Then it goes straight to the body.

One pump is not very efficient. Blood pressure drops in the gills and blood moves slowly round the body. This is fine for a fishy way of life.

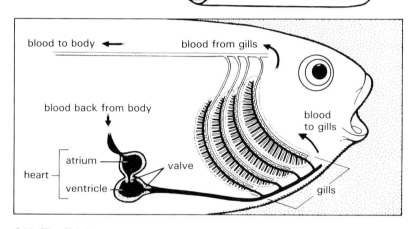

S32 The fish heart – one pump

A double pump – the mammalian heart
In mammals there are two pumps. One sends blood to the lungs, the other sends blood to the rest of the body. The right pump and its tubes twist around the left pump and its tubes.

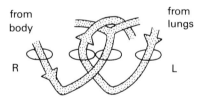

the circles represent one-way valves

S33 Blood flow patterns in a double pump

A great deal of blood passes through the heart, but its muscles are so thick that they need their own blood supply. Blood for the heart muscles travels through the coronary arteries. Blockage of one of these causes a heart attack.

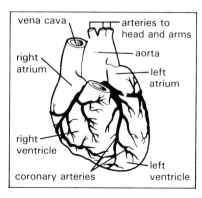

This means that an area of muscle cells run out of fuel and oxygen, stop contracting and die. This kind of heart problem is called a coronary thrombosis. A thrombosis is a clot. (More later.)

S34 The mammalian heart and its own blood supply

Design Specification –
pump for human body

Must

work without maintenance for 70 years or more

be self-lubricating

be self-regulating

normal rate 50–70, b. per m. must cope up to 200 beats per minute

normal volume pumped 5 litres per minute, must cope up to 40 litres per minute

The heartbeat
First stage

The diagram shows the relaxation phase in the heartbeat. The chambers of the heart fill with blood, which flows from

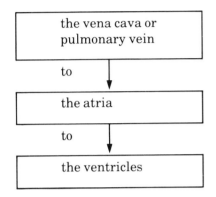

the vena cava or pulmonary vein

to

the atria

to

the ventricles

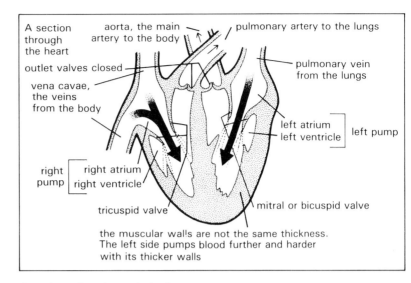

A section through the heart

aorta, the main artery to the body

pulmonary artery to the lungs

outlet valves closed

pulmonary vein from the lungs

vena cavae, the veins from the body

left atrium
left ventricle

left pump

right pump

right atrium
right ventricle

tricuspid valve

mitral or bicuspid valve

the muscular walls are not the same thickness. The left side pumps blood further and harder with its thicker walls

S35 A section through the heart

To prevent blood flowing back into the ventricle from the arteries, the aortic and pulmonary valves shut. As they slap shut they make a 'lub' sound. Heart murmurs occur when valves do not shut properly and blood seeps through.

Second stage
The atria contract

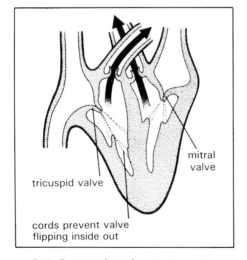

mitral valve

tricuspid valve

cords prevent valve flipping inside out

S36 Contraction phase, stage 3

Third stage
The ventricles contract and push blood up the aorta and the pulmonary arteries. The 'dub' sound of the heartbeat is the tricuspid and bicuspid valves slapping shut to prevent blood flowing back into the atria. The two sets of pumps beat together. The rate at which the heart beats is under the control of the nervous system and adrenalin. It changes as the result of exercise, anger, excitement and so on. The basic rate depends upon the pacemaker, a bundle of cells in the right atrium.

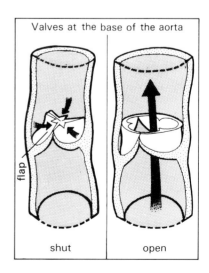

Valves at the base of the aorta

flap

shut

open

S37 The flaps of the valves fill up like pockets and block the way out from the heart

What is blood?

Blood is made up of plasma, red blood cells, white blood cells and platelets. Plasma is a straw-coloured liquid, mostly water, which does many jobs. Red blood cells transport gases. White blood cells and platelets defend the body.

Blood is not isolated in its blood vessels. Some plasma leaks out – and is then called tissue fluid. There is about twice as much tissue fluid in the body as there is blood.

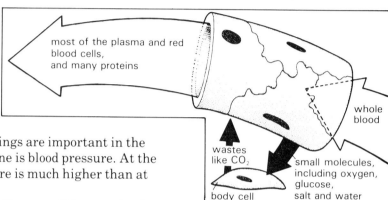

S38 Blood components

Leaking plasma carries small molecules, such as oxygen and glucose, in solution to body cells. Most of the tissue fluid seeps back into the capillaries, together with dissolved wastes like carbon dioxide.

How does this return happen? Two things are important in the capillaries which loop around cells. One is blood pressure. At the beginning of such a loop, blood pressure is much higher than at the end of the loop.

The other important thing is osmosis. Because of the proteins in the blood, water tends to move into the capillary by osmosis. When plasma leaves the capillary, large molecules tend to be left behind and so become more concentrated in the blood.

S39 Capillaries leak

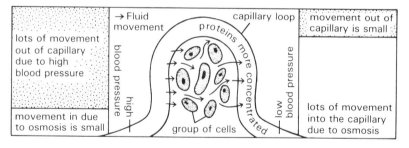

S40 Movement in and out of capillaries

At the start of the capillary loop, blood pressure is more important than osmosis, so the tube leaks. At the end of the loop, blood pressure is much less important than osmosis, so water and small molecules move back into the blood.

Not all the extra tissue fluid goes back into the capillaries. Some is picked up by tiny lymph vessels. The liquid is now called lymph. It moves slowly through the lymph system, and collects white blood cells which help combat infection. Eventually lymph rejoins the blood in the vein at the base of the neck. Blocking the lymph system causes swelling.

The answer to 'What is blood?' is not simple. Blood is a body fluid that happens to flow in blood vessels, but it is connected to other body fluids and could not do its job without them.

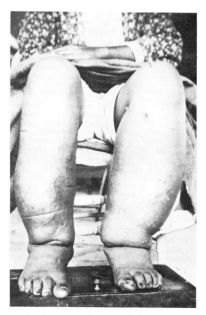

S41 The lymph vessels in this man's leg have been blocked by a parasitic worm. This tropical disease is called elephantiasis.

Summary and questions

Summary
The blood system of large, active animals like mammals consists of a pump, blood vessels and blood. The heart is a double pump – half sends blood to the lungs and the other half to the body. Each pump is made up of two parts, the atrium and the more powerful ventricle, with valves to make sure blood doesn't flow backwards. The arteries are large muscular blood vessels leading from the heart, the largest being the aorta. The veins, which have thinner walls, return blood to the heart. Capillaries form a link between arteries and veins. They allow some blood to leak out and, as tissue fluid, to bathe the body cells.
Most tissue fluid soon returns to the capillaries, but some enters the lymph system. This rejoins the blood system at a vein in the neck. In this way the various body fluids form a connected system.

Questions

1. Match the description with the name. Write out full sentences.

Name	Description
(a) The heart	are tubes leaving the heart.
(b) Arteries	is a pump to keep blood moving.
(c) Veins	link larger blood vessels.
(d) Capillaries	return blood to the heart.

2. Draw a diagram of the heart showing the ventricles contracted. Label the following: aorta, vena cava, left atrium, right atrium, left ventricle, right ventricle, pulmonary vein, pulmonary artery, open valves, closed valves.

3. Explain how
   (a) one-way valves in a vein work
   (b) blood vessels control the way organs and tissues in the body get the blood they need
   (c) a double-pump heart (like yours) is more suitable for a large, active animal than a single-pump heart (like a fish's)

4. Make a poster advertising the heart as a pump.

5. What is the importance of the following in the blood system?
   (a) pacemaker
   (b) aorta
   (c) atrium
   (d) coronary artery
   (e) lymph

6. If the pacemaker in someone's heart is faulty, as the result of disease, it can sometimes be replaced by an artificial pacemaker which provides small electrical shocks to the heart muscles.
   (a) One kind of artificial pacemaker causes the muscles to contract 70 times a minute. This is about right for normal activities. What problems might a person with one of these have if they wanted to climb mountains or take part in a game of football?
   (b) Some people have problems with the link between the ventricles and the pacemaker (in the atrium), which otherwise works normally. They may be able to have an artificial pacemaker which picks up the natural rhythm of impulses from the tissue in the atrium and passes them on to the ventricles. Why is this kind of artificial pacemaker better than the one in part (a)?

7. In 1732, Stephen Hales inserted a narrow glass tube into a blood vessel in a horse's leg. This narrow tube was attached to a much longer glass tube by a goose's trachea (windpipe). Blood shot up the tube to a height of nine feet and stayed there, going up and down a little in a rhythmical manner.
   (a) What kept the blood up?
   (b) Why did it go up and down a little?
   (c) What could you use instead of the trachea?
   (d) Today we measure blood pressure with a sphygmomanometer, and many people are very concerned if they have 'high' blood pressure. Find out why.

Blood cells

Portrait of a red blood cell

Shape: a flattened disc – thinner in the middle. They are flexible for squeezing through capillaries.

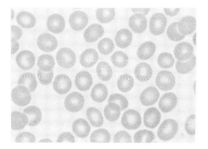

S43 Red blood cells

Size: 125 of them in a line stretch about 1 mm.

Number: you might have 25 million million of them.

Age: 4 months at most – millions are born and die every day.

Made in: bone marrow of adult humans.

Disposed of: in the spleen or the liver. Most haemoglobin is recycled (used again).

Made of: a membrane bag full of haemoglobin solution. There is no nucleus to leave more room for haemoglobin.

Job: haemoglobin picks up oxygen in the lungs, and drops it off in body tissues. Haemoglobin also helps carry carbon dioxide back to the lungs.

Not enough of them: you have anaemia. This can be the result of shortage of iron or Vitamin B12, though there are many causes. In any case, the patient is pale and breathless – oxygen is not getting to the tissues fast enough.

S42 Red cells enlarged

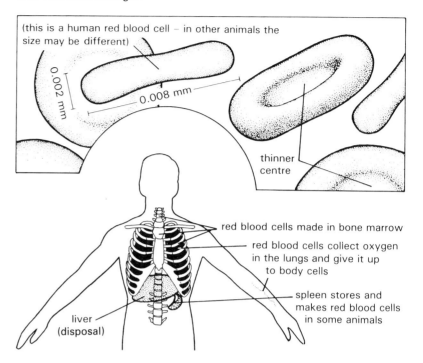

(this is a human red blood cell – in other animals the size may be different)

0.002 mm
0.008 mm
thinner centre

red blood cells made in bone marrow
red blood cells collect oxygen in the lungs and give it up to body cells
spleen stores and makes red blood cells in some animals
liver (disposal)

S44 Places in the life of a red cell

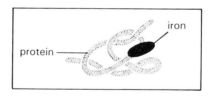

iron
protein

S45 Haemoglobin is made of protein and iron

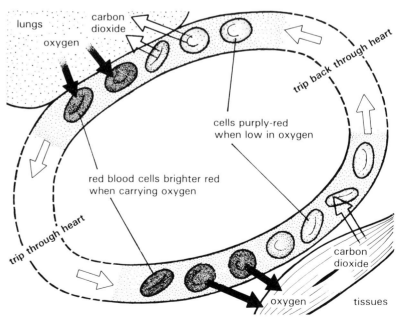

lungs
carbon dioxide
oxygen
trip back through heart
cells purply-red when low in oxygen
red blood cells brighter red when carrying oxygen
trip through heart
carbon dioxide
oxygen
tissues

S46 A red blood cell's job routine

Portrait of a white blood cell

Shape: varies – there are several kinds of white blood cells. They can change shape, and wriggle out of capillaries.

Size: varies from the size of a red blood cell to three times the size.

Number: about 1/700 as many as red blood cells.

Age: from a few days to several years.

Made in: thymus, bone marrow, spleen and lymph system.

Made of: membrane, cytoplasm and nucleus, with special abilities.

Job: body defence. There are two main groups. Large ones absorb invaders like bacteria. Small ones make antibodies. Antibodies react with the surface of an invader and make it easier to absorb and destroy it.

When things go wrong. A person without enough of them has no resistance to disease. Leukaemia happens when white blood cells multiply uncontrollably – so it's a type of cancer. The dividing cells do not become mature white blood cells and do not defend the body.

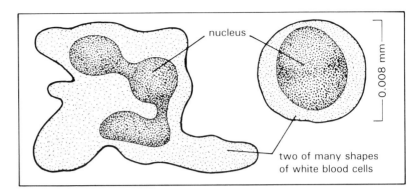

S47 White blood cells

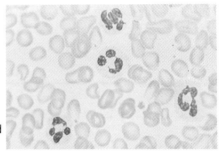

S48 White cells plus some red cells

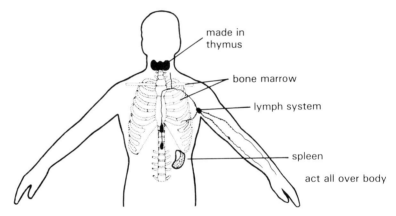

S49 Places in the life of a white cell

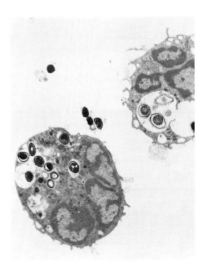

S50 This white blood cell will surround and destroy the bacteria. It may die in the process.
Pus is dead and living white blood cells, bits of skin tissue and bacteria.

167

More about blood

Wound healing
Wounded people sometimes bleed to death, but usually they don't. The body has an efficient repair system.

Cut blood vessels rapidly constrict. If they are small enough, they become plugged with blood platelets. A more secure plug is quickly formed, as shown in the diagrams.

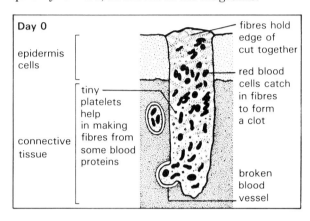

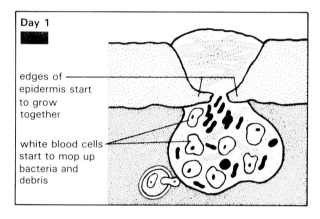

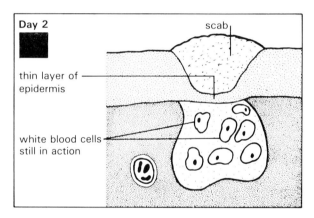

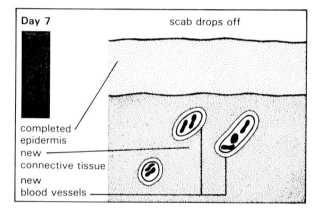

S51 Section through skin showing wound healing

A bruise is the result of blood vessels breaking inside the body, spilling blood under the skin.

Problems
Clots are useful as long as they do not spread beyond the area where they are needed. There is a system of proteins which breaks up clots, but if it does not keep up with the clotting system there can be problems. Clotting inside blood vessels – thrombosis – can be dangerous because clots can block important blood vessels. In a coronary thrombosis the blood vessels which supply the heart muscles are blocked. Haemophilia is a rare disease in which the blood does not clot at all.

Blood and heat transport

Some animals do not produce much heat. Their body temperature tends to be the same as the temperature of their surroundings. When it's hot they are hot. When it's cold so are they – and they slow down. Other (warm-blooded) animals eat more and make heat from some of the energy in the food. They can keep moving fast all the time, but only if heat is available all over the body.

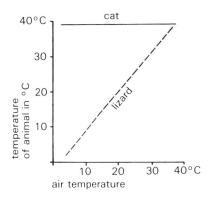

S52 Not all animals can control their body temperature

Heat is produced by the liver and muscles. Heat production can be increased when necessary, for example by shivering. Blood spreads the heat around the body.

Control of body temperature involves the blood vessels to the skin, since this is where most heat is lost. The more hot blood there is flowing near the skin surface, the more heat is lost. Muscle cells in the walls of arterioles determine which capillaries the blood flows through.

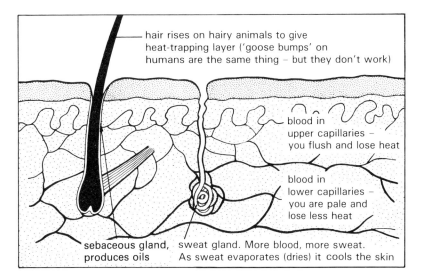

S53 A section through skin highlighting its job in temperature control

Warm-blooded animals do not keep the whole of their body at the same temperature. In people the centre of the body is kept steady at about 37°C, but the hands, feet and skin are allowed to be cooler.

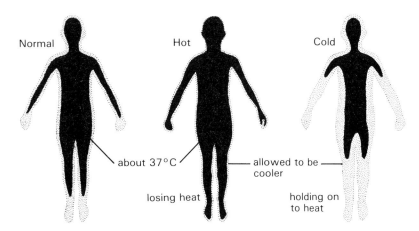

S54 Hands and feet are useful

The skin with its blood supply is not the only way organisms control their temperature, but it is very important.

Plasma and water

Plasma is mainly water, but dissolved in it are proteins, sugars, salt and lots of other substances. It is imporant that plasma is of the right concentration. Why?

	plasma concentration	the cell
(a)	same as cell	stays same size as normal
(b)	more concentrated than cell	cell shrinks due to water loss by osmosis
(c)	less concentrated than cell	cell swells due to water gain by osmosis

S55

Look at it from a red blood cell's point of view. Remember osmosis? Normally the situation is as shown in Fig. S55a. When animals are very dehydrated (dried out), blood gets thick, and red blood cells can't work properly. Humans are very ill when they lose 1/10 of their body water (b).

When an organism is dry and then drinks a lot of water suddenly, case (c) can happen. Desert animals like camels cope better than people. Their bodies can lose three times more water than ours, and their red blood cells do not burst if they drink a lot of water fast.

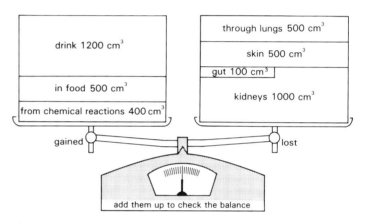

S56 Human daily water balance

In general an organism must gain each day the amount of water it loses. (Growing organisms need extra water, as they need extra everything else). The diagram (Fig. S56) shows a possible water balance for a human for one day. Your water balance is probably different. Your size, the air temperature and how much you drink are just a few of the sources of variation.

Questions

1. How is blood involved in keeping a mammal's body at a steady temperature? Write a limerick beginning
   'There was a young reindeer called . . .'
   as part of your answer.

2. (a) Animals like frogs are often described as cold-blooded. Why do you think this is misleading?

   (b) In very cold conditions, people sometimes lose fingers or toes because the blood supply has been cut off for so long (frostbite). This isn't too great, but the alternative is worse. What is the alternative and why is it worse?

   (c) James Bond staggers out of the desert. He has walked many miles in the blazing heat. He begs for a drink – a big drink – of water. Do you give him lots of water or a little? Why?

Transplants

Replacing a diseased organ by a healthy one seems like a good idea, but transplants are difficult. Even in a simple case – blood transfusions – patients used to die.

In 1900 Karl Landsteiner discovered why – and transfusions became safer. The answer lay in **blood groups**. Your blood group is decided by one or two of the proteins you have in your red blood cells. You may have **antibodies** in your plasma for the red cell proteins you haven't got.

If you mix blood from two similar groups, nothing happens.

If you mix blood with plasma which has the wrong type of antibodies, they clump the red blood cells. The cells are destroyed and capillaries are damaged, as they are blocked by the clumps.

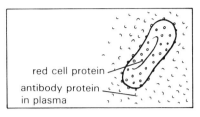

S57 Blood proteins matter

Right antibodies don't react with red cell protein	
Wrong antibodies react with red cell protein. Red cells stick together	

S58

If your blood group is	you have these red cell proteins	but **not**	and your plasma has these antibodies	these antibodies clump blood cells from	so you can only receive blood from
A	A	B	anti-B	B and AB people	A and O people
B	B	A	anti-A	A and AB people	B and O people
O	neither	A and B	anti-A and anti-B	A, B and AB people	O people
AB	A and B	neither	neither	nobody	anybody

Blood cells are soon replaced by the recipient's own cells. Transplants which have to last longer have greater problems.

The small differences in the proteins of the donor and recipient tissues trigger the recipient's defence system. White blood cells normally make antibodies to attack invaders like bacteria. They can also make them against the cells of a transplant. This may take a few days or weeks, and during this time a transplant patient is given treatment to prevent the white blood cells from acting. The patient is defenceless against disease and has to live in near-sterile conditions. Donors are chosen so that chemical differences are as few as possible. At the moment only a few organs, such as kidneys, can be transplanted. Rejection is likely – the recipient's defences destroy the transplant.

The cornea is special, as it has no blood supply and is not affected by the defence system. Undamaged corneas can be used to repair damage to the front of the eye. They are taken from people who have given permission for their eyes to be used after death.

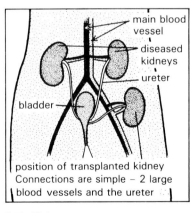

position of transplanted kidney
Connections are simple – 2 large blood vessels and the ureter

S59 Kidney transplants

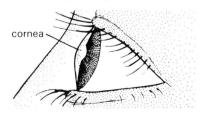

S60 The cornea is a special case

171

Immunization

Once you've had some diseases, you don't catch them again – you're **immune**. Part of the body defence system which formed to fight the disease remains ready for action after the disease is over. The next time they're needed, antibodies form quickly instead of after several days. The disease organism does not have a chance to multiply and make you ill (Fig. S61).

weakened strains can be used to immunize against	
smallpox	polio
TB	rabies

dead micro-organisms can be used in defence against		
cholera		flu
measles	rabies	polio

Immunization involves giving the body a dose of the disease-causing organism in weakened or dead form. No illness results but the defence system is triggered. If an immunized person later meets the same disease organism the defence system acts at once – the organism doesn't have a chance.

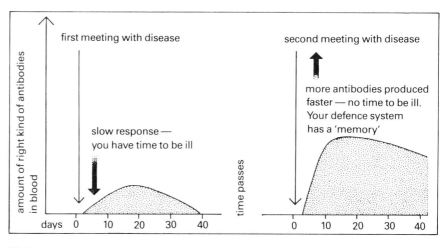

S61

Immunization doesn't always work, but one big success story is smallpox – a disease which once killed up to half the people who caught it. It looks as though a programme of immunization run by the World Health Organization has wiped out this disease completely – but only time will make this certain.

It has been a long struggle. The ancient Chinese partly protected themselves by using a weak strain of smallpox which they introduced by a scratch in the skin. Edward Jenner improved the technique in 1796. There was a folk story that people who had had cowpox, a mild disease caught from cattle, did not catch smallpox. Jenner tested the idea on a young man – James Phipps – who did not catch smallpox after the inoculation of cowpox. The idea eventually caught on after a lot of resistance. Immunization is also known as vaccination, after Jenner's discovery. Vaccinus is the Latin word for cow.

Improvements in immunization against smallpox seem to have been successful, but just one smallpox victim could start an epidemic. People gradually lose their immunity, and they aren't having smallpox vaccinations any more.

S62

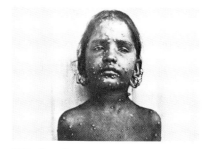

S63 Smallpox victim

Waste disposal

Organisms produce a number of unwanted materials as part of their body chemistry. Getting rid of them (and getting rid of excess materials taken in) is called **excretion.**

T1 Plant waste disposal

Plants have few excretion problems. They tick over more slowly than animals, and wastes build up slowly. Unlike animals they can

(a) re-use waste nitrogenous materials

(b) use up the waste product of respiration (CO_2) in photosynthesis.

In **animals,** excretion involves getting rid of a number of waste materials. The diagram (Fig. T2) shows the routes used by mammals.

Undigested food leaving as faeces doesn't count in excretion, as it has never been part of the body – just passing through.

Kidneys keep the osmotic balance of body cells stable.

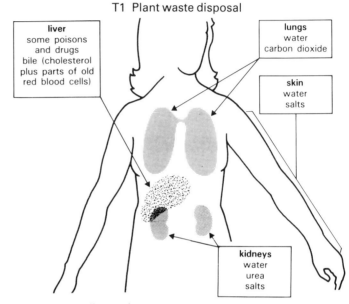

liver
some poisons
and drugs
bile (cholesterol
plus parts of old
red blood cells)

lungs
water
carbon dioxide

skin
water
salts

kidneys
water
urea
salts

T2 Animal waste disposal

The kidneys are important in varying water loss. They are also important in animals which have to get rid of extra water. Fresh-water fish have blood more concentrated than pond or river or lake water.

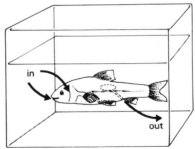

Water enters by osmosis. Kidneys get rid of extra water as urine – otherwise fish would swell.

However, kidneys can cause problems. Salt-water fish have blood less concentrated than sea water.

They lose water by osmosis. They also lose some through the kidneys, though they only produce enough urine to get rid of wastes.

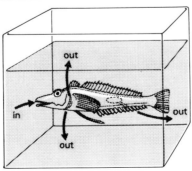

These fish drink salt water and pump the salt out through the gills. The left-over water makes up for losses.

We live on land, where water loss is always a problem – so why do we have kidneys, and how do they work? Read on to find out.

T3 Kidneys and regulating the osmotic balance of cells

Kidneys

The cells of an animal's body live in water, whether the animal does or not. Regardless of what the animal eats, the cells must have a stable environment – maintained (in mammals) mainly by the kidneys. Kidneys do three things at once.

(a) they control the amount of water in the body
(b) they control the amount of salt and other minerals in the body
(c) they excrete (get rid of) urea and other wastes containing nitrogen.

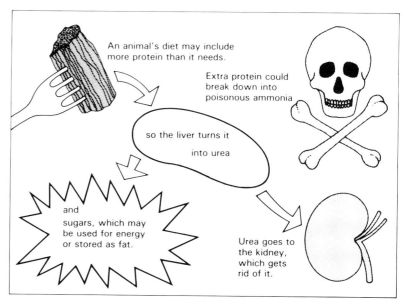

T4 The story of urea

Kidneys produce a concentrated urea solution, called **urine** (pee), which trickles down tubes to the bladder for short-term storage.

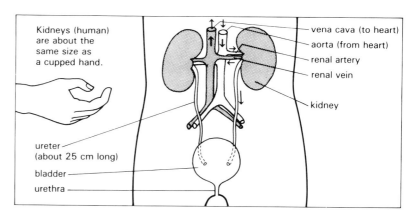

T5

Kidneys are fragile, but one normally functioning kidney is enough to keep the body healthy.

Cut in half, a kidney is dark red. A lot of blood flows through it and is processed by it – 70 litres an hour.

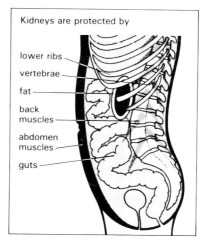

T6

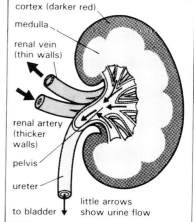

T7 Section through a kidney

Under a microscope, the medulla and cortex are a confusing mass of tubes. These tubes are capillaries plus the kidney tubules – **nephrons**.

Straightened out, each nephron would be 40 mm long.

They are *very* thin. Each kidney contains about a million nephrons.

Each nephron is folded up.

The Bowman's capsule surrounds a knot of blood capillaries – the **glomerulus**. Blood pressure forces water and smaller molecules into the nephron.

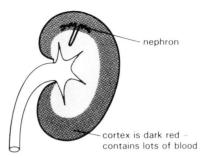

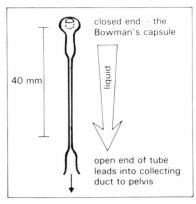

T8 Section through a kidney to show the position of nephrons

T9 The main parts of a nephron

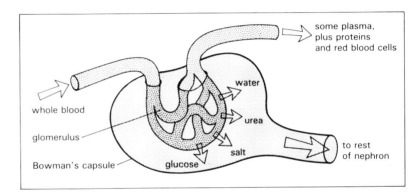

T10 The start of a nephron

As the liquid moves through the nephron, tubule cells collect useful items – glucose, most of the salt and minerals, and water. These are returned to the blood. Capillaries wind around the tubule.

The tubule cells can vary the amount of salt and water they retrieve. Drinking a lot results in lots of dilute urine, because the tubules take back less water. If there is too much salt in food, the tubules take less salt back into the blood. A water shortage means a smaller amount of more concentrated urine, as the body holds on to its water.

In any case, the body gets rid of its urea (though some urea may take several trips through the kidney before it is removed). Fig. T12 just shows what happens, not what it looks like.

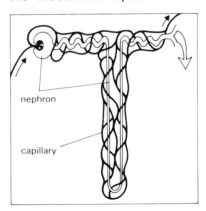

T11 A nephron with its capillaries

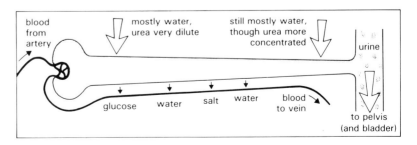

T12 The same nephron straightened and shortened. The width of the tube indicates how much liquid is in the tube at a particular point.

Summary and questions

Summary

Blood consists of the following:

(a) plasma – a watery solution which transports heat, dissolved food, wastes and gases round the body. It also transports proteins, which include antibodies and some hormones

(b) red blood cells – important in the transport of gases, especially oxygen

(c) white blood cells – involved in defending the body from invaders like bacteria

(d) platelets – which, along with some of the blood proteins, are important in clotting.

Blood must be of the right concentration, otherwise osmosis can damage cells.

The water balance of an organism is always important and the kidney is especially vital in providing a suitable concentration of body fluids to bathe cells. The kidney is also important in getting rid of nitrogen waste in the form of urea made by the liver. Urea and water and a little salt form urine which is excreted. The excretion of other wastes often involves the same organs as water loss.

Questions

1. Write this out – filling in the blanks.
   By far the most common of the two types of cells in blood are the _____ blood cells. White blood cells are involved in _____ the body, while red blood cells transport _____ from the _____ to the _____ _____, and transport carbon dioxide back again. _____ blood cells remain in capillaries, but _____ blood cells can leave these vessels. Red blood cells contain _____ made of protein and _____ but have no _____. White blood cells do have a _____, although the shape may be unusual.

2. (a) Water moves in and out of a fish through the gut lining and the gills. Why not the rest of the fish's surface?
   (b) How much water is gained and lost by a human each day, according to the text? (It's just an average.)
   (c) What would probably happen to the amount of urine produced if a person (i) drank six large cups of tea? (ii) lay all day in the sun without drinking any extra liquid? (iii) drank just over a litre of liquid during the day? (iv) ate several large slices of water melon?
   (d) Why do you think the text says that cells live in water?

3. (a) Draw a diagram of the outside of a kidney.
   (b) Label the tubes to it and from it.
   (c) Say what the tubes contain and how the contents differ from each other.

4. Carbon monoxide is produced by car engines and cigarettes. It reacts with haemoglobin and will not come unstuck (unlike CO_2 or O_2). Once this has happened, the haemoglobin is no good for transporting other things. What do you think would happen to a person who had breathed in (i) a little carbon monoxide (ii) a lot of carbon monoxide? Why?

5. Dave cuts himself and the blood spurts out in bright scarlet bursts. Pete cuts himself, but the blood is darker and flows out smoothly. (Both have cut their arms.)
   (a) One of them has cut through an artery and one a vein. Who has done what? Explain your answer.
   (b) You want to reduce bleeding enough to give the clotting mechanisms a chance to work. You take different kinds of action in the two cases. Which of the following methods would you use in Pete's case? Why?
   (i) See if you can find a pressure point between the wound and the heart where the blood vessel can be flattened against a bone. Press there.
   (ii) Raise the limb in the air.
   (c) Briefly describe what happens once bleeding has slowed enough for clotting to start.

6. Draw a diagram of
   (a) a red blood cell
   (b) a white blood cell
   Show how big each cell is. Where are the cells made? Which is likely to live longest?

Theme 4 Development of organisms and continuity of life

Growth

Growth usually means getting larger – an increase in size. It involves making or eating food, and turning the food material into the stuff we are made of. We can look at the growth of single cells or organisms or populations (groups of organisms).

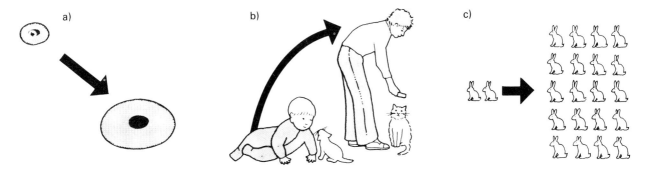

U1 (a) Cells, (b) organisms and (c) populations grow

There are different ways of growing.
Something may grow until it reaches a particular size and then divide into two (Fig. U2).

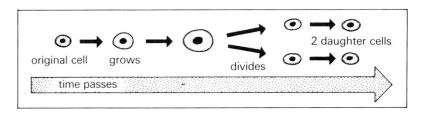

U2

Or an organism may grow for a while and then stop. Only parts reproduce (divide) (Fig. U3).

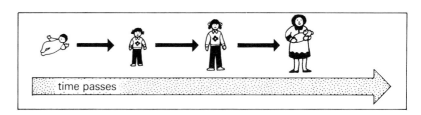

U3

Sometimes only part of an organism grows – this is especially true of plants. (Fig. U4).

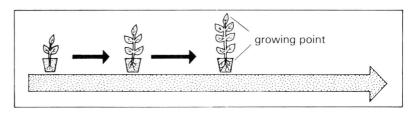

U4

Growing often means changes in shape too (Fig. U5).

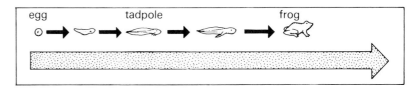

U5

Measuring growth
The way growth is measured depends a lot on what is being measured. Here are some guidelines.

Counting
Counting numbers of organisms (in a population) or cells gives an idea of growth because it tells us how fast things can multiply (Fig. U8).

Sometimes counting the parts of an organism is a measure of growth – like counting the rings in a tree stump.

This only works if there is any change of numbers as time passes and things get larger. It doesn't work for things like the legs of a starfish.

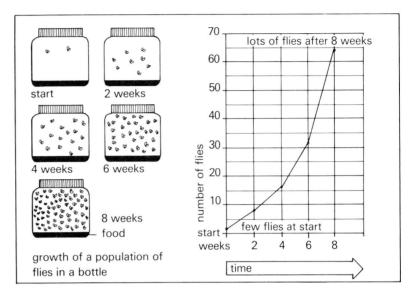

U6 Measuring growth by counting

Height or length
This includes all the kinds of things which are measured with a ruler (Fig. U7).

There are snags. What if two leaves grow to the same length, but one is much wider than the other (Fig. U8)?

leaves may start the same length, and end the same length, but B has grown more

measure breadth as well as length (or surface area)

U8

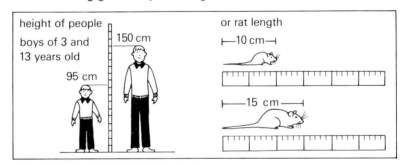

U7 Measuring growth by measuring increase in length

Mass
This measures the amount of material added in growth.

Wet mass is when a living organism is weighed – water and all . Using wet mass an organism's growth can be followed over time (Fig. U9).

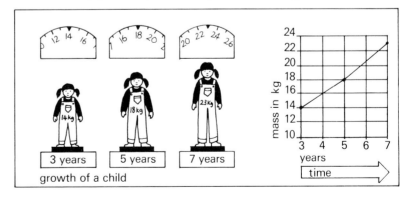

U9 Measuring growth by measuring mass changes

Dry mass is the mass of all the dry material in an organism. Water is removed by drying in an oven until all the water is gone – so that further heating makes no difference to the weight. It shows just how much extra protein, carbohydrate and so on is gained in growth. There is one big disadvantage – the organism has to be dead and can grow no more.

179

Differentiation

For many organisms, growth has three parts (Fig. U10).

1. Cells **divide**.

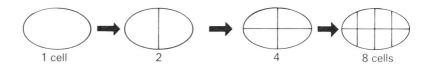

2. Cells **grow**.

3. Cells **differentiate**. They change their shape in order to do particular jobs.

a flat cell which might be part of the skin

U10

If cells didn't differentiate, large organisms would be a collapsed heap of jelly. In other words, they couldn't exist.

There are many types of possible cell.
Animals have muscle cells and nerve cells, among others (Fig. U11).

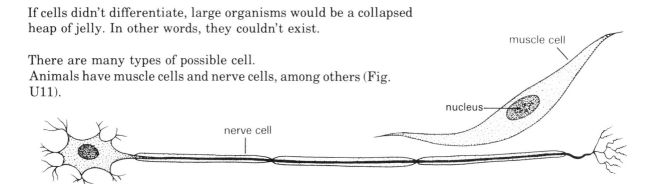

U11 Animal cells

Plant cell types include palisade cells and guard cells. (Fig. U12).

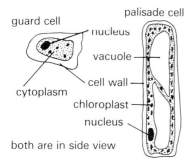

U12 Plant cells

If you look through a microscope at the growing tip of a root, the three stages can be seen (Fig. U13).

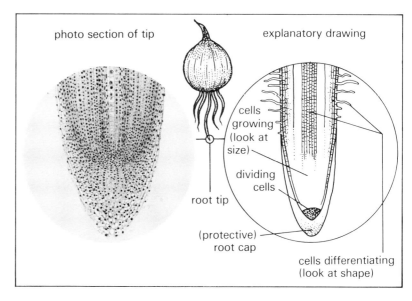

U13 Growing tip of a root

180

Groups of the same kind of cells are known as **tissues**.

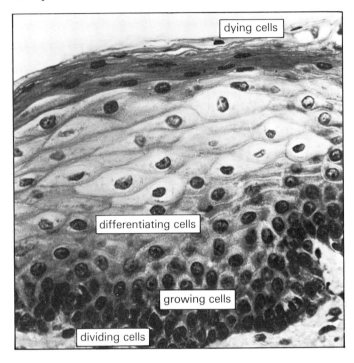

U14 Growing skin tissue

Groups of tissues working together to do a particular job are called organs. Plant organs include flowers, leaves and roots. Animal organs include guts and lungs.

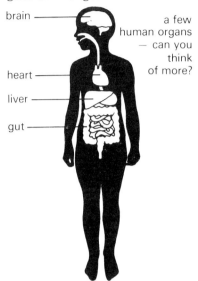

U15 A few human organs

a) Organisms

b) are made up of organs

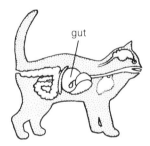

An important part of growth is the formation of the right organ in the right place at the right time (Fig. U17).

c) which are made up of tissues

the gut consists of several kinds of tissue (muscle, skin and gland tissue)

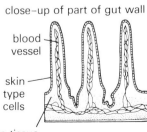

d) which are made up of cells

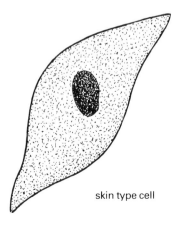

skin type cell

U17 The cow shows a mistake in development – an extra leg. Perhaps cells divided at the wrong time; perhaps some cells differentiated into bone and muscle cells instead of skin cells. The next page or so is about cell division and how it is controlled

U16

Cells - a reminder page

Plants and animals are made up of cells. Animal and plant cells are similar in many important ways.

They have a thin layer (a **membrane**) round them, made of protein and fat. The membrane controls what goes in and out of a cell.

Much of the inside of the cell is **cytoplasm**, which is where most chemical reactions happen. For example, in the cytoplasm glucose is broken down to release energy and proteins are made. Cytoplasm feels like jelly but is more complicated.

There is a **nucleus**, which contains the instructions for running the cell. The nucleus has a membrane around it.

There are other structures in cytoplasm besides the nucleus. For example there are tiny bags of enzymes called mitochondria. Mitochondria do the hard work of respiration for cells.

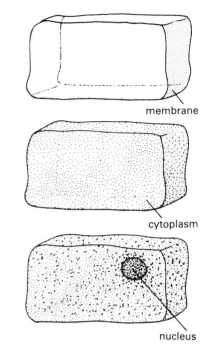

U18 Building a cell

Cells can be all kinds of shapes depending on the job they do. In books, an animal cell is often drawn as a circle and a plant cell as a square. This may be because it's easy to prepare cells like these to look at under a microscope. Don't be fooled. Cells vary in shape a good deal.

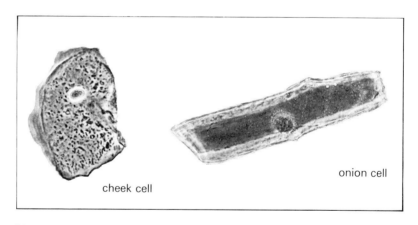

U19 Animal and plant cells are different

There are real differences between plant and animal cells (Fig. U19).

Plant cells have a cellulose cell wall outside the membrane. Many have vacuoles – membrane bags full of salty or sugary solution. Palisade cells have smaller membrane bags full of chlorophyll (chloroplasts). However, lots of plant cells don't have them. For example, the cells in the roots don't.

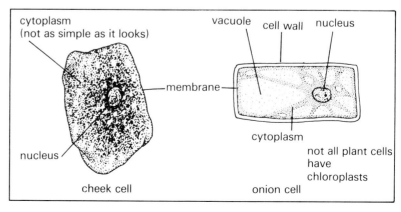

U20 Interpreting Fig. U19

The nucleus

The nucleus organizes chemicals into cells. It is the 'recipe' for the cells. Cooking recipes give the ingredients and mixing instructions for food such as cake. Different recipes (sets of instructions) produce different kinds of cake.

The cell acts as its own 'cook' as the instructions from the nucleus are followed by the cytoplasm.

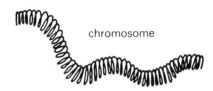

chromosome

U21 Around this page is a line. Here is a line of the same length coiled up. It is much easier to see.

The instructions for a cell are long thin molecules. Normally these molecules are uncoiled in the nucleus and can't be seen.

Just before a cell divides, the instruction molecules coil up and can be seen. They are called **chromosomes** (Fig. U22).

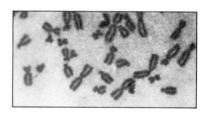

U22 Human chromosomes

Most cells in an organism have the same number of chromosomes. This means that the cells in the organism in Fig. U23 have six chromosomes. The cells have all the instructions needed to make all the cells in the organism. Different types of cell happen when different bits of the instructions are followed.

These cells have only 6 chromosomes so it's easier to see what is happening.

Bands on chromosomes show which instructions are used in different kinds of cell.

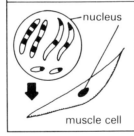

nucleus

muscle cell

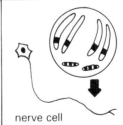

nerve cell

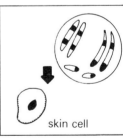

skin cell

U23 Cells in the same organism have the same chromosomes

Different kinds of organism have different numbers of chromosomes. They may be different sizes. This is not surprising – kinds of organisms are different because they have quite different sets of instructions.

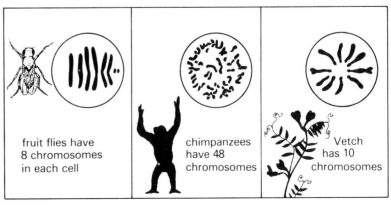

fruit flies have 8 chromosomes in each cell

chimpanzees have 48 chromosomes

Vetch has 10 chromosomes

A very important part of cell division is the division of the nucleus.

U24 Different organisms have different chromosome numbers

Mitosis - cell division

Between a fertilized egg and an adult organism are many cell divisions. Whenever an organism needs repair there are more cell divisions.

Every division turns one cell into two. The two cells each have a complete set of chromosomes. Chromosomes are copied (doubled) before every division – otherwise cells would soon have only bits of the instructions they need.

Mitosis is the way in which two complete sets of chromosomes muddled up in one cell are sorted into two groups – one complete set in each new cell.

The diagrams on the opposite page show the position of chromosomes at particular stages of mitosis. The chromosomes move from one stage to another all the time. Try making pipe-cleaner chromosomes and taking them through mitosis. The cells in Fig. U25 have four chromosomes but the same things happen if there are lots of chromosomes

After mitosis the rest of the cell divides, and cell division is over. It usually takes several hours. The new cells can grow and divide or perhaps differentiate.

U25 After mitosis both 'daughter' cells have the same number of chromosomes

Looking for cells dividing
Green plants have growing points where cells are dividing rapidly.

Cut off a growing point and it takes time for a plant to recover. Grass grows as fast as you mow the lawn because the cutter does not chop off the growing point.

In animals, cells may be dividing anywhere in the body – skin cells, cells lining the gut, kidney cells are among those that are always being replaced. Your body produces hundreds of millions of new cells every day. The process slows down as you get older.

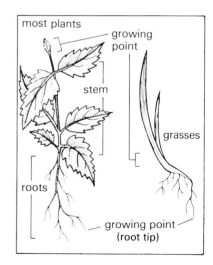

U26 Growing points in plants

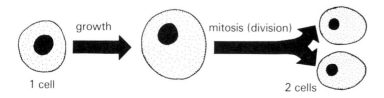

1 cell   growth   mitosis (division)   2 cells

U27 To summarize

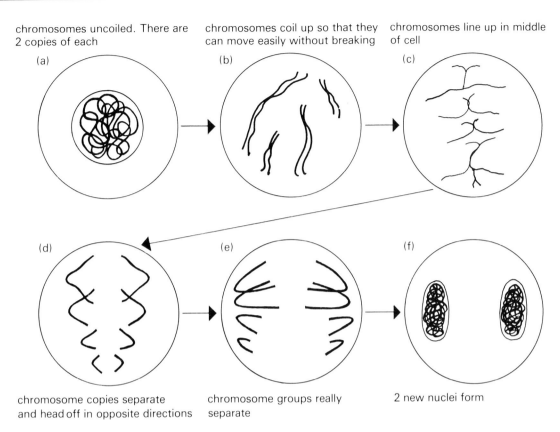

(a) chromosomes uncoiled. There are 2 copies of each

(b) chromosomes coil up so that they can move easily without breaking

(c) chromosomes line up in middle of cell

(d) chromosome copies separate and head off in opposite directions

(e) chromosome groups really separate

(f) 2 new nuclei form

U28 Mitosis

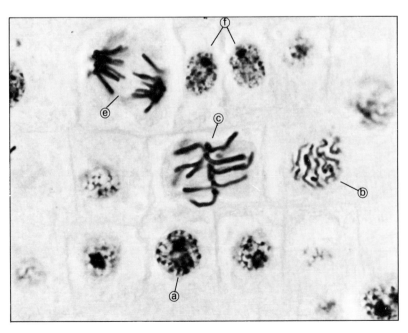

U29 Mitosis in dividing plant cells. The letters refer to the stages drawn in Fig. U28 above.

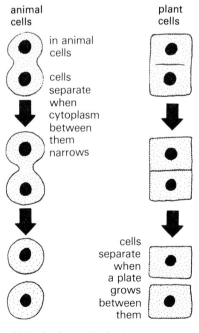

animal cells

plant cells

in animal cells

cells separate when cytoplasm between them narrows

cells separate when a plate grows between them

U30 At the end of mitosis, the daughter cells separate. Animals and plant cells separate slightly differently.

Controlling mitosis (cell division)

Cells usually divide at just the right rate for growth and repairs.

Skin cells

Skin cells usually divide just fast enough to replace dead cells which flake off. If skin is cut, the cells in the area start to divide faster to fill in the cut. When the cut heals, the cells go back to their normal division rate.

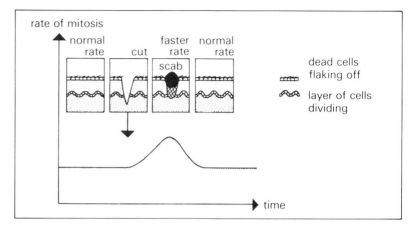

U31 Skin cells divide faster when a cut is healing and then go back to normal

Some cell divisions are controlled by chemicals from glands, others by whether light is present or not. Also, mitosis is often slower when cells have others all around them. The cell membrane is the part of the cell touching other cells. It may be because they have peculiar cell membranes that some cells divide too fast.

Cancer cells are such cells. Uncontrolled cell divisions often produce a lump – a tumour. Cancer tumours grow fast and destroy other tissues. (Some tumours are benign – non-cancerous. They are slow growing lumps which do not destroy other tissues.)

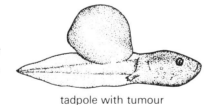

tadpole with tumour

U32 Uncontrolled mitosis can produce lumps (tumours)

Cancer cells do not do any of the jobs needed to keep an animal healthy and alive. When they replace normal cells, they can kill an animal.

Normal cells can change into cancer cells for many reasons.

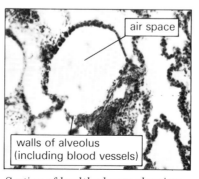

Section of healthy lungs showing alveoli

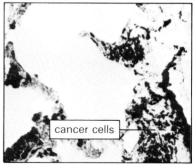

The same kind of tissue, but with cancer cells

U33 Cancer cells look abnormal and behave abnormally

A change from normal to cancer cell can be triggered by

1. **Chemicals** – like cigarette smoke, asbestos, even hair dye. There are many chemicals that may be involved.

2. **Radiation** – like ultra-violet light, X-rays and radiation from radioactive materials.

3. **Viruses** – these are simple, small living things. They have been found to trigger some cancers

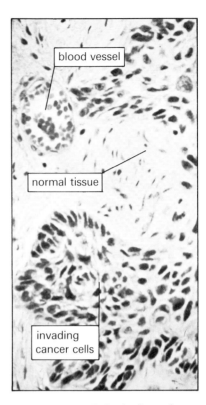

U34 Cancer cells in the bronchus wall (an early stage)

A cancer can start in many places in the body. Some are easier to spot than others. If a tumour is spotted early enough, it can often be removed or the cells killed by chemicals or radiation. If it's not found soon enough, some cancer cells may have broken away from the main tumour. These cells can travel around the body in the blood and start cancers elsewhere in the body. It can be very difficult to find and treat these secondary cancers.

Cancer cells are not so very different from normal cells. Their cell division controls have gone wrong somehow. Perhaps research into the way mitosis is usually controlled will help us to understand this group of killing diseases.

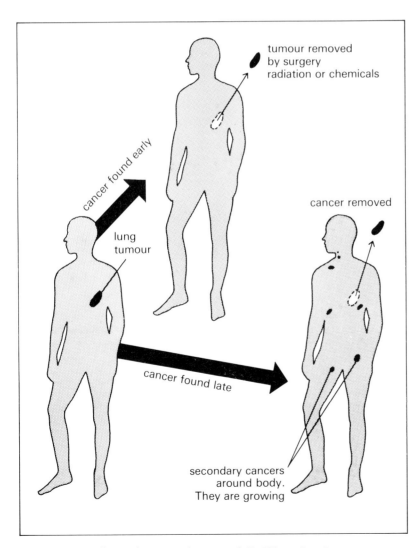

U35 Cancer cells can be treated successfully if found early

Summary and questions

Summary
Cells, organisms and populations can all grow – get larger. There are several ways of measuring growth.
In normal development:
1. cells increase in size;
2. cells divide by mitosis in a controlled manner;
3. cells differentiate – become specialized.
Cancer happens when growth is not normal.

Questions

1. What would you measure if you wanted to follow the growth of
   (a) a young brother or sister from one month to one year.
   (b) the population of guppies in a fish tank.
   (c) a sycamore seedling for its first two years.
   Give one reason for your choice in each case.

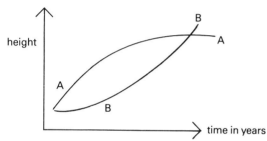

U36

2. This graph shows the growth of two organisms. What does it tell you about them? It isn't really a very helpful graph as so much information is missing. What other information should the graph include?

3. Explain what each of the following words means: growth, population, chromosomes, differentiation, mitosis, cancer.

4. Which of the following statements is true and which false? Write out the true ones and a corrected version of the false ones.
   (a) When cells are differentiating, they are dividing.
   (b) Palisade and muscle cells are examples of cells after differentiating.
   (c) If you want to find dividing plant cells, it would be sensible to examine shoot and root tips.
   (d) Only plant cells can divide by mitosis.
   (e) Only plant cells have cellulose cell walls.
   (f) During mitosis, the membrane around the nucleus disappears.

5. You are looking at a group of dividing cells on a slide. You have to decide whether they are plant or animal cells. There are several clues. Give one connected with the structure (shape and make up) of the cells. Give another connected with the way the cytoplasm divides.

6. Anya prepares cells from two places in a plant and looks at 50 cells from each place. She counts the number of cells at each stage shown in Figs. U28 and U29. Draw a graph showing her results. Which sample came from an actively growing area and why?

sample	stage a	stage b	stage c	stage d	stage e	stage f
A	17	6	5	4	7	12
B	41	2	1	1	0	5

7. This cell is part-way through mitosis.

   U37
   (a) Copy it into your book and label the membrane, cytoplasm and chromosomes.
   (b) At the end of mitosis, there will be two cells. How many chromosomes will each of them have in this case?
   (c) Draw a diagram to show the stage before the one shown.
   (d) Draw another diagram to show what happens next.

8. (a) Bob is worried about 'catching' cancer from a friend who is in hospital being treated for lung cancer. What advice would you give Bob and why?
   (b) Ros had a lump which has recently grown on the back of her hand. It doesn't hurt but she is a bit worried about it. What would you advise her to do and why?

Patterns of growth - from egg to adult

Many-celled animals and plants grow from a single cell (a
fertilized egg).

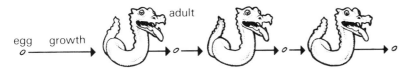

V1

This repeat pattern is often drawn as a **life cycle** (a circle) –
maybe to save space. It doesn't mean that the adult comes from its
own egg.

This section is about how eggs are produced, how they are
fertilized and the pattern of growth once the egg is fertilized.
There are three main patterns of growth 'from egg to adult' to
look out for.

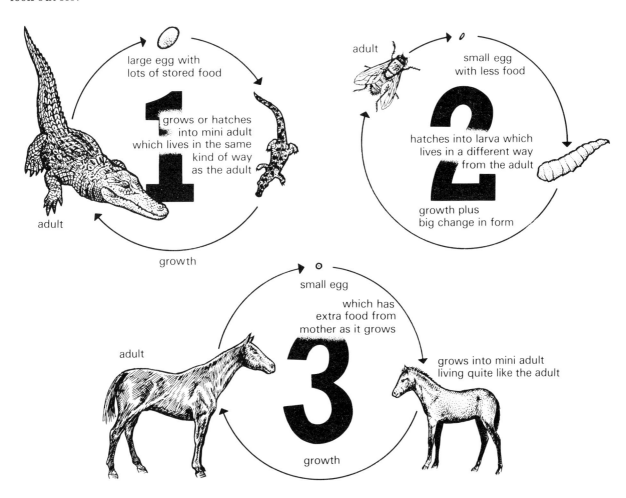

V2

189

Sexual reproduction in plants

Sexual reproduction is all about two sex cells or **gametes** meeting and fusing. The actual moment when the cells join (**fertilization**) tends to get lost in the preparations and results, even in plants. Still, it's what all the fuss is about.

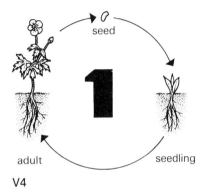

V4

The sex cells in plants are the ovule (egg) and the pollen (male cell).

Gametes are made in reproductive organs, which may be
(a) part of the same flower e.g. tulip
or (b) different flowers, e.g. hazel

Male cells
Pollen is made in stamens, the male organs. **Stamens** consist of an **anther** and a **filament**.

Pollen is made in the anther, which splits open when ripe to release the dust-like pollen. Pollen coats are very tough. By looking closely at a grain of pollen (an electron microscope is best) you can tell which type of plant it came from.

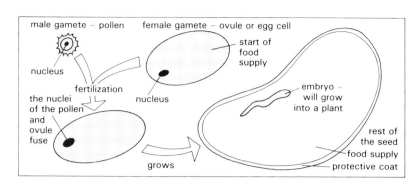

V3 Pollen plus ovule equals seed

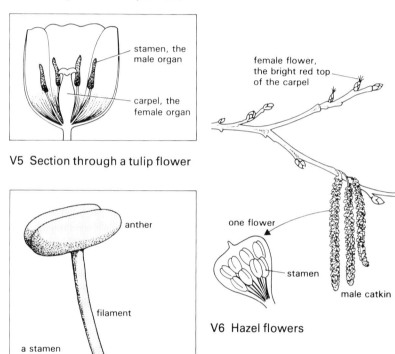

V5 Section through a tulip flower

V6 Hazel flowers

V7 The parts of a stamen

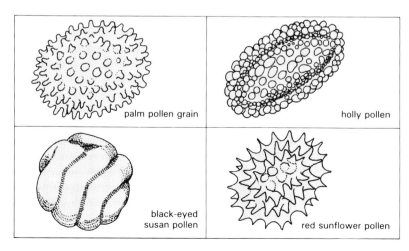

V8 Different types of pollen

190

Female cells

Female sex cells, the ovules, are made in an ovary which is part of a carpel. Carpels are female sex organs.

Carpels consist of a **stigma**, a **style**, an **ovary** and one or many **ovules**, arranged in various ways. All the parts come in a lot of different shapes and sizes. The stigma is often sticky to trap pollen.

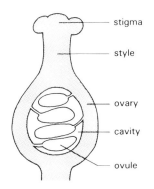

V9 A section through a carpel

Problem

getting pollen to the ovule. Plants have come up with so many solutions that they have a double-page spread to themselves – 'More on pollination', over the page.

Fertilization

Once the pollen grain has arrived on the stigma it splits and a tube starts to grow down through the stigma and style. The pollen tube only grows well if the pollen is from the same kind of plant as the carpel.

When it reaches the ovary, the pollen tube grows towards an ovule and enters it. It is hard to see what happens in fertilization, but it seems that the tip of the tube breaks and a nucleus from the pollen tube meets a nucleus in the ovule and joins up with it.

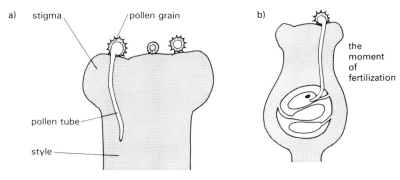

V10 Fertilization in section

The ex-ovule grows into a seed – an embryo plus its food supply. Stamens and petals die. The ovary grows to form a fruit, and the top of the flower stalk may also be involved in helping the seed travel from the parent plant and survive.

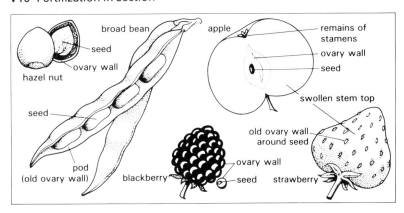

V11 Various seeds

191

More on pollination

There are all sorts of methods of transporting pollen from stamen to stigma. Flowers are usually adapted to one way or another. Pollen travels by **water** in a few plants like Canadian pond weed. There are more kinds of plants whose pollen travel by **wind** – examples include nettles, dock, trees with catkins, oaks and grasses.

Watch out for:
1. large amounts of small light pollen
2. small scentless flowers, often green
3. feathery stigmas – they have large surfaces to catch pollen
4. large anthers hanging out on long filaments so that pollen is easily blown away
5. flowers held above leaves or produced before leaves are out.

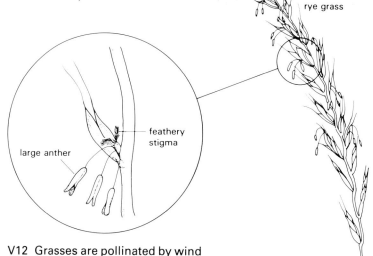

V12 Grasses are pollinated by wind

Animal pollination is also common. The flowers are quite different. They attract animals which carry pollen from flower to flower on their bodies.

(a) The flower provides something the animals want – usually food, such as extra **pollen** to eat or **nectar** to drink. Nectar is a sugary liquid which animals like bees turn into honey.

(b) The flower signals to the animals. It pays to advertise!

(c) The flower is constructed so that as an animal collects food, it brushes against the stigma and stamens. This means it picks up pollen, and pollen already on it from another flower rubs off.

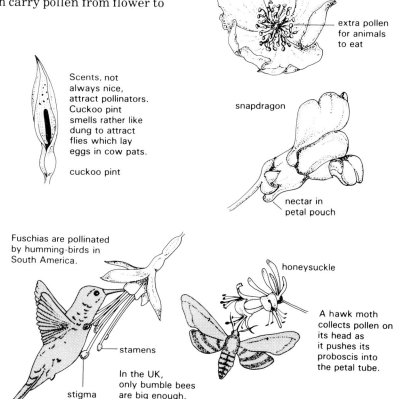

V13 Animal pollinated flowers

Self pollination

In all the flowers we have seen so far, pollen travels from one flower to another, often on a different plant. This is called **cross-pollination.**

Self-pollination happens when pollen from the stamens fertilizes an ovule in the same flower. This is less chancey but it reduces variety, and many plants have ways of avoiding it. For example, in rose-bay willowherb, stamens and carpels are not ripe together, so self-fertilization is avoided.

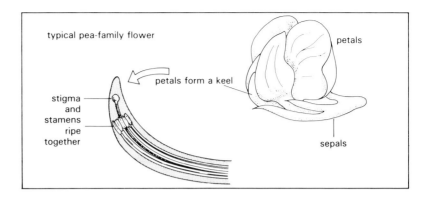

V14 An example of a self-pollinated flower

In some plants, pollen will not grow on the stigma of the flower that produced it. This is self-sterility. Broad beans and peas have lost their self-sterility, and they often self-pollinate. Other plants self-fertilize when there are few insects around to carry their pollen.

Plants from many parts of the world can grow in Britain, but they may not be able to breed here. They may only be pollinated by one insect, which isn't found in Britain. The fig is an example.

V15 Fig

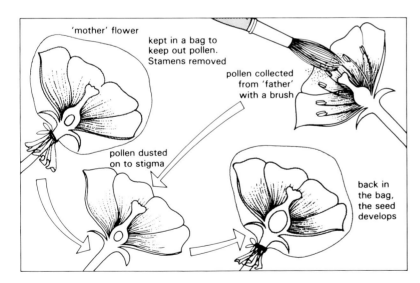

V16 Breed your own

We may control pollination to produce new plant varieties. Pansies are the result of cross breeding three varieties of violet.

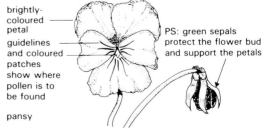

V17 Pansies are insect pollinated

Seed to adult plant

Many green plants start their offspring off with a supply of food –
as a seed.

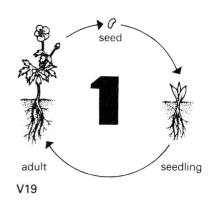

V19

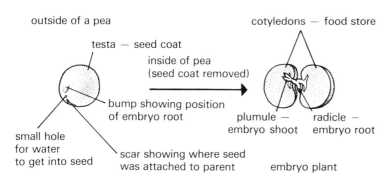

V18 Parts of a seed

Many seeds have a **dormant** phase when the embryo plant inside
doesn't grow – say over the winter. Apple pips have to be cold for
a time before they can grow. It looks as though many seeds need a
spell of cold before dormancy can be ended. The next stage is
germination, when the embryo grows into a seedling. Figure
V20 shows three stages in the germination of a pea.

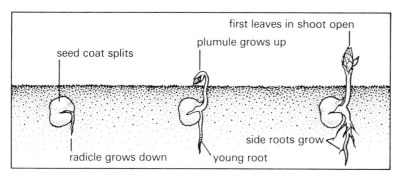

V20 Germination of a seed

The seedling will grow in size and eventually flower when
conditions are right – the cycle is complete.

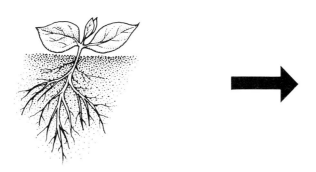

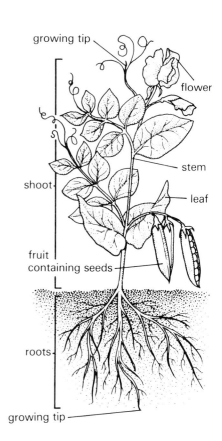

V21 Seedling to adult

Summary and questions

Summary
Flowers are organs of sexual reproduction. They consist of stamens, which are male and make pollen, and carpels which are female and contain ovules or egg cells in an ovary. Carpels also have a stigma, and a style which joins ovary and stigma. Pollination is the transfer of pollen from stamen to stigma. It is usually the result of wind blowing the pollen, or of animals, especially insects, carrying pollen on their bodies. Once on the stigma, pollen grows a pollen tube down to an ovule. Fertilization occurs when pollen and ovule join and form a seed. Flowers also have petals which may be brightly coloured to attract insects. They have an outer layer of sepals (usually green) which protect the delicate bud, and later often support the petals.

Questions

1. Match up the part of the flower from column A with what it does in column B. Write out complete sentences.

A	B
The anther	is the part of the carpel which receives pollen.
The filament	protect buds and support petals.
The stigma	is the part of the stamen which makes pollen.
The style	may help to attract insects.
The ovary	holds up the stigma.
Petals	holds up the anther.
Sepals	is the part of the carpel which contains the ovule.

2.

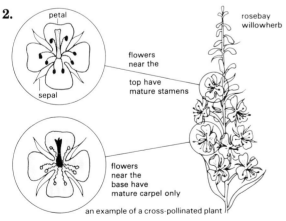

V22

Do you think this flower is cross-pollinated or self-pollinated and why?

3. Make an advertisement for a flower of your choice (or design an ideal flower). The advertisement should bring out why your flower is so good at getting pollinated.

4. Copy out this diagram. Draw it large enough to fill half a page. Label everything which has an arrow pointing to it.

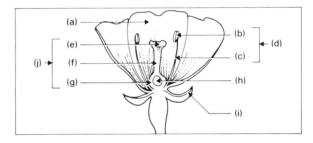

V23 Section through a flower

5. This table compares wind-pollinated and animal-pollinated flowers. Fill in the gaps.

	Wind-pollinated	Animal-pollinated
pollen is		small and often sticky
the amount of pollen produced is	even larger than in animal-pollinated flowers	large
petals are	small and green	
scent is		
nectar is	not made	
stamens are		various sizes and shapes. They are often held up
stigmas are	often feathery, with a large surface to catch pollen	
an example is		a rose

195

Sexual reproduction in animals

Sexual activity in animals, as in plants, is aimed at fertilization – bringing together male and female sex cells or gametes to produce a cell which can grow into a new organism.

Sperm – male gametes

Sperm travel. They are small – you need a microscope to see them. They have tails which thrash around to move them along. They are produced in large numbers as many do not survive or are lost.

snake

man

frog

rat

whale

hen

0.09 cm

V24 Sperm from different animals

Sperm vary in shape and size – but not much.

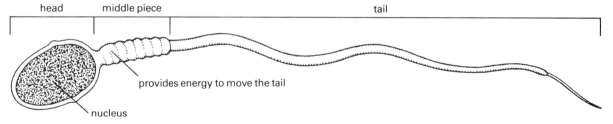

head middle piece tail

provides energy to move the tail

nucleus

V25 An enlarged sperm

Eggs – female gametes

Eggs contain food to start the embryo off in life. They are much larger, don't move, and are produced in smaller numbers.

Unlike sperm, eggs vary in size – to some extent it depends on whether the embryo develops outside the body or not.

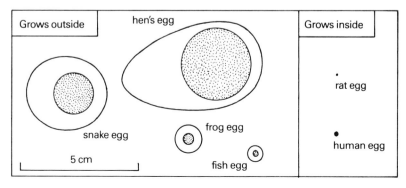

Grows outside hen's egg Grows inside

snake egg

frog egg

fish egg

5 cm

rat egg

human egg

V26

The place where an embryo develops does not have to be the same as the place where fertilization happens. There are three variations.

Fertilization	Embryo grows	Example	
outside	outside	and fish	**must** have water for reproduction
inside	outside	and birds, reptiles, butterflies and so on	doesn't need water. Unless there is a lot of parental care, most eggs get eaten
inside	inside	really just mammals, and the odd fish and snake. Do hedgehogs do it? Yes, but very carefully with flattened spines	protection in the womb during early development gives the embryo a good start in life

V27

a) The male frog's throat amplifies croaks to attract females

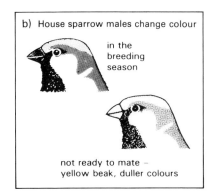

b) House sparrow males change colour in the breeding season

not ready to mate – yellow beak, duller colours

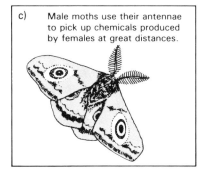

c) Male moths use their antennae to pick up chemicals produced by females at great distances.

V28 Making fertilization more likely

Many female animals are unwilling to mate without a special pattern of behaviour – courtship – which overcomes other behaviour patterns.

This prevents a waste of energy and eggs. It is all geared to finding the best mate of the right species and sex at the right moment.

Ways of bringing the sexes together vary. Many animals use chemical signals (Fig. V28c).

Others use sound – like birds and frogs (Fig. V28a).

'I'm ready to mate' can be said with colours (Fig. V28b).

Courtship displays often sort out which males will father most of the next generation.

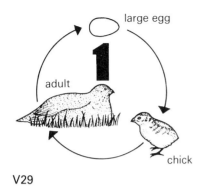

V29

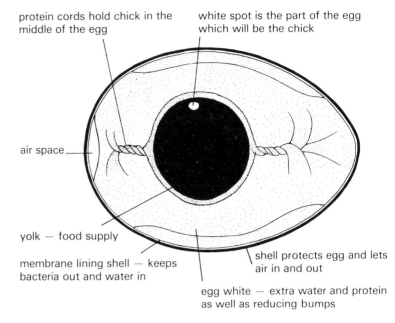

protein cords hold chick in the middle of the egg

white spot is the part of the egg which will be the chick

air space

yolk — food supply

membrane lining shell — keeps bacteria out and water in

shell protects egg and lets air in and out

egg white — extra water and protein as well as reducing bumps

V30 Parts of a bird's egg

Chicks can often feed themselves as soon as they hatch – especially those from eggs with large yolks.

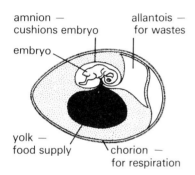

amnion — cushions embryo

allantois — for wastes

embryo

yolk — food supply

chorion — for respiration

V31 Section through an egg showing the membrane bags around the chick

In its private pond, the bird's egg grows into a chick. During this time, it's called an **embryo.** Embryos soon start to develop the organs of an adult.

As it grows, the chick embryo needs a larger respiratory surface. Membranes grow out from the embryo and line the shell.

After three or four weeks the chick pokes into the air space and takes its first breath. It chips its way out of the shell with its egg tooth. The young bird changes little except in size after hatching.

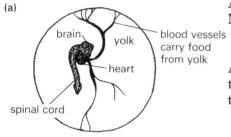

(a)

brain

yolk

blood vessels carry food from yolk

heart

spinal cord

very young embryo — only the basic organs

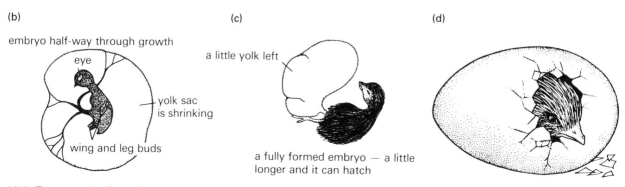

(b)

embryo half-way through growth

eye

yolk sac is shrinking

wing and leg buds

(c)

a little yolk left

a fully formed embryo — a little longer and it can hatch

(d)

V32 The growth of a chick embryo

Egg to adult - butterflies

A butterfly spends the later part of its life as a flying adult looking for a mate. It spends the early part as a crawling larva – eating hard and growing.

Eggs are laid on the food plant. Over a few days (or weeks in some cases) the single egg cell develops into a **larva** or **caterpillar**, which chews its way out. Its first act is to eat its eggcase – and then its plant – steadily and very nearly without stopping.

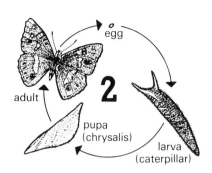

V33

Over the next few weeks it grows rapidly – perhaps to 3000 times its mass at hatching. Being an insect, it has a chitin skin which doesn't grow. From time to time it must moult. It may shed its skin five or more times.

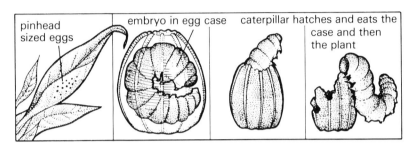

pinhead sized eggs

embryo in egg case

caterpillar hatches and eats the case and then the plant

V34 The egg hatches

A caterpillar has an ideal body for feeding – but not for reproduction. It changes enormously when it becomes a butterfly with reproductive organs and a different life-style. This event is called **metamorphosis**.

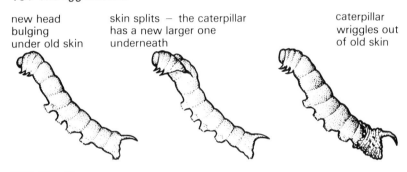

new head bulging under old skin

skin splits – the caterpillar has a new larger one underneath

caterpillar wriggles out of old skin

V35 Moulting

The last larval moult produces a **pupa** or chrysalis. There is then a pause – perhaps 10 days, perhaps over winter. The pupa looks unchanging, but inside it caterpillar tissues are broken down and put together again as adult butterfly tissues. Eventually the pupa case splits. Metamorphosis is over and the **adult** emerges.

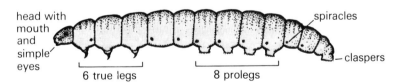

head with mouth and simple eyes

spiracles

claspers

6 true legs

8 prolegs

V36 Parts of a caterpillar

The adult flies off in search of a mate. It may live a few days or a few months, but the only food it takes is nectar – for energy, not further growth.

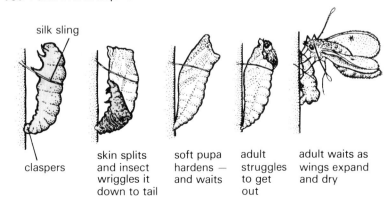

silk sling

claspers

skin splits and insect wriggles it down to tail

soft pupa hardens – and waits

adult struggles to get out

adult waits as wings expand and dry

V37 Metamorphosis

199

Egg to adult-frogs

Another group that undergo metamorphosis are the frogs (and toads). Adult frogs are meat-eaters who can live on land. Their tadpoles are plant-eaters who must remain in water. It's quite a change.

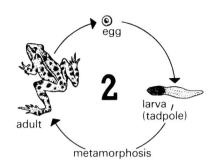

V38

Eggs are laid in water. The tadpoles hatch after a few days and soon start to eat. They are herbivores – interested in pond weed.

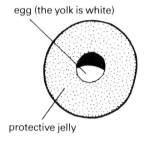
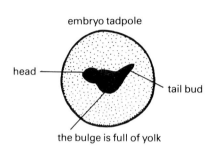

free swimming tadpole

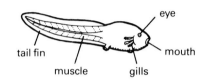

Some changes in metamorphosis are easy to see. Others go on inside the tadpole.

hind legs appear

The froglet then grows – catching insects and worms for food until its ready to breed.

gills disappear inside, front legs grow through gill slits

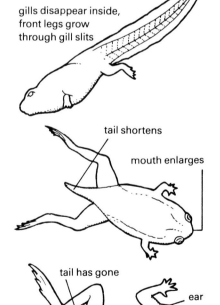

tail shortens

mouth enlarges

What changes as the tadpole becomes an adult? – The answer is – pretty well everything. This table summarizes a few of the changes.

tail has gone

ear

Tadpole		Adult frog
Gills for water	Breathing	Lungs for air (plus skin)
A herbivore – has a long gut to digest plants	Gut	A carnivore – short gut to digest meat
Tail fin	Moving	No tail. Legs for land and webbed feet for swimming
Thin	Skin	Thicker for land life
No eyelids needed	Sight	Has eyelids

eye position has shifted

V39 The development of a tadpole

Questions

1. Some insects have a life cycle which shows **incomplete metamorphosis**. The egg hatches into a **nymph**, not a larva. The nymph is similar to the adult but smaller, and it has no wings or reproductive organs. As it grows it moults. Over a number of moults, wings and reproductive organs appear and grow.

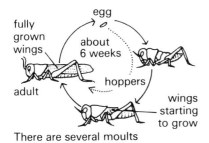

V40 Life cycle of a locust

The drawings shows the life cycle of a locust. Is this complete or incomplete metamorphosis? Give a reason for your answer. Why do locusts have to moult?

2. Explain how the following animals find a mate: (a) moths, (b) sparrows, (c) frogs, (d) a dog or a cat.

3. Many animals go through courtship 'dances' – a 'step' by one animal triggers its partner to respond. Only suitable partners get it right, and one false step means no mating. In some cases these 'dances' keep the pair together. This can be important if rearing the young takes the efforts of two parents, and is commonest in animals like birds and mammals. Albatrosses have a 'dance' which leads to mating and makes them a long-term pair. (See Fig. V41.)
   (a) Why do you think albatrosses go through such an elaborate courtship?
   (b) Describe the albatross 'dance' in your own words.

4. Mix and match. Write out your answers in full sentences beginning with column A and finishing with the correct phrase from B.

A	B
Yolk	is another word for pupa.
The plumule	is the stage when a caterpillar changes (metamorphoses) into an adult butterfly.
A pupa	are lost when a tadpole metamorphoses into a frog.
Gills	is the food supply for an embryo.
Maggots	is an embryo shoot found in a seed.
Chrysalis	is the larva of insects such as bluebottles – like a caterpillar without legs.

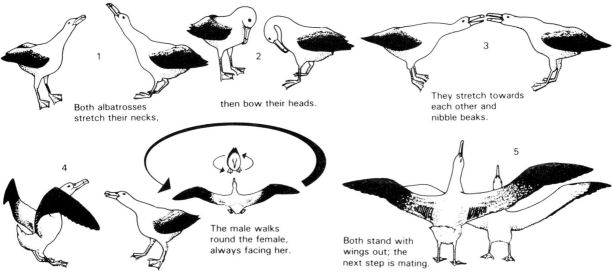

Both albatrosses stretch their necks,

then bow their heads.

They stretch towards each other and nibble beaks.

The male walks round the female, always facing her.

Both stand with wings out; the next step is mating.

V41

Egg to adult - mammals (part one)

Mammals manage without metamorphosis because their small eggs go through the embryo stage inside the mother.

The embryo must develop until the animal can survive alone – then it is born. We can look at changes in the whole animal: or we can look at just one part of it.

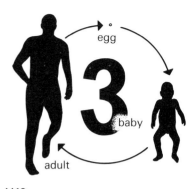

V42

An important stage in any life cycle is fertilization, when a sperm meets an egg cell and they fuse to start a new life. In mammals and birds this happens inside the mother, and few egg cells are wasted. In frogs and fish fertilization happens outside, in the water. Many eggs are never fertilized, and many young fish and tadpoles are eaten before they can grow to adulthood. Fish and frogs may have to produce hundreds or thousands of eggs to allow for wastage.

Internal fertilization needs quite complicated sexual organs to make sure that sperm manage to reach the egg.

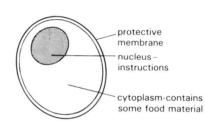

protective membrane
nucleus – instructions
cytoplasm-contains some food material

V43 A human egg enlarged

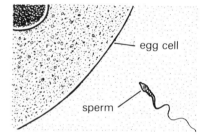

egg cell

sperm

V44 Just before fertilization

Male reproductive system

The male reproductive organs are for making sperm and getting them into the female. The most noticeable bits of the apparatus are the **penis** (in Latin it means sword) and the **scrotum**, a rather wrinkled skin bag containing the **testes** where sperm and male hormones are made. In many animals the penis is protected inside the body when not in use, but most keep their testes hanging below them where it is cool. Sperm soon die at normal body temperatures.

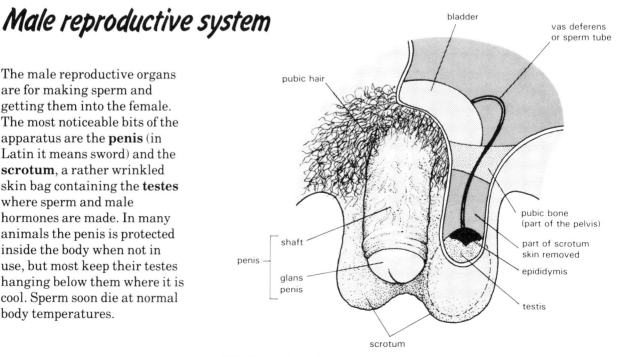

bladder
vas deferens or sperm tube
pubic hair
shaft
penis
glans penis
scrotum
pubic bone (part of the pelvis)
part of scrotum skin removed
epididymis
testis

V45 Front view of the human male reproductive organs

Inside the testis are many coiled tubules which join up to form the epididymis. This opens into the vas deferens or sperm tube. The walls of the tubules are lined with cells which divide and become sperm at a rate of 50 000 a minute. From here it may take sperm 3 weeks to reach the vas deferens, as the main tube of the epididymis is 6 metres long in man.

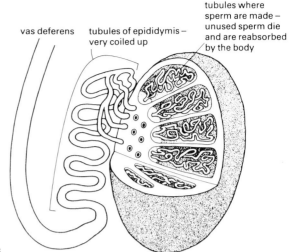

V46 Inside a testis

A limp penis is not much use for getting sperm into a female. Aroused by touch, sight, even imagination, the penis stiffens and increases in size as blood pours into the spongy tissue faster than it leaves. Further stimulation results in an ejaculation when the sticky white semen leaves the penis. Semen is only one-tenth sperm – the rest is liquid made by the seminal vesicles and prostate glands. Its job is to provide food and protection for the sperm. Man normally produces an amount between 0.5 cm³ and 6 cm³ in one ejaculation containing some 400 million or so sperm.

At orgasm, the muscles of the various tubes and the pelvis contract together and force out semen. Afterwards the penis goes limp as blood flows out of the spongy tissue.

In animals other than man there are some interesting variations on the penis – fold-up ones (bulls), penises with bones inside (sea-lions), long ones (hedgehogs), penises with spines (cats), forked ones (kangaroos) and so on.

V47 Section to show the male reproductive organs

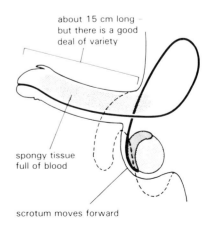

V48 An erect penis

203

Female reproductive system

In mammals, the female reproductive organs produce eggs (the female gametes) and provide a safe place for the early growth of offspring. Most of the organs are protected inside the body. The few parts you can see are involved in making sure the penis ends up in the right place.

The **clitoris** has many nerves and is very sensitive. It is usually rubbing the clitoris which causes female orgasm.

The **labia** are flaps which fill up with blood and swell a little. They help guide the penis.

The **vagina** is a muscular tube. When a woman is sexually excited the muscles relax (to fit the penis) and the vagina is lubricated with fluid. During orgasm the vaginal muscles gently relax and contract round the penis.

Inside the body are the **ovaries** where eggs (and sex hormones) are produced and the **uterus** where the embryo grows.

The ovaries, unlike the testes, produce very few gametes. Usually one egg is released each month in women between 10 and 50 – though this varies a lot. A woman produces about 400 mature eggs in a lifetime.

To avoid wasting eggs, each month the uterus is prepared to care for an embryo. This means it is all too easy for most women to become pregnant if they have sex. Whether they have an orgasm or not makes no difference to fertilization.

If fertilization does not happen, the lining of the uterus breaks down and the blood-stained tissues pass out through the vagina. This is menstruation, and it takes a few days. It's also known as the menstrual period. Menstruation is only one part of the changes which take place during a month. More on page 151.

The view from outside

pubic hair

clitoris

labia

entrance to the urethra (tube leading to the bladder)

entrance to the vagina

anus

V49 Human female reproductive organs – the view from outside

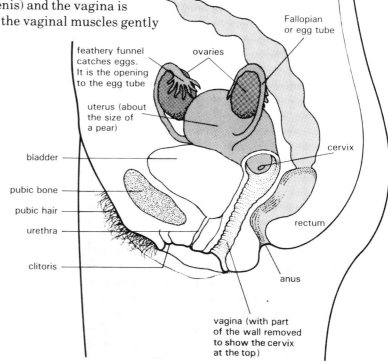

Fallopian or egg tube

feathery funnel catches eggs. It is the opening to the egg tube

ovaries

uterus (about the size of a pear)

cervix

bladder

pubic bone

pubic hair

urethra

clitoris

rectum

anus

vagina (with part of the wall removed to show the cervix at the top)

V50 Section showing the female organs in side view

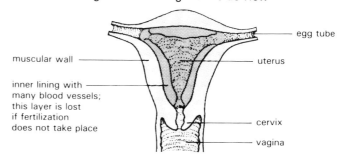

egg tube

muscular wall

uterus

inner lining with many blood vessels; this layer is lost if fertilization does not take place

cervix

vagina

V51 The inside of the uterus has a lining which is lost and replaced each month

Fertilization

In sexual intercourse, the penis fits into the vagina and sperm are released close to the opening of the cervix. The sperm swim up through the uterus to the Fallopian tubes to fertilize the egg.

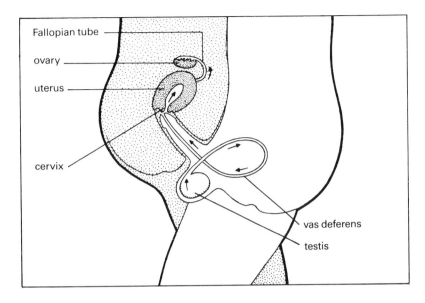

V52 Intercourse

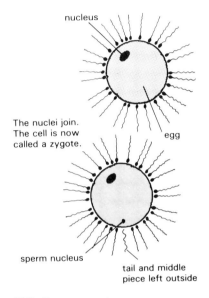

The nuclei join. The cell is now called a zygote.

sperm nucleus

tail and middle piece left outside

V53 Sperm meets egg

Perhaps one million sperm make it through the cervix into the uterus after an ejaculation. Only a few thousand arrive, thirty minutes later, at the entrance to a Fallopian tube. Even so, any egg in the tube becomes surrounded by a cloud of sperm – only one of which fertilizes the egg.

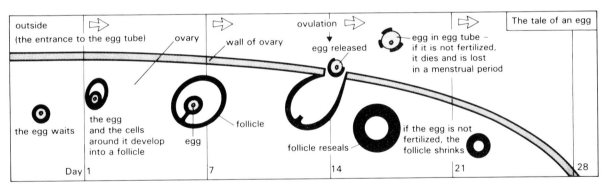

V54 The egg's story

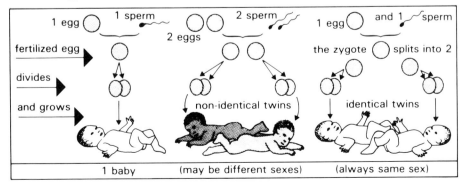

V55 Suppose there is more than one egg?

Controlling fertilization

Understanding how fertilization happens means we can begin to control it. Hormones which control ovulation can be used to increase family size. Fertility drugs cause eggs to be released from the ovary. It is difficult to judge the dose which will release the right number of eggs.

V56 Given a fertility drug, a sheep may produce four lambs instead of one or two

Other sex hormones are used in the pill, which prevents eggs being released from the ovary – as long as it is taken regularly. The pill is one of several ways sperm can be prevented from reaching an egg (contraception).

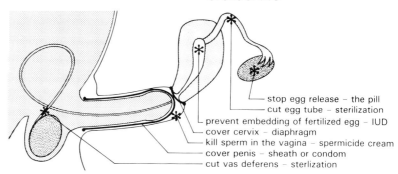

- stop egg release – the pill
- cut egg tube – sterilization
- prevent embedding of fertilized egg – IUD
- cover cervix – diaphragm
- kill sperm in the vagina – spermicide cream
- cover penis – sheath or condom
- cut vas deferens – sterlization

V57 A very safe couple

It is now possible to choose not to have children, or to choose when to have them and how many. The type of contraception should be chosen carefully. Some contraceptives can only be got from a doctor, and medical advice is useful anyway. For example – do all methods work equally well? The answer is no.

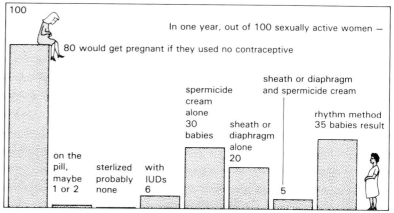

In one year, out of 100 sexually active women –

80 would get pregnant if they used no contraceptive

on the pill, maybe 1 or 2

sterilized probably none

with IUDs 6

spermicide cream alone 30 babies

sheath or diaphragm alone 20

sheath or diaphragm and spermicide cream 5

rhythm method 35 babies result

V58 The effectiveness of various contraceptive methods

It looks as though sterilization is safest if you don't want children. In men it is particularly quick and easy. However, you should be sure you're not going to change your mind. Sterilization can sometimes be reversed, but not always.

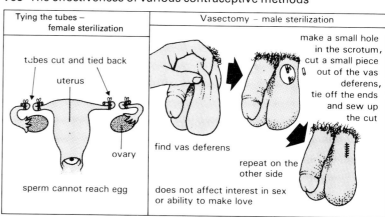

Tying the tubes – female sterilization

tubes cut and tied back

uterus

ovary

sperm cannot reach egg

Vasectomy – male sterilization

make a small hole in the scrotum, cut a small piece out of the vas deferens, tie off the ends and sew up the cut

find vas deferens

repeat on the other side

does not affect interest in sex or ability to make love

V59 Sterilization

IUDs are useful because once they are in place they can be more or less forgotten. Some women cannot use them as they sometimes cause bleeding or cramps. IUDs work best in women who have had children.

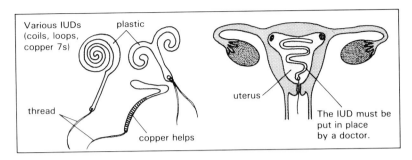

V60 Various IUDs (coils, loops, copper 7s)

Barriers like sheaths and diaphragms are convenient for many people, but they are not very effective without a spermicide cream or foam placed inside the vagina to kill sperm. And even a small hole in the sheath or diaphragm makes it useless.

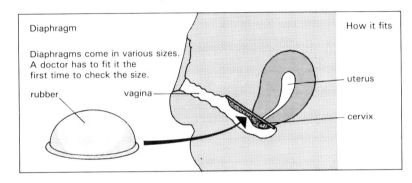

V61 Diaphragm

The egg is only in the tubes for a few days each month. The rhythm method relies on not making love during these days. For it to work, you must be able to find out which they are. Women who have regular cycles can work out when they ovulate by keeping a record of their body temperatures. Not all women have regular cycles, and this makes the method risky. It is mostly used by people whose religion does not allow them to use other methods of contraception.

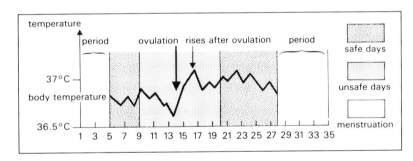

V62 Rhythm method

Each of these methods of contraception has advantages and problems. People use other ways to try to avoid pregnancy, but they work even less well. 'Just the once', doing it standing up or jumping up and down afterwards don't help a bit. It's very important to take proper precautions.

Question

1. What method of contraception would you advise for the following people?
   (a) a couple who have three children and think that's plenty
   (b) someone who hasn't a steady lover but who wants to be safe if an opportunity turns up
   (c) a woman who has one child and wants to wait a few years before having another
   (d) a young couple not ready to start a family
   Give a reason for your suggestion in each case.

2. Look at Fig. V58 which shows the effectiveness of various methods.
   (a) Which method apart from sterilization is the safest and why?
   (b) Which method is the least safe and why?

207

VD

Venereal diseases (VD) are caused by organisms which specialize in travelling from person to person through areas of thin damp skin. These are the areas which come into contact during sexual activity. Sex to the VD organisms is an opportunity to travel, to enter a new host by way of mouth, anus or sexual surface. The organisms range in size from visible pubic lice (crabs) to microscopic organisms like Candida (a yeast causing thrush) to the very small indeed (viruses like those causing AIDS).

Two common types of VD are gonorrhoea (clap) and syphilis (pox); both caused by microscopic organisms.

Both diseases can be cured completely it treated early enough. They can unfortunately be caught again – and again. The graph (Fig. V65) gives a rough idea of how common they are compared to measles. There are probably many more cases of gonorrhoea as not everyone comes for treatment – which is free. It's a pity they don't, as gonorrhoea is increasing.

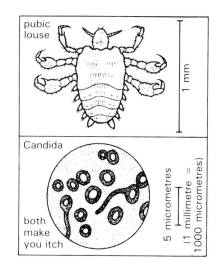

V63 Two causative organisms

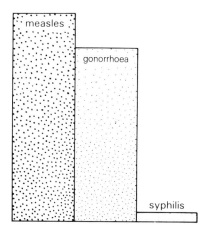

V64

Many people are shy or embarrassed, especially about telling their lovers. Would you prefer to be told or not if there was a chance you had VD?

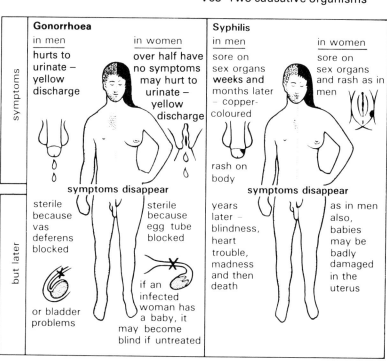

V65 Gonorrhoea and syphilis summary

Questions

1. The organisms which cause gonorroea and syphilis die as soon as they are not protected by the warmth and dampness of the body. Knowing this, do you think is it possible to catch VD from a lavatory seat?

2. Far more people catch gonorrhoea than syphilis in England, although both are easy to treat. Why do you think there is less syphilis around?

3. During the last day or so, David has noticed that he has leaked a little yellowish goo and that his privates itch. It doesn't quite fit with the symptoms for gonorrhoea in this book but he is a bit worried – especially as he's been to a party lately where he could have picked up a dose. What should he do, and why? Would you? Why?

Summary and questions

Summary
Animals signal that they are ready to mate in many ways, including scents and songs. Many show courtship patterns which help to get as many eggs as possible fertilized. People have some control over fertilization – fertility drugs increase the chances, contraceptives reduce them. Human sexuality has become more relaxed now that pregnancy is a matter of choice, but there are problems such as the increase in venereal disease.

Male and female reproductive organs fit together in sexual intercourse in order to place sperm – male sex cells – well inside the female's body. Sperm are made in the testes and pass out of the male's body in a fluid – semen – through the penis during ejaculation. The penis fits into the female's vagina, so the sperm have only a small distance to swim to enter the uterus. They cross the uterus and travel along the Fallopian tubes towards the ovaries where eggs are stored. If there is an egg in the Fallopian tube, fertilization takes place. The fertilized egg travels to the uterus and embeds in the lining. If fertilization does not take place, the lining breaks down and is lost as part of the monthly menstrual cycle.

Questions

1 Write this out, filling in the blanks.
In animals, _____ gametes are sperm which must _____ towards the eggs. Sperm are made in the _____ which they leave by a tube called the _____ _____ which leads into the urethra, which goes down the middle of the _____. This organ fits neatly into the female's _____, provided enough preparation has been made. The internal organs of the female are the uterus and the _____, which contain the eggs. They are linked by the _____ tube and it is in this tube that _____ takes place. Sperm must swim through the _____ and across the _____ to reach the egg – from the sperm's point of view an enormous distance.

2. Explain the difference between each of the following pairs:
   (a) egg and sperm
   (b) penis and clitoris
   (c) vas deferens and urethra (in males)
   (d) testes and ovary
   (e) fertilization and sexual intercourse
   Give as much information as you can. Then describe the similarities between each pair.

3. Explain how
   (a) a penis becomes erect
   (b) the uterus is prepared each month for a possible pregnancy
   (c) twins – a boy and a girl – might happen
   (d) the female's reproductive system prepares for intercourse

4. (a) Two fluids pass down the penis. What are they?
   (b) How do the plumbing arrangements in the female differ from those in the male?

5. Both testes and ovary are inside the body in an embryo. A boy's testes move into the scrotum just before birth. Look at the male reproductive system and suggest a way in which its layout supports the idea that testes change their position.

6. You are given a hollowed-out pear, a cardboard tube, two plums and two straws. Make a model of the female reproductive organs.

7. How would you explain to a young brother or sister the facts of life? Include in your explanation any pictures you might use.

Egg to adult - pregnancy and birth

The fertilized egg is moved by the beating of the cilia (small hairs) of the cells of the Fallopian tube. It drifts slowly down into the uterus and embeds itself in the uterus lining.

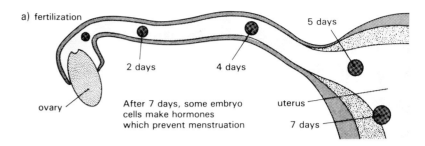

a) fertilization

2 days   4 days   5 days

ovary

After 7 days, some embryo cells make hormones which prevent menstruation

uterus

7 days

Food and oxygen first come from the uterus wall. The wall has got ready for pregnancy by becoming soft, thick and full of blood vessels. The embryo tucks itself into the wall which grows around it. Projections grow out to increase the area where the surface of the embryo's tissues touches the mother's (Vitamin E is needed for this to be successful).

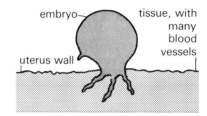

b)

about day 7, the human embryo digs itself into the uterus wall

embryo — tissue, with many blood vessels

uterus wall

V66 Following fertilization

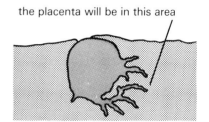

c) it is nearly buried by day 10

the placenta will be in this area

The embryo grows and needs more food and oxygen. For this it has to have a large surface in contact with the mother. This surface is provided by the **placenta**. Mammals who don't have placentas have to give birth to their young when they are only partly developed. Kangaroos and opossums are like this.

The placenta in humans is soup-plate-sized. In it the blood of mother and young flow very close together, but do not actually mix.

Protection is provided by the mother's body as the embryos grow in the **uterus** or **womb** – a muscular bag. The diagram shows a human with one embryo. Many animals have two **uteri** and many embryos.

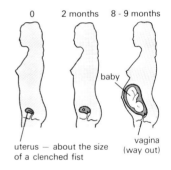

0   2 months   8 - 9 months

baby

uterus — about the size of a clenched fist

vagina (way out)

V67 The mother's body protects the embryo

Extra protection is provided by membrane bags filled with liquid. These surround and cushion the embryo – like an enclosing waterbed.

placenta

V68 Rat embryo in its membranes

Development

In the uterus, the embryo develops from a simple ball of cells into the complex organism we call a baby. This time is known as **gestation** or **pregnancy.** On the whole, the larger the animal the longer the pregnancy.

Long pregnancies sometimes, but not always, end in well-developed young.

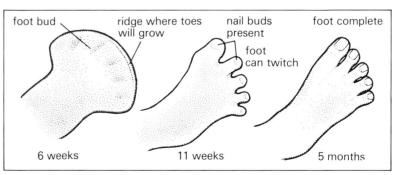

foot bud   ridge where toes will grow   nail buds present   foot complete

foot can twitch

6 weeks   11 weeks   5 months

V69 The development of a foot

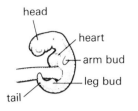

head
heart
arm bud
leg bud
tail

human embryo at 4 weeks

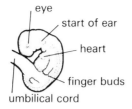

eye
start of ear
heart
finger buds
umbilical cord

5 weeks

6 weeks

has now started
everything found
in an adult
and is called
a foetus

8 weeks

V70 The development of the whole organism

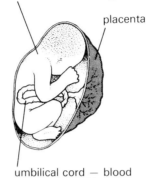

5 month baby (foetus) in its membrane bags

placenta

umbilical cord — blood travels along this between baby and placenta

V71

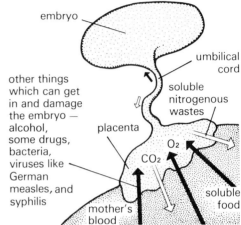

embryo

umbilical cord

soluble nitrogenous wastes

other things which can get in and damage the embryo — alcohol, some drugs, bacteria, viruses like German measles, and syphilis

placenta

O_2

CO_2

soluble food

mother's blood

V72 The placenta

Birth

In humans, pregnancy usually lasts 9 months. If the baby is lost early, it is known as a **miscarriage**. At least half of the miscarriages happen because the embryo is not normal in some way.

At the end of pregnancy there is another problem – how to get quite a large baby out. It's solved with a lot of hard work – **labour**. The pelvis, which, in humans at least, has supported the baby, stretches to let the baby out.

Muscles of the abdomen wall and the uterus combine to push the baby out. The uterus in particular is made of powerful muscles. They work up strong contractions which eventually result in the birth of the baby.

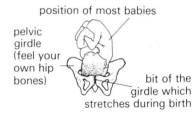

position of most babies

pelvic girdle (feel your own hip bones)

bit of the girdle which stretches during birth

V73 The position of most babies at birth

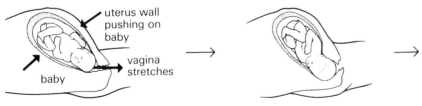

uterus wall pushing on baby

vagina stretches

baby

hands are supporting, not pulling

V74 Birth

The baby is flexible at this stage and in most animals slides out quite easily.

Following the baby is the 'afterbirth' – the placenta. Many animal mothers eat it. This may be to make sure the blood doesn't attract hungry carnivores, or to avoid wasting useful materials like iron.

Once born, the baby soon takes its first breath and uses its own lungs. Blood stops flowing along the umbilical cord, which can be cut. There are no nerves in the cord, so this doesn't hurt. The baby is, more or less, on its own – although mammals do care for their young until they are really able to be independent.

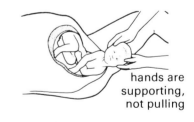

V75

Egg to adult - childhood and adolescence

2 years

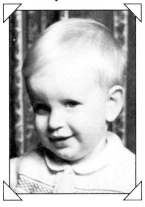

	female	male
height	0.9 m	0.9 m
mass	11 kg	12 kg
% of final mass	20%	12%

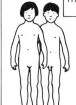

hand key

- ☐ before birth
- ▨ up to one year
- ■ 1 - 2 years
- ▦ 2 - 5 years

The bones can all go on growing for years

This shows the order in which the bones of the hand harden. Changes like this are affected by such things as food – or lack of it. Remember rickets and kwashiokor? Parental care or the lack of it is also very important and affects the whole growth of the child.

6 years

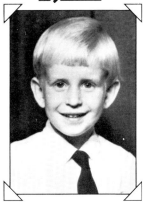

	female	male
height	1.1 m	1.1 m
mass	19 kg	20 kg
% of final mass	33%	30%

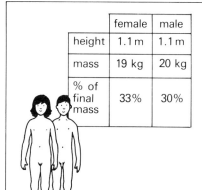

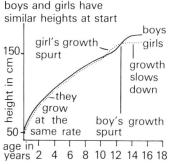

boys and girls have similar heights at start

girl's growth spurt — boys

girls — growth slows down

they grow at the same rate

boy's growth spurt

height in cm: 50, 150

age in years 2 4 6 8 10 12 14 16 18

We could put all the figures on a graph – a summary of growth.

10 years

	female	male
height	1.3 m	1.3 m
mass	31 kg	31 kg
% of final mass	53%	45%

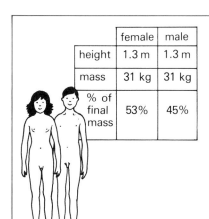

Adolescence is part of growing up. It includes **puberty**, which is when a person becomes able to have children. Girls produce eggs and begin to menstruate at around 13. Menstruation is the monthly shedding of the uterus lining. The whole body changes – body hair, breasts and pelvis grow. So does pubic hair and the reproductive organs.

14 years

ADOLESCENCE

	female	male
height	1.5 m	1.6 m
mass	49 kg	49 kg
% of final mass	85%	75%

Boys tend to start puberty later than girls. The penis and testes grow, the shoulders broaden, body and pubic hair also grows. The voice breaks. Boys produce mature sperm around 14. Puberty takes many years to complete.

18 years

	female	male
height	1.6 m	1.7 m
mass	57 kg	65 kg
% of final mass	98%	92%

All the figures are averages. There is a lot of variety in the population.

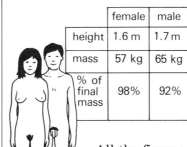

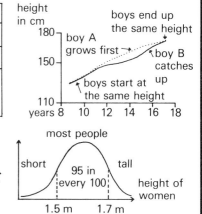

height in cm
180
150
110
years 8 10 12 14 16 18

boys end up the same height
boy A grows first
boy B catches up
boys start at the same height

most people
short — tall
95 in every 100
height of women
1.5 m   1.7 m

22 years

ADULT

	female	male
height	1.6 m	1.7 m
mass	58 kg	70 kg
% of final mass	100%	100%

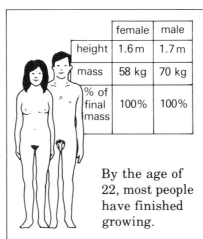

By the age of 22, most people have finished growing.

Growth changes are controlled by body chemicals called hormones. As the hormones change over the years, adolescents may suffer for a time from problems such as skin trouble and heavy sweating. Hormones also affect behaviour and may make people moody – making a tough time of life more difficult.

Adult to the end

The graph shows changes in height as a person grows older. There are also changes (at different times) in such things as body mass, sexual activity, life-style, mental abilities and health.

The graphs showing such changes are nearly always averages. They give a picture of a population, not of one person in particular.

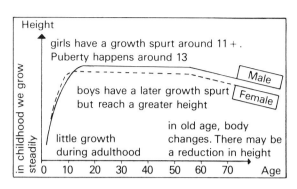

V76 Height changes with age

People change their life-styles as they **become adults**. They move away from home, start work and often have families. Their bodies change, too.

Young adults are at a peak. They are very fertile. They are at their strongest, their reaction rates are fastest, and their memories can only get worse as nerve cells die. They also take risks. If they die at this age it will probably be in an accident.

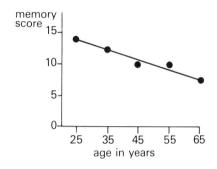

V77 Memory changes with age

V78

Middle age brings responsibilities and a more settled way of life. The body is beginning to work less well – body processes slow down, and a few stop. In women, the ovaries stop producing hormones and eggs. This is the **menopause**, which happens between the ages of 45 and 55. Menstruation stops, and for a time the change in hormone levels can have irritating effects. Menopause does not signal the end of a woman's sex life – just the end of her reproductive years.

Often people let themselves get too fat. Years of carrying around extra body mass puts strain on the joints. Later this produces diseases like osteoarthritis.

The extra body mass can kill people in middle age. Overloading the heart may well provoke a heart attack or another problem of the blood system.

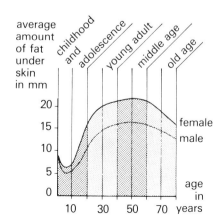

V79 Fat storage and age

Today, more and more people reach **old age** and face its changes.

If you know an old person you feel you can talk to, ask them about old age and perhaps death. They may be very happy to talk about it but be careful. Write a description of your conversation including how you feel about what was said.

Think of an old person you know. Make your own list of age changes. You may include lined skin, weight loss, age spots, loss of teeth, white hair, stooping, large joints, poor eyesight and problems with moving and memory (among others). These are all clear signals that the body no longer works properly.

People show such changes at different ages – some are roaring around enjoying life 20 years after others have given up.

Eventually, for everyone, there comes a **time to die**. People who know they are dying go through many phases – shock, refusing to believe it, anger, depression and grief – before they can face it in a way that is right for them and the way they have lived. Would you prefer to know you were dying? How would you feel about being kept alive by machines? Doctors use the death of the brain as a guide to the death of a person, but it is sometimes difficult to decide these days.

V80 Skull changes with age

Lifespan
Most animals have the same number of heart beats in their life – it's the speed of beats that varies. Small animals have a fast heart beat and a short life. Large animals have a slower heart beat and a longer life. For our size and heart rate we live three times as long as we should. No one knows why.

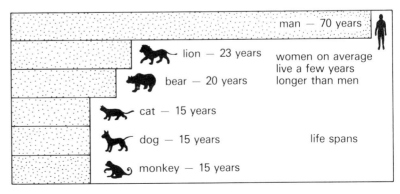

man — 70 years

lion — 23 years

women on average live a few years longer than men

bear — 20 years

cat — 15 years

dog — 15 years

life spans

monkey — 15 years

V81 Lifespans

215

Questions

1. Copy this out and fill in the gaps.
   On the whole, small animals have a _____ pregnancy compared to larger animals. Another word for pregnancy is _____, which refers to the length of time the _____ grows inside the mother's _____. There it is protected and provided with _____ and _____. These are obtained from the mother, where the embryo's blood and the mother's blood flow close together in the _____. Just before birth is a period called _____ when the mother's body prepares to push the baby out. Once born, humans grow and develop for many years – through childhood to _____ and sexual development, to adulthood and lastly _____.

2. How does
   (a) an embryo in the womb get rid of waste materials?
   (b) the hardening of the bones in the hand allow for growth after birth?
   (c) the timing of puberty in boys and girls differ?
   (d) the growth of an early developer differ from that of a late developer?
   (e) the life span of a human come as a surprise to a biologist who has been studying the life spans of other animals?

3. Use the information about people at the ages of 2, 6, 10, 14, 18 and 22 years to plot the following graphs:
   (a) increase in height of boys and girls
   (b) increase in body mass in boys and girls
   (c) the percentage of the final body mass at each age
   Look at the growth graphs in the text for clues on how to set this out.

4. Marsupials are animals which give birth to very undeveloped young. The first weeks of the baby's life are spent attached to a nipple in the mother's pouch. What does the nipple provide? And the pouch? The kangaroo is a marsupial. The water opossum, which spends a lot of time swimming, is another. The opening to the mother's pouch is closed tight by a muscle. The young don't drown, but they do have to tolerate high concentrations of a certain gas. Which one?

5. Consider the information in Fig. V82
   (a) Which animals have gestation periods which are the same length?

   (b) What happens to gestation periods as animals get larger?
   (c) Explain what is meant by 'gestation period'.

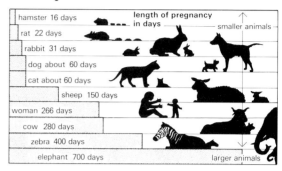

V82 Length of pregnancy in days

6. Read the following life stories. Draw life cycle diagrams for each organism. Say whether the pattern is type 1, 2 or 3.
   (a) Adders are snakes. They lay about 14 large eggs with leathery shells. From the eggs hatch snakes which are small versions of the adult snake.
   (b) Dolphins live in the sea. They produce one baby dolphin at a time. The young develop within the mother for several months. After birth the mother feeds the young dolphin on milk and keeps an eye on it. The baby dolphins are well able to swim.
   (c) Toads lay many eggs enclosed in strings of jelly. In water, the eggs hatch into larvae (the plural of larva) which swim around using their tails. They change gradually into adult toads with lungs, no tails, and legs.

7. An abortion occurs when a child is born before it is able to survive outside the womb. When this happens naturally it is called a miscarriage. It may happen for various reasons – for example, if the mother has an accident or the foetus is very abnormal. People sometimes choose to have an abortion, perhaps if the pregnancy is unwanted, or tests show that the baby is going to be abnormal. Do you think people should be able to have abortions whenever they want to? Give your reasons.
   (Don't write anything until you have tried to find out more information about abortion, and discussed the problem with other people. Boys should ask girls how they feel about the subject.)

Review questions

1. Indian corn or maize originally came from South America but it grows well in Africa. In Africa, there are areas where people eat maize and little else. They develop a skin disease called pellagra. The people who took the maize to Africa had no reason to expect this as the South American Indians were healthy. Their diet included tomatoes and green peppers. What important nutrient do you think is missing from maize?

2. Old people's bones often become brittle – they are less likely to have trouble if their diet includes milk each day. What mineral shortage causes the problem of easily broken bones?

3. Over 2000 years ago, a group of nomads in the Middle East used to cook an ox like this. They cut the flesh off the bones and put it in the rumen (one of the stomachs), along with a little water. They hung the rumen over a fire made of the bones. In fact, the ox was made to boil itself. What does this tell you about the size of the ox's rumen? Why do oxen need stomachs like this?

4. Cholera bacteria live in the gut. So do a number of other animals such as the tapeworm. Can you give one reason why the gut is a good place to live? What problem would organisms living there have to solve?

5. To make 1 kilogram of glucose, a green plant needs about the amount of energy used by a TV set running for 15 hours. Where does the plant get its energy from? That kilogram of glucose contains about 400 grams of carbon – where does the plant get that from?

6. You are going to do a photosynthesis experiment. You plan to use a starch test to check whether a plant has been photosynethesizing. Before the experiment, you keep the plant in the dark for two days. Why?

7. Mangrove trees grow in swamps, often on a coast. Some of their roots have side roots which come up out of the mud and water they grow in. These side roots have spongy tissue in them full of air. What is the job of these roots and why are they needed?

8. Draw and label a diagram of mammalian lungs. Use coloured arrows to show the path of air in and out of them. Explain how air is cleaned (filtered) as it enters the lungs.

9. True or false – say whether each sentence is true or false. Write out the true sentences as they are and a corrected version of the false ones.
   (a) A crocodile has a life cycle like that of a frog.
   (b) Animals which have small eggs always produce them in very large numbers.
   (c) In the growth of a bird embryo the brain and heart develop very early.
   (d) In a seed the plant embryo consists only of an embryo root called a radicle.
   (e) When seeds start to grow they are said to be dormant.
   (f) Caterpillars eat the eggs they hatch from.
   (g) In a mammalian embryo, the eye develops before the heart.

10. Make a table to compare the changes of adolescence and old age. Try and put in at least 6 differences – here is one to start you off.

Adolescence	Old age
Considerable increase in height	Slight decrease in height

217

Population growth

A **population** is a group of organisms of the same kind.

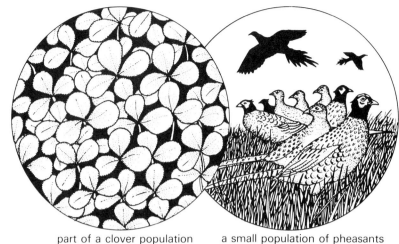

part of a clover population   a small population of pheasants

W1 Sample populations

Populations grow by increasing in numbers. This happens when there are more births than deaths.

Populations can also increase by immigration (organisms arriving from outside).

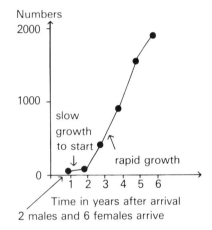

population shrinks	population stable	population grows
births deaths		

W2 Three population patterns

If organisms arrive in a new area and conditions are good (and nothing happens to stop it) the population grows slowly for a while, and then increases rapidly.

W3 The increase in pheasant numbers on Protection Island, Washington – an example of immigration

Growth is slow to start because there are few organisms to breed. Once there are lots of pheasants, or people, or clover plants, they can reproduce more rapidly. This kind of rapid growth is called **exponential growth**.

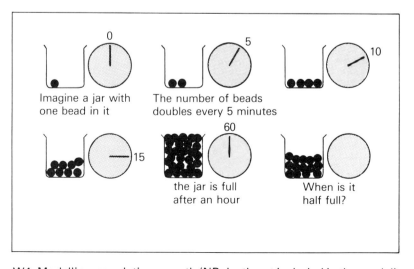

Imagine a jar with one bead in it

The number of beads doubles every 5 minutes

the jar is full after an hour

When is it half full?

W4 Modelling population growth (NB death not included in the model)

Stabilizing

The graph on the opposite page shows the growth of a pheasant population. The growth was starting to slow down when the scientists stopped counting. Probably it became stable, with births equalling deaths, like the population of yeast cells in the graph on the right. Many populations are more or less stable.

A population becomes stable when:
(a) there is a limited amount of something important, like food or space; or
(b) the organisms are eaten as food, as fast as new ones are born; or
(c) a combination of (a) and (b). Anything which slows and stabilizes the growth of a population is called a **limiting factor**.

In any case, **deaths equal births**.

Sometimes organisms die off faster than they are born and a population shrinks. The reindeer on an Alaskan island ate all the food on the island and starved. The population of Sei whales off South Africa disappeared because the animals were caught by whalers.

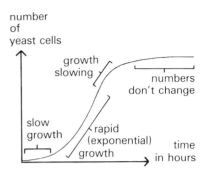

W5 Change in yeast population growing in a lab

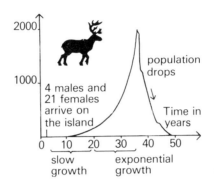

W6 Number of reindeer on an island off Alaska

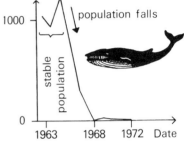

W7 Number of Sei whales caught off South Africa

How do people fit in?

Population growth varies from country to country. In some places population size is stable – in others it is increasing very fast. The human population of the world as a whole may soon run out of space, food energy or raw materials. As you can see from the graph, total population growth is still exponential. Many more people are born each year than die. To stabilize the population, either
(a) fewer (a lot fewer) babies must be born; or
(b) many more people must die each year.

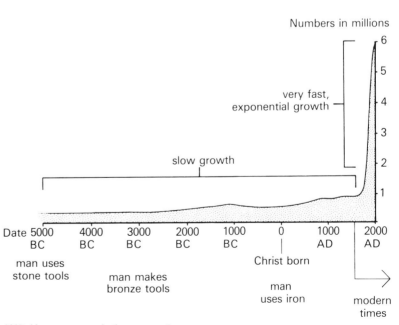

W8 Human population growth

Question

List the factors which limit or **stabilize** the growth of a population

Community growth

A **community** is a group of many kinds of organisms in an area. The way a community grows and changes depends upon what happens to all the organisms in it.

On the next few pages are stages in the growth of communities in the three environments opposite – a sandy dune, a tip (it could be a land slide) and a pond. Each environment has its own problems for organisms to cope with. For example, there is little proper soil on the dune or the tip for plants to grow in.

All the same, there is a similar pattern of changes in each environment. They are summarized on the right for a model pond.

W9 Small part of a pond community

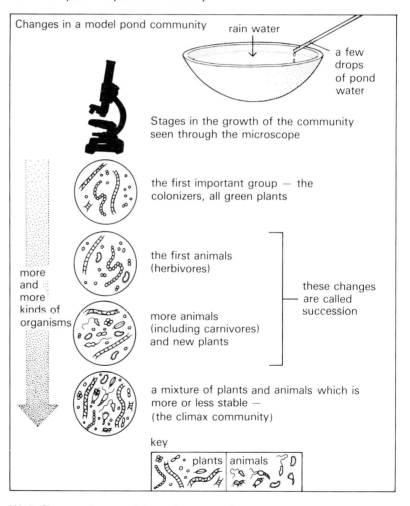

W10 Changes in a model pond community

The original pond water contained a mixture of organisms. The rain water was only suitable for some of them – the plants – to grow in at first. Very small numbers of animals may have survived in protective coats (perhaps in suspended animation) until there was enough food for them. Organisms this small are easily blown from place to place. They can survive as long as they have tough, waterproof coats. Some may have arrived at the model pond like this.

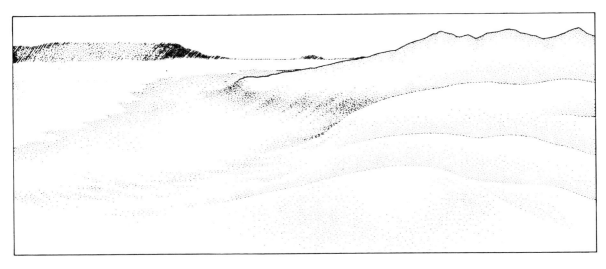

W11

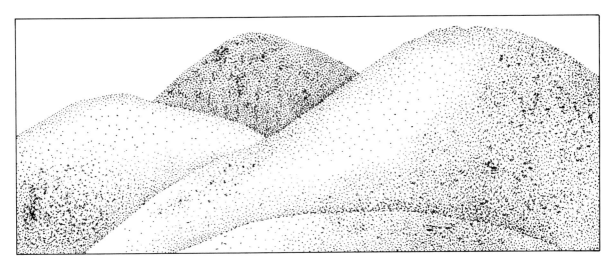

W12

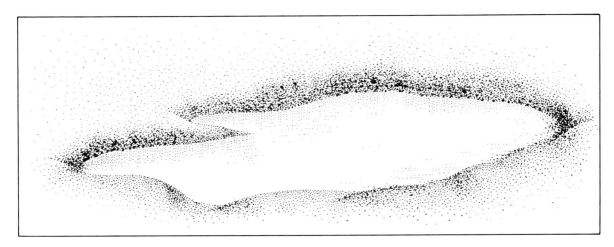

W13

Community growth - colonizers

Colonizers are the first organisms – the founders of a community. They are the food-making plants (though animals soon follow).

The sand dune
Loose sand piles up against almost anything to start a dune. It can blow away again too – unless held together by the roots of plants like marram grass and sea-couch grass.

Marram is a major dune grass. It has large leaves which can roll up to save water.

Dead dune plants decay and start to make the sand more fertile. As a result the sand starts to turn grey.

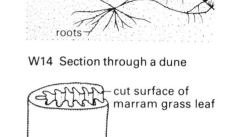

W14 Section through a dune

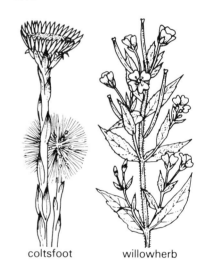

W15

The tip
Again the colonizers are tough, often small, plants. The type of plant depends on the tip. Only a few plants are adapted to the acid or high metal conditions of some tips. Some grasses are found and also plants like willowherbs and coltsfoot, the sort of plants often found on waste lands. They have many seeds and grow fast. After death these colonizers also decay and add to the soil.

coltsfoot   willowherb

W16 Tip colonizing plants

The pond
The pond already has its own community of organisms but it may not always stay a pond. If it silts up (fills with mud) a new land community may grow up.

The first 'land' organisms are likely to be marsh grasses, reeds and sedges which have their roots in water. Their remains help to build up less wet areas for later plants.

Colonizers arrive in a new area in many ways. Seeds can be blown by the wind, or carried by water or by animals. Animals may walk, swim or fly – or hitch a ride.

W17 People make use of marsh conditions when they grow rice

sea couch grass nearer
sea because it can
cope with salt spray

marram grass on
highest dunes

W18

lots of bare patches still

Yorkshire fog grass

cocksfoot grass

W19

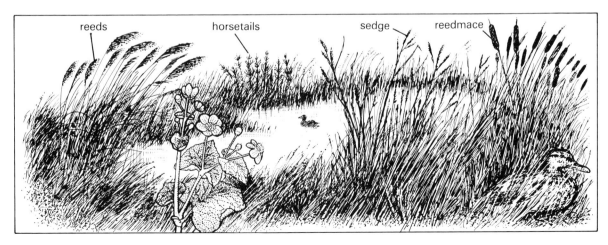

reeds   horsetails   sedge   reedmace

W20

Community growth-succession

Succession happens as a community changes. The colonizers change their environment. For example, as they die, their rotting bodies make the soil more fertile. Species disappear and are replaced by new ones which flourish in the changed conditions. Usually there are more types of plants and animals as time goes by.

The dune
As the dune soil becomes more fertile, flowering plants appear – like sea holly, wild carrot and wild thyme. There is a moss which screws itself up to save water. The grasses change and gradually brambles and shrubs like aspens, elder and hawthorn appear.

screw moss

in damp weather   in dry weather

W21

The tip
On the tip, like the dune, there are fewer open spaces, more soil and more kinds of plants. There may be a cover of grasses, with brambles, broom and hawthorn as well as smaller plants.

Growth on old tips may be very slow indeed. In some places, trees are planted on tips to speed up the greening process. It helps keep the tips steady, too.

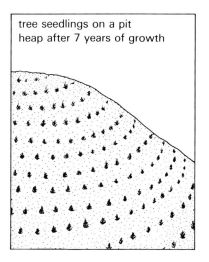

tree seedlings on a pit heap after 7 years of growth

W22 Tree seedlings on a pit heap after 7 years of growth

The pond – now a marsh
Again larger plants are arriving. Willow and alder seedlings grow on the soil (no longer mud). Areas may become meadow land with plants like buttercup and lady's smock.

For more plants – or at least help with finding out what they are – try:
Concise British Flora in Colour – Keble Martin (Michael Joseph/Sphere). This has drawings.
Trees of Britain – Roger Phillips (Ward Lock/Pan)
Wild Flowers of Britain – Roger Phillips (Ward Lock/Pan)
   These are both all photographs, arranged according to the time of year.
and
Plant Communities (*Penguin Nature Series*) – Anne Bulow-Olsen (Penguin)

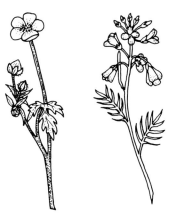

buttercup   lady's smock

W23

W24

W25

W26

Community growth-climax

A **climax** (or balanced) community is the final group of organisms found in a particular area, when things are more or less stable. The type of climax depends on the environment as a whole.

The dune
The dune area may eventually be covered by large trees. Whole oak forests based on sand are common on the Dutch coast. In England, pine trees are often planted by man.

W27 You can follow all the changes by taking a walk from the edge of the sea inland

The tip
Tip areas may take a long time to reach a climax, and even then the organisms may be few and small. Coal tips hundreds of years old may have only tiny woodlands with sycamore, hawthorn and elder trees – all small, short-lived trees. Tips from copper mines thousands of years old may have only a few scrappy plants in an area where the normal climax is oak forest. The traces of copper in the soil mean that most plants cannot grow there. For them the land is poisoned.

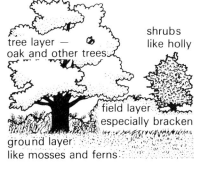

W28 Same tip with 30 years of growth (grasses and pines)

The marsh
The marsh area may well end up as alder woodland, or it may go on to support the larger, heavier oak woods (Fig. W29) – with all the other plants and animals found in such woods. It depends on how wet the area is.

shrubs like holly

tree layer — oak and other trees

field layer especially bracken

ground layer like mosses and ferns

W29

To sum up

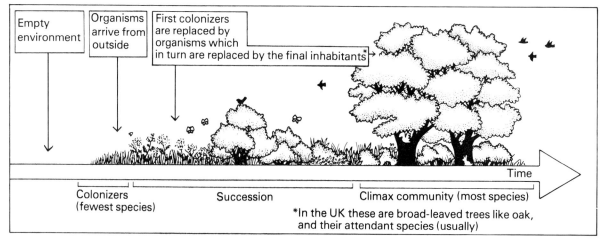

Empty environment

Organisms arrive from outside

First colonizers are replaced by organisms which in turn are replaced by the final inhabitants*

Time

Colonizers (fewest species)

Succession

Climax community (most species)

*In the UK these are broad-leaved trees like oak, and their attendant species (usually)

W30

W31

W32

W33

Climax communities in the United Kingdom

Two thousand years ago most of Northern Europe was covered in trees. For most soils forest was the natural climax community. England today looks very different – largely because of our activities. Trees have been cut down for building, or for fuel (and useful ones have been planted). Land has been cleared for planting crops, and grazing animals have been introduced (Figs W34 and W35).

W34 Natural forest

W35 Farmland in the UK

Changes can easily be caused by man – for example, when a grazing animal is introduced or removed. Rabbits were brought to England for their meat by the Romans. The rabbits eat tree and shrub seedlings. They caused places like the Downs to be mainy grassland (Fig. W36). In the 1950s many rabbits were killed by myxomatosis, and as a result there were big changes (Fig. W37).

W36 The Downs as grassland

W37 Scrub taking over

Many plant communities look as though they are natural climaxes because they are very old and people are used to them. Areas like the Norfolk Broads were man-made (actually dug!). They need constant care if they are not to change. They are **artificial climaxes** (Figs W38 and W39).

W38 The Norfolk Broads – where people go

W39 A Broad which has been left alone

So how do I recognize a climax community?

The test is to leave an area and see if it changes. With trees, though, you might have to wait a lifetime or so before you could be sure it was stable. There are virtually no natural climax communities in the UK. A few bogs, very isolated and too wet for trees, are natural climaxes. There are one or two bits of almost undisturbed coast, and a few small woodland areas. That's it. Such areas of special scientific interest are very precious.

Summary and questions

Summary
Populations of organisms grow and stabilize or die away. Communities change as populations of different organisms grow and disappear or remain. The first organisms in a new area are the colonizers and they are followed by a changing sequence of organisms as the environment (especially the soil) changes. This is succession. Left alone, a final stable climax community is reached which is made up of many varied organisms. Man in the UK often interferes with the natural climax which would be a mixed woodland in most areas.

Questions

1. Copy this out and fill in the blanks.
   In a new area, for example a deserted tip, the first organisms to arrive are called _____. They are _____ because they can make their own food. These early arrivals are replaced as time goes by, and large plants such as _____ grow. These changes are called a _____ and end in a _____ community which is _____. The process usually takes many years.

2. Trace the graph of population growth of pheasants on Protection Island. (It's on page 218.) Add these labels:
   (a) exponential growth
   (b) growth starting to slow
   Draw a dotted line to show what you think would happen to the population over the next few years. Give a reason.

3. Explain what is meant by the following (give an example in each case): limiting factor, stable population, artificial climax.

4. Explain the difference in the meanings of the following pairs:
   population and community
   exponential growth and stability
   colonization and succession
   a natural climax community and a garden community

5. What do you think is the best way to stabilize the human population? You'll need to discuss this and do some research on your ideas. What are the snags in people's ideas?

6. True or false? Write out the true sentences in the next column as they are and write a corrected version of the false ones.

   (a) Sei whales all over the world have been wiped out by man.
   (b) Colonizers are usually animals because these can walk or fly to a new area.
   (c) As organisms die, their bodies rot and help to form soil, which gets more fertile as time goes by and so allows different kinds of plants to grow well.
   (d) Marram grass has short roots and stems which help stop sand blowing away on dunes.
   (e) An oak woodland climax includes many kinds of trees, shrubs and herbs as well as oak trees.
   (f) The death of rabbits due to myxomatosis made no difference to the Downs.

7. Oak trees either have only male flowers, or only female flowers. They can't pollinate themselves. On an island, some kilometres from the mainland, is a single oak tree with female flowers. It produces fertile acorns, and eventually there is a small oak wood on the island. Can you suggest how the first oak might have been pollinated?

8. The answers to these questions can be found by looking at the various graphs in this section.
   (a) How long after the arrival of pheasants on Protection Island was population growth slow? (Fig. W3)
   (b) In which year (of the ones shown) was the population of Sei whales highest? (Fig. W7)
   (c) What was the largest (about) number of reindeer on the Alaskan Island? (Fig. W6) How many times did the population multiply before the numbers crashed?

9. Tell the story of the dune or the tip or the pond as it developed towards a climax.

229

Adaptation

Organisms fit well into the world in which we live. They survive because their body structure, the way their bodies work and their behaviour are suited to coping with the problems of living in their environment. There have been many examples of adaptation so far.

Adaptations allow cacti to use what water there is and protect them against heat and drought. Sometimes rather different organisms solve the problems in similar ways – they have similar adaptations.

X1

Solving movement problems

(a) Adaptations for moving in air

They all have light bones which support a large surface.

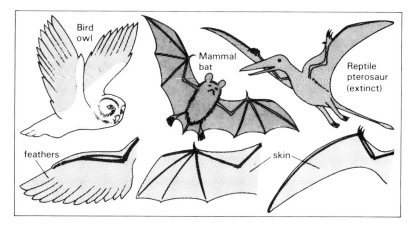

X2 Adaptations for flying

(b) Adaptations for moving in water

They all have a streamlined shape and use limbs as paddles.

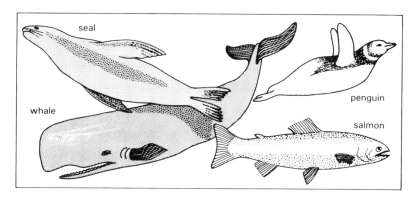

X3 Adaptations for swimming

Related organisms can have adaptations for different ways of life.

Beaks adapted to eating different foods

Question

Look at Fig. X4 and explain how each bird is adapted to its diet.

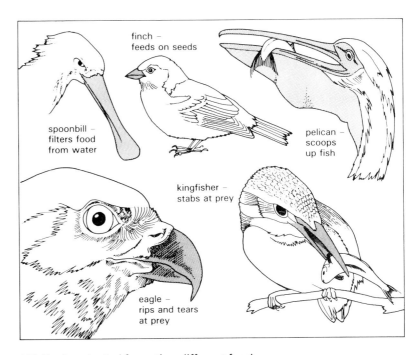

X4 Beaks adapted for eating different foods

How do they (and we) get to be like that? Much of the rest of this book tries to answer this quesion – and explain why some possibilities don't happen.

X5 Unnecessary adaptations!

231

Parasites

Parasites are organisms which live on or in another organism – the host. (They include some worms, single-celled organisms, fungi, and many more.) It is a one-sided relationship. The host provides food (and shelter) and in return is harmed by the parasite.

Parasitic lice can do damage in more than one way. The host loses blood. The parasite may carry disease, and it makes holes where bacteria can attack.

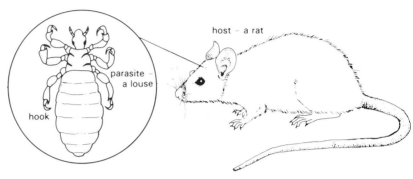

X6 A parasitic louse and its host

A well-adapted parasite does not do too much damage, though. It is not a good idea to kill the host that feeds you.

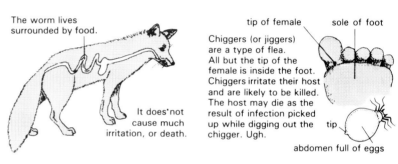

X7 Well-adapted parasite – roundworm

X8 Less well-adapted parasite – chigger

The adaptations of a parasite depend upon where it lives. Many can only survive in one place in one kind of host.

For example: large roundworms are common in the guts of people all over the world. Their eggs leave the body in faeces. If the eggs get into drinking water or on dirty hands they can be swallowed, and so start life in a new host. Infection is very likely if sewage treatment is poor or absent.

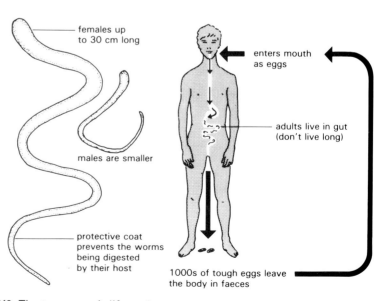

X9 The tapeworm's life cycle

Some gut-living worms have extra adaptations. Tapeworms have hooks and suckers at the head end of their ribbon-like bodies to hold on to the gut wall. The rest of the body is an egg-making machine. Who needs a gut in a food-filled environment?

the 'head' of a tapeworm

hooks

suckers

a small tapeworm as tapeworms go

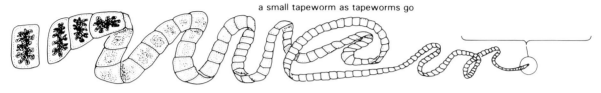

X10 A small tapeworm as tapeworms go

Tapeworms have an extra step in their life cycle, which helps them to find new hosts. They produce many eggs, a few of which are eaten by a secondary host. The eggs develop into bladder worms in the muscles of the secondary host. If the muscles (meat) are eaten raw or undercooked, the bladder worms survive and develop into adult tapeworms in the gut. (Have you ever eaten a rare steak?)

Some tapeworms have fish, pigs or dogs as secondary hosts.

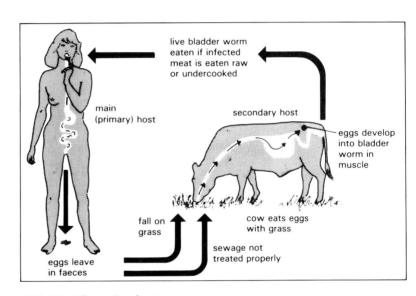

live bladder worm eaten if infected meat is eaten raw or undercooked

main (primary) host

secondary host

eggs develop into bladder worm in muscle

fall on grass

cow eats eggs with grass

sewage not treated properly

eggs leave in faeces

X11 The life cycle of a tapeworm

Parasites gnaw into other parts of the body and often do a lot of damage. They may live in blood, lymph, muscles, brains and so on. Adaptations include ways of fooling the host's white blood cells – and solving the transport problem.

The blood sucked up by this mosquito might contain malaria parasites – hitching a lift to the blood of a new host.

X12 Some mosquito species transmit disease organisms as they suck blood

Adult parasites often seem very dull. They sit there, feeding through their skin and reproducing. They haven't got much in the way of a nervous system, or means of moving, or sense organs. *But* they have a successful way of life – there are probably more of them than of all other types of organisms put together.

Variety

Organisms show lots of variety in their adaptations. There are many types of plants and animals.

X13

There is variety among organisms of the same species. (See Fig. X14.)

There is even variety among parts of the same organism. (See Fig. X15.)

X14

Questions

1. List the organisms in Fig. X13. Group them in two different ways.
   (a) Sort them out according to where they live (water, land or air). What features do the organisms share because of where they live?
   (b) Sort them into groups according to some other relationship. What features did you use to sort them and why?

2. Look at Fig. X15. Would you expect the leaves to be different colours as well as different shapes? Give a reason for your answer.

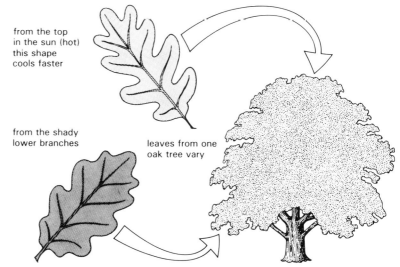

from the top in the sun (hot) this shape cools faster

from the shady lower branches

leaves from one oak tree vary

X15 Variety in oak leaves

New adaptations are based on variety which already exists. It looks as though organisms pass on to their children the variety they **inherited** from their parents.

The pups' ears (Fig. X16) will prick up like the parents' ears when they are older. Their tails will stay long unless they are cut.

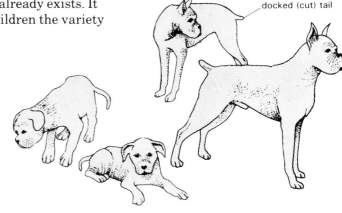

X16 A boxer family

It can be hard to sort out how much of the variety is due to the effect of the **environment** on an organism, and how much is inherited. Experiments can help.

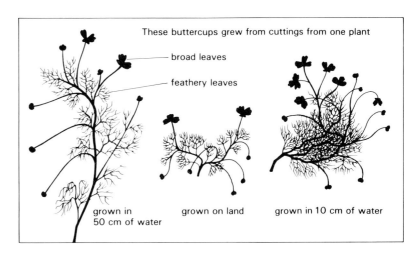

X17 Differences may be due to environment

It is sometimes possible to show how much of the differences between organisms is due to inheritance.

However, it isn't always possible to tell – real life is complicated.

Try this problem (Fig. X19) on your friends. Do they all take the same time to do it?

Do you get your intelligence from the way you are brought up? or inherit it from your parents? or both? Nobody is sure.

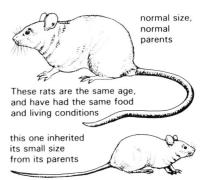

X18 Differences may be inherited

X19 Does everyone take the same time?

Gametes, chromosomes, variety and sex

Being able to reproduce is an important feature of living things. They can do it in two quite different ways, and these give different amounts of variety in the offspring.

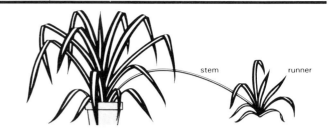

X20 Spider plant

Asexual reproduction is reproduction without sex. It involves only one parent and no sex cells. It has advantages – offspring get a good start in life, since they are fed by the parent for quite a long time.

Some plants send out runners. Potatoes reproduce asexually. 'Spuds' are tubers – the swollen ends of underground stems. Plant a tuber and it'll grow into a new potato plant. Some plants reproduce by budding. So do some animals. The buds break away. Some organisms reproduce both sexually and asexually.

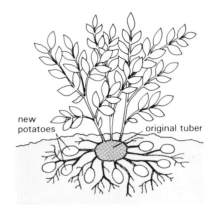

X21

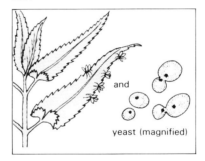

X22 Bryophytum leaf with buds

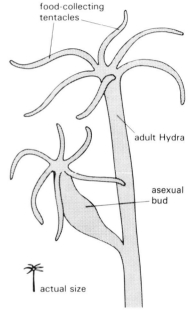

X23 Hydra lives in water and is related to jellyfish and coral

Sexual reproduction involves the meeting of two sex cells – a sperm and an egg.

Sperm (pollen in plants) and eggs (ovules) are known as gametes. In plants flowers can be either male or female, or both male and female. In most animals the sexes are separate (though animals like earthworms and snails have both male and female organs). Many animals reproduce sexually but not all. Some organisms reproduce both sexually and asexually.

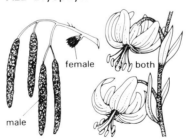

X24 Sexual organs of plants

X25

To summarize
Sexual reproduction produces varied offspring. Organisms produced asexually inherit exactly the same structure from the parent. If they do grow differently, it is because their environments are different.

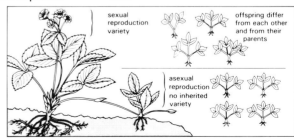

X26 Summary

Why does sexual reproduction provide variety?

In many ways the members of a family are alike – they have the same number and kinds of legs, ears, lungs and toes. There are often family likenesses in small details. If plants and animals always budded asexually off their parents like strawberry plants, the members of a family line would be exactly the same. This doesn't happen. Hair colour or allergies may be different. A list of family differences may be quite long. How does sexual reproduction produce all the differences and all the similarities?

X27 An Edwardian family

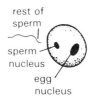

X28 Fertilization

We know that the nucleus is important – only the nucleus of a sperm (or pollen grain) enters the egg at fertilization (Fig. X28).

Inside a dividing cell, rod-like chromosomes can be seen. The chromosomes carry all the instructions for the growth of a new organism.

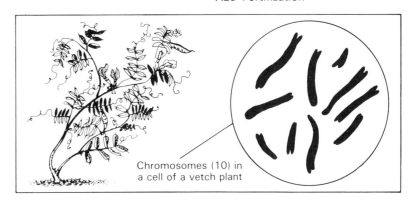

Chromosomes (10) in a cell of a vetch plant

X29

Whatever the number (different in different species) a gamete has half as many chromosomes as an ordinary body cell (Fig. X29).

| | Number of chromosomes in | | |
	egg cells	sperm or pollen cells	body cells
Hawkweed	4	4	8
Sedge	21	21	42
Hen	18	18	36
Humans	23	23	46
Kangaroo	6	6	12

X30

The chromosomes in a body cell can be sorted out into pairs – which fits with the idea that half came from one parent, half from the other. Each body cell has two complete sets of chromosomes, one set from each parent (Figs X29 and X30).

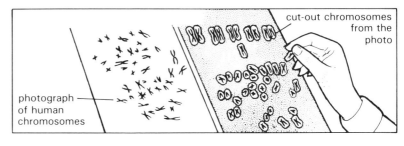

cut-out chromosomes from the photo

photograph of human chromosomes

X31 Sorting out human chromosome pairs

237

What are chromosomes made of?

The short answer to this question is 'protein and DNA'. A longer answer might be: **Proteins** – which may help to give the chromosome its structure (by providing a framework for the DNA) and help control the action of DNA; and **DNA** (d̲eoxyribose n̲ucleic a̲cid). DNA is a molecule which acts as a plan for the cell. In a similar way, a recipe is a plan for a cake but not the cake itself.

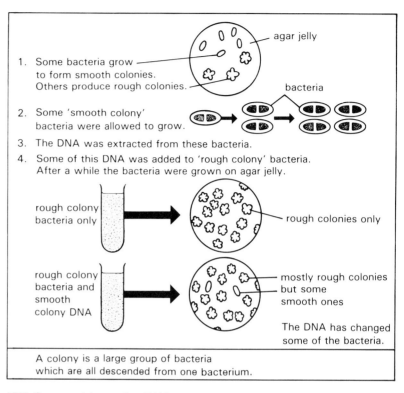

1. Some bacteria grow to form smooth colonies. Others produce rough colonies. — agar jelly

2. Some 'smooth colony' bacteria were allowed to grow. — bacteria

3. The DNA was extracted from these bacteria.

4. Some of this DNA was added to 'rough colony' bacteria. After a while the bacteria were grown on agar jelly.

rough colony bacteria only → rough colonies only

rough colony bacteria and smooth colony DNA → mostly rough colonies but some smooth ones

The DNA has changed some of the bacteria.

A colony is a large group of bacteria which are all descended from one bacterium.

X32 Some evidence that DNA controls cells

DNA is a very long thin molecule (Fig. X32).

It does two essential things supremely well.
1. It can copy itself accurately. This is important every time a cell divides.
2. It can be 'translated' as proteins by the cell. The proteins can be enzymes, or ones which are important to the structure of a cell. The proteins a cell makes decide what kind of cell it is. All the cells together decide the characteristics of an organism.

The length of DNA which codes for a protein is the section of a chromosome we call a gene.

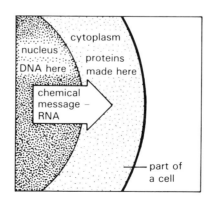

cytoplasm
nucleus
DNA here
proteins made here
chemical message – RNA
part of a cell

X34 The DNA in chromosomes tells the cell what proteins to make

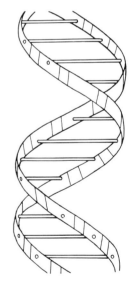

X33 DNA is a long molecule made of 2 twisted strands

The DNA in each chromosome contains the instructions for many different characteristics. For example, in human beings, everything that goes to make males and females different is controlled by just one of the twenty-three pairs of chromosomes. It is the same in many other animals.

Males are said to be XY and females XX – mostly because of the shapes of the sex chromosomes. The X and Y chromosomes are made up of the genes which control sexual development (among other things).

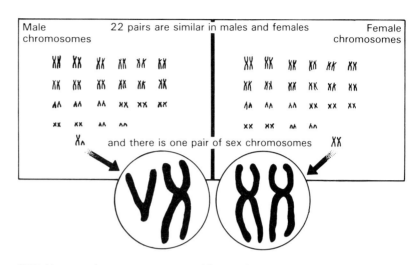

X35 Human chromosomes sorted into pairs

People still cannot choose the sex of their children, but we do know how sex is inherited.

From the mother (XX). The egg contains twenty-two 'body' chromosomes and one sex chromosome. It can only be an X chromosome. So all eggs have an X.

From the father (XY). Sperm also have twenty-two body chromosomes. Half the sperm have an X sex chromosome. The rest have a Y chromosome.

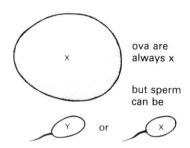

X36 Gametes and sex chromosomes

If one of the sperms reaches the egg first and fertilizes it, the result is a girl.

But there are just as many sperms, and if one of them arrives first the result is a boy.

In small families there may be more boys than girls just by chance. In the whole population, equal numbers of boys and girls might be expected. In fact slightly more boys than girls are born, though we are not sure why.

Boy babies are more delicate and more of them die than girl babies, so the numbers balance by the end of childhood.

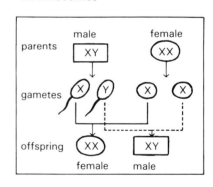

X37 Diagram to show how sex is inherited

Very rarely, mistakes happen and a sperm or egg either has an extra sex chromosome or no sex chromosome. People born with the wrong number of sex chromosomes are usually sterile – they cannot have children themselves. It would be nice to help people with genetic mistakes by somehow providing 'working' genes to replace faulty ones, but genetic engineering has a long way to go before we can do that.

Genetic engineering involves using biological tricks to snip out of a cell's DNA a section which codes for a protein we need. This DNA is put in another cell (at the moment this is usually a bacterium) which is allowed to multiply and make the protein we want. As this book was being written, there was a lot of interest in making insulin (a hormone needed by diabetics) and interferon (the body's chemical defence against viruses). By the time you read this page, I am sure much more will be possible.

Gamete formation - meiosis

Sex cells are not the result of mitosis like ordinary body cells. After mitosis the daughter cells have the same chromosomes as the parent cells.

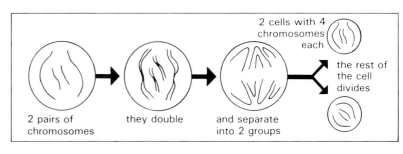

X38 Mitosis in a cell with 4 chromosomes

Sex cells are produced by a process called meiosis which happens in the sex organs. After **meiosis** or **reduction division,** each daughter cell has half the chromosomes of the parent cell. The daughter cells may be male or female gametes, depending on whether they are in an ovary or testis (or stamen).

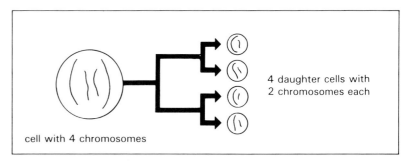

X39 Meiosis

Each of the daughter cells has one of each type of chromosome. Fertilization produces a cell with two full sets of chromosomes.

One interesting result of meiosis is that all the gametes produced are different. Before looking at meiosis in more detail in order to explain how this happens, you need to know a little more about chromosomes.

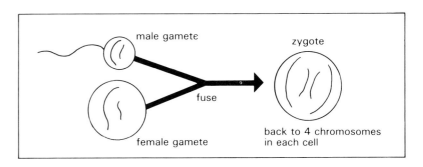

X40 Fertilization

Chromosomes and genes

We have only twenty-three pairs of chromosomes to carry the instructions for the whole human body. Each chromosome carries the information for many chemical reactions. For example, we believe that the instructions for making both salivary amylase and the Rhesus blood antigens are part of the same chromosome. The instructions for a particular trait or characteristic are called a **gene**. There are genes for eye colour, blood type and so on.

You have two copies of each gene, one in each of a pair of chromosomes. They may be identical or they may have slightly different effects. For example, you have two genes for eye colour, but one might be for blue and one for brown eyes. (More later.)

One copy of each gene came from your father, the other from your mother.

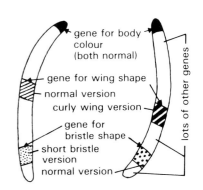

X41 A pair of chromosomes from the cell of a fruit fly

Meiosis in more detail

For each cell that divides, meiosis results in four gametes. The chromosomes double, and then divide first into two groups and then again so there are four groups.

In the diagrams, the dark-coloured chromosomes are from the father's side.

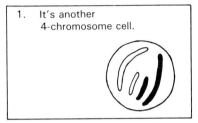

1. It's another 4-chromosome cell.

2. The chromosomes double.

3. Pairs of chromosomes lie alongside each other.

4. They twist around each other and exchange bits of chromosome material (and so exchange genes).

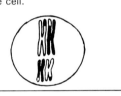

5. They move to the middle of the cell.

6. Pairs of chromosomes separate – this is the first division.

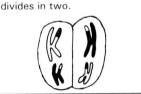

7. The rest of the cell divides in two.

8. The chromosomes move to the middle of the new cells

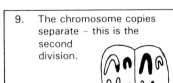

9. The chromosome copies separate – this is the second division.

10. The rest of the cells divide.

X42 The stages of meiosis

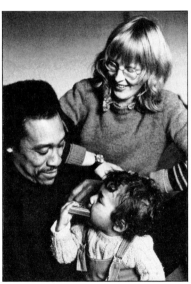

X43

The sex cells are a mixture of the chromosome material of both parents.

As humans have forty-six chromosomes, not four, in their normal body cells, it is not surprising that one set of parents can produce very different children. However, each one has all the information to grow into an adult human.

Summary and questions

Summary
Chromosomes are rod-like bodies in the nucleus of each cell which carry the instructions for making new cells. They are made of protein and DNA. During meiosis, the number of chromosomes in a cell is halved. As the result of meiosis, gametes are produced. A gene is a section of DNA which codes for a protein and so for a characteristic of the organism. In gametes, genes have been shuffled, which means that the offspring in a family differ from each other and from their parents.

Questions

1. Do you think it would be a good idea if people were allowed to choose the sex of their babies? Give your reasons.

2. Fill in the numbers and write out the passage below.
   Human body cells have _____ chromosomes. Of these, _____ are sex chromosomes. Organisms have different numbers of chromosomes. For example, a kangaroo has _____ chromosomes in each body cell. Gametes always have _____ the number of chromosomes found in a body cell.

3. Explain the connection between
   (a) a chromosome and a gene
   (b) meiosis and gametes
   (c) sex and sex chromosomes

4. Explain why
   (a) organisms which reproduce asexually have the same chromosomes as their parent
   (b) you would expect equal numbers of boys and girls to be born (though in fact more boys are born than girls)

5. The cucumbers we eat are from unpollinated flowers – fertilized seeds produce bitter cucumbers. Bananas don't have fertilized seeds in them either. New banana plants grow from suckers, like strawberry plants. All these plants reproduce sexually or asexually? Will the offspring be the same genetically as their parents or not?

6. Here is a description of mitosis. Rewrite it for meiosis, replacing the underlined phrases if necessary and adding anything you think is important.
   Mitosis is the type of cell division which produces ordinary body cells. It can happen in many places in an organism. The daughter cells are identical with each other and with the parent cell. First the chromosomes double. Then the copies separate into groups at opposite ends of the cell. The cytoplasm of the cell divides to form two daughter cells. These can then divide again or become active body cells such as muscle cells.

7. Think of a family you know (mother, father, two or more children). Make a list of similarities between the children which you think might be inherited. Make a list of differences between the children. How can you explain the differences?

8. A cell undergoes meiosis. If it is in a testis, four sperm cells result. If it is in an ovary, only one of the four cells produced becomes a mature egg cell. Why do you think this is? (Hint: size.)

9. Grafting is used with fruit trees, vines and others to combine different root and shoot systems. A variety (A) with poor fruit but tough roots can be joined to one (B) which has small roots but sweet fruit, to get an ideal combination (from our point of view). Will the seeds the grafted plant produces grow into plants like A or plants like B or a mixture of both? Explain your answer.

Genetics 1

We can't see genes but we can see their effects. Studying the visible patterns of inheritance and trying to explain them is called **genetics**. The patterns were first explored using organisms like Drosophila (the fruit fly), mice or corn – not human beings. Why?

Drosophila (and smaller organisms)	Humans (and large animals)
You can control which fruit fly mates with which.	People do **not** like having mates chosen for them in order to do an experiment.
Fruit flies breed when 14 days old – you can look at many generations in a short time.	It takes years before the next generation is produced.
Fruit flies have hundreds of offspring. This means the results you get are less likely to be just chance.	Families are small so chance is important.
Sharp differences in appearance are easy to study genetically.	Shades of colour, height and so on are difficult to study.
Lots of fruit flies can live in a small space. They're easy to handle.	Take up a lot of room.

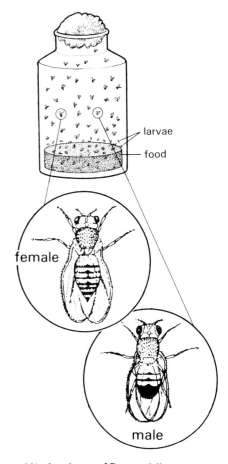

Y1 A culture of Drosophila

From organisms like Drosophila we have learnt to understand inheritance. There have been many experiments – here is one of them.

Start with pure-bred flies. A pure-bred organism comes from a long line of individuals which have bred true for a characteristic. For example, if we mate two pure-bred short-winged flies then all their offspring will have short wings.

A A pure-bred long-winged fly mates with a pure-bred short-winged fly.

B All the hundreds of offspring have long wings.

C Two of these are mated. For every three of their offspring with long wings, there is one with short wings.

How can this be explained – what happened to 'short wings' in the middle? Turn over to find out.

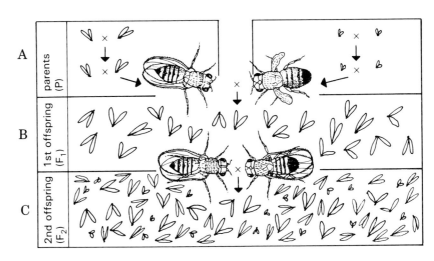

Y2 A Drosophila breeding experiment

243

Genetics 2

The explanation goes like this. We know that offspring inherit
half their genes from each parent. Suppose there is a gene for
wing length and it comes in two versions: **N** is the version
for normal wing length and **n** is the version for short wings.
Each gamete is Ⓝ or ⓝ and each adult has two copies of the
gene – one from each parent.
We can explain what we see like this:

Parents are **NN** and **nn.** Their gametes are Ⓝ and ⓝ, and the
first offspring (F1) must be **Nn.**

The effect of n is hidden by **N**.

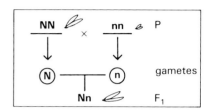

Y3 The first generation

But what happens if we do some breeding?

Each of the F1 parents is **Nn.**
They each have Ⓝ and ⓝ gametes.

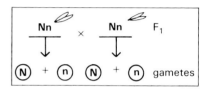

Y4 The next generation

There are four possible combinations by chance:

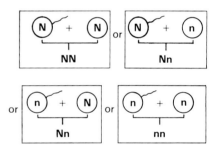

Y5 The possible combinations for
fertilization

or use a Punnet square to work it out:

sperm / eggs	N	n
N	**NN**	**Nn**
n	**Nn**	**nn**

Y6 Summarizing Fig. Y5 as a
Punnet square

So F2 (second offspring) are three long-winged flies to every one
short-winged fly.

This 3 : 1 ratio is a sign that both parents have a mixture of
genes.

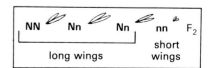

Y7 The F2 generation

Genetics has some useful words – handy for keeping explanations and questions short.

Word	Meaning	Fruit fly examples
Homozygous	The two versions of a gene are the same.	**NN** and **nn** flies were homozygous for wing length
Heterozygous	The two versions of a gene are different.	**Nn** were heterozygous flies.
Recessive	A gene which can be hidden by another. Its effects are only seen in a homozygote.	**n** is a recessive gene.
Dominant	A gene which hides another. Its effects are seen in both homozygotes and heterozygotes.	**N** is a dominant gene.

Coleus plant example

Coleus plants can have deep-lobed leaves or shallow-lobed leaves.

If a cross is set up between **homozygous** shallow-lobed and deep-lobed plants then the offspring is deep-lobed. The deep-lobed gene (**L**) is dominant over the shallow-lobed gene (**l**).

shallow-lobed plant

deep-lobed plant

Y8 Two Coleus variations

The cross is shown in Fig. Y9. The offspring are **heterozygous.**

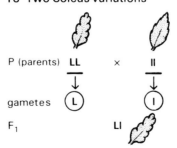

P (parents) **LL**   ×   **ll**

gametes (L)   (l)

F₁   Ll

Y9

A Punnet square showing the effect of crossing two F₁ heterozygotes looks like this:

Question
How many F₂ plants would have deeply lobed leaves?

pollen / ovule	L	l
L	LL	Ll
l	Ll	ll

Genetics 3

Some more useful words

Genotype and phenotype

genotype – the genes an organism has

phenotype – what it looks like (the effect of its genes)

LL and **Ll** Coleus plants have the same phenotype but different genotypes.

Inheritance of albinism example (Fig. Y10)
A normal man (Dave) marries an albino woman (Sue). (Albino means having no colour in the skin. White mice with pink eyes are albino). The gene for albino (**c**) is recessive compared to the gene for normal colour (**C**). All Dave's sperm must have **C** genes and all Sue's eggs must have **c** genes.

Kids (F₁) must be normal-coloured as they have one dominant gene for colour.

Mary can have an albino child if she marries a man who also carries an albino gene. This is not very likely, as the albino gene is not common. If she does, there is still only once chance in four that a child will be albino.

Another way of working out Mary's children:

sperm \ eggs	C	c
C		
c		

With all the possible combinations filled in:

sperm \ eggs	C	c
C	CC	Cc
c	Cc	cc

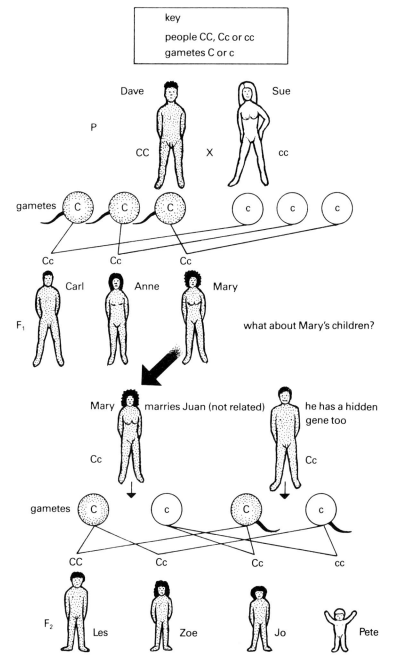

Y10 Albinism in a human family

Explaining a family tree

In the family tree in Fig. Y12, all the shaded people (like A) have six fingers. The others have five. The things to note are: six-fingered people (A) can have five-fingered children (F); and as long as one parent has six fingers (D), some of the kids have six fingers (I and K). So a good guess is that the six-finger gene **F** is dominant over the five-finger gene **f**. Capital letters are used for dominant genes. A is probably heterozygous. Fill in the family tree and see if it works.

Y11 Among the Amish people in the USA, people are sometimes born with 6 fingers

A family tree

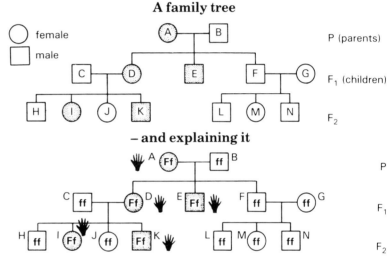

Not all genes work as simply as the ones we've looked at. Sometimes neither version of a gene is dominant – the heterozygote looks like a mixture. This is called **incomplete dominance**. Here's an example.

Y12

Frizzle feathers among poultry show incomplete dominance (Figs Y13 and Y14).

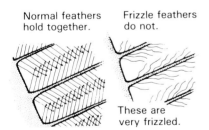

Normal feathers hold together.

Frizzle feathers do not.

These are very frizzled.

Y14 Why feathers frizzle

Monohybrid crosses (all the ones we've discussed so far) involve only one set of genes. Things get very complicated when more genes are involved in one characteristic.

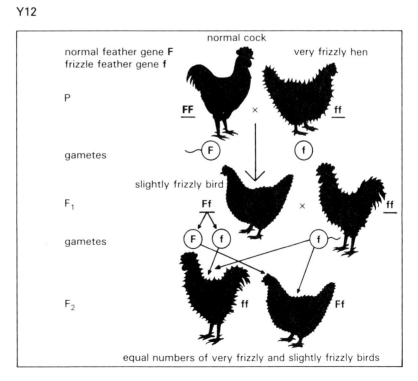

Y13 An example of incomplete dominance

247

What Mendel did

Mendel was an Austrian monk who worked over 100 years ago. He discovered the basic laws of inheritance. In his monastery he did many experiments with garden peas. The choice of plant was fortunate – garden peas normally self-pollinate and usually breed true (that is, they are homozygous) and they have clear-cut characteristics. Mendel carefully cross-pollinated his true-breeding peas. The table shows some of his results.

Y15 Gregor Mendel

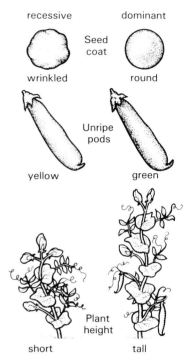

Y16 Peas' characteristics

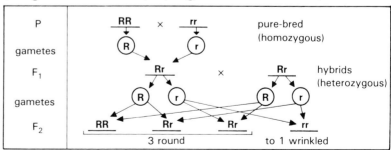

Y17 Section through a sweet pea

Mendel did not know about genes, but he worked out that his results could be explained by an organism inheriting 'factors' (genes) from its parents.

He used the idea of dominant and recessive factors to explain the way some characteristics – like wrinkled seeds – disappeared in the F_1 mixtures or **hybrids**.

P (pure-bred)	F_1 (hybrids)	F_2
round × wrinkled	all round	5474 round + 1850 wrinkles or about 3 : 1
green pods × yellow pods	all green	428 green + 152 yellow or about 3 : 1
tall × short	all tall	787 tall + 277 short or about 3 : 1

Y18 Some of Mendel's results

(**R** – gene for round coat)   (**r** – gene for wrinkled coat)

Y19 An explanation for the cross between round and wrinkled seeds

Mendel sent his results to a Swiss botanist who did not think they were important. No one realised how important his ideas were until other people investigating the same ideas using fruit flies. Mendel was dead by then.

Summary and questions

Summary

For any characteristic an organism has at least two genes – one from each parent. They may be the same (homozygous) or different (heterozygous). Versions of a gene which always show their effects are dominant. Versions of a gene which can be hidden are called recessive. Genotype refers to the genes an organism has, phenotype to the way it looks. The original work was done by Mendel using garden peas. Like other useful organisms for studying genetics, peas reproduce quickly, are no trouble and have clear-cut alternative characteristics. The best way to get on top of genetics is to do lots of problems.

Questions

1. Explain the difference between the following pairs:
   (a) fruit flies and elephants as suitable organisms for genetic studies
   (b) hybrid and pure-bred organisms
   (c) homozygous and heterozygous organisms
   (d) recessive and dominant versions of a gene
   (e) the way coleus leaf edges are inherited and the way frizzle hen feathers are inherited
   (f) genotype and phenotype (use examples)

2. Look back to Fig. Y10 – the family with an albino mother.
   (a) Name all the homozygous people in this family.
   (b) Name all the heterozygous people in this family. Which people have the same genotype as Dave?
   (c) What genes must a person have to be albino?
   Look at Fig. Y12 – the family where some people have six fingers.
   (d) Which is recessive – the six-finger version of the gene or the five-finger version?
   (e) Give the letters of two people who are heterozygous for this gene. Give the letter of a person with the same genotype as B.
   (f) How many children does F have? How many are boys?

   (g) How many grandchildren does A have? How many are girls? Where did E inherit the **f** gene from? and the **F** gene?
   Look at (Fig. Y13) – the chicken feathers.
   (h) What genes does a slightly frizzly bird have? Is the frizzle or the non-frizzle feather gene dominant?
   (i) What do you get if you cross a slightly frizzly bird with a very frizzly bird?
   (j) What do you get if you cross a slightly frizzly bird with a normal bird?

3. (a) A pure-breeding black bull is crossed with a pure-breeding red cow. Their offspring are all black. Choose letters to represent the genes and draw a diagram which explains this cross. Which version of the colour gene is recessive? Which animals are heterozygous for this gene?
   (b) Two curly-winged Drosophila are mated. Their offspring are 341 curly-winged and 110 normal-winged flies. How could you explain this?

4. (a) In cattle, a horned animal crossed with a hornless animal sometimes produces only hornless cattle. Is horned or hornless the dominant gene? Choose letters for the horned and hornless versions of the gene and write out the cross. Which animals are heterozygous?
   (b) Sometimes, though, a horned animal crossed with a hornless animal produces equal numbers of horned and hornless animals. Can you explain what has happened?

Mutations-genetic change

Mutations are changes in genetic material. Sometimes large parts of a chromosome are affected, sometimes the change is within one gene.

Nearly all mutations are harmful. This is hardly surprising, as the existing genes of an organism already work well together. Missing genes, extra genes and changed genes are almost bound to upset the system. It can mean death.

A few mutations are useful to the organisms in which they happen. Our distant ancestors did not look like us, judging by their fossilized bones. As useful mutations happened, organisms gradually became more like those living today.

Mistakes in genes can happen anyway, but more mutations happen when an organism is exposed to radiation or chemicals like mustard gas and LSD. Mutation in body cells may result in a cancer. Mutations in cells which become gametes mean that the mistakes can be passed to offspring – genetic diseases may result. This is very worrying as humans are using more sources of radiation (nuclear bombs, nuclear power stations) and more new chemicals which can get into our food or the air we breathe. It is for this reason that pregnant women should be X-rayed as rarely as possible.

Genetic diseases
An example – sickle-cell anaemia (Fig. Y22).
A person with sickle-cell anaemia has red blood cells which become drawn out and cannot carry oxygen properly round the body. It is caused by a mistake in a gene involved in making haemoglobin – usually called Hb^S. The normal gene is Hb^N.

Here (Fig. Y23) is a family in which the parents are both heterozygous for this gene. Dominance is incomplete.

There are many genetic diseases, such as cystic fibrosis, phenylketanuria and Huntington's chorea. Most are unpleasant, and if their names are unfamiliar it is because mostly they are rare.

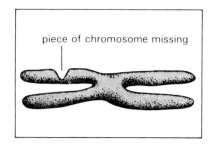

Y20 Human chromosome with a visible mutation

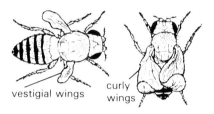

Y21 These fruit flies have mutations which would mean their death in the wild

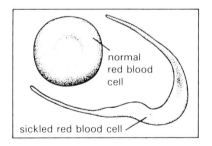

Y22

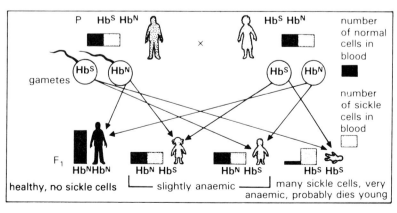

Y23

One special group of mutations are the **sex-linked** ones where changes happen in the X chromosome. The result is interesting. If a man has the mutated gene as part of the X chromosome the effects will show, as the Y chromosome hasn't got a gene to make up for the deficiency. If a woman has one X chromosome with a mutation, and one normal one, she appears to be normal – but she is a **carrier**. A woman only shows the effects if she has two damaged X chromosomes.

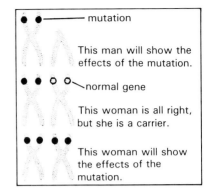

Y24 Mutations of sex chromosomes

Colour-blindness is a fairly common example. Sex chromosomes have genes for characteristics besides sex. The ability to see colour is one of them. Here is a family in which the mother has a hidden gene for colour-blindness. Her sight is normal.

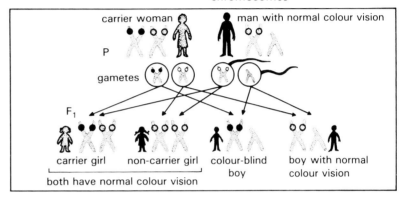

Y25 The inheritance of colour blindness

The clues to sex linkage are:
(a) It is nearly always males who suffer.
(b) They only suffer from sex-linked diseases because their mothers are carriers. From their fathers they inherit a Y chromosome which isn't affected.
(c) You can only tell that a woman is a carrier if she has sons who are affected.

A famous sex-linked disease is haemophilia. Haemophiliacs – 'bleeders' – have blood which doesn't clot properly. They often die young. It is a rare disease, but Queen Victoria was a carrier for it, perhaps as the result of a mutation in a gene in one of the X chromosomes she inherited from her parents. She passed it on to her children, and the gene spread through several European royal houses. It no doubt affected history.

Y26

Using genetics-people

There is always a small risk of having a handicapped child, but no one would deliberately have one.

Genetic counselling helps couples to decide how great the risk is for them. Perhaps someone comes from a family in which haemophilia is known (Fig. Y27).

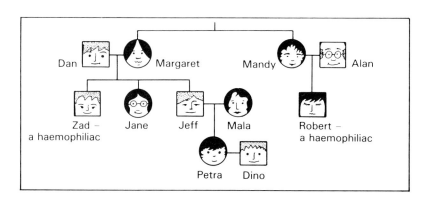

Y27

Petra is worried – is she a carrier for haemophilia? Should she risk having children? In fact she is clear – her X chromosomes must both be normal. If Jeff had inherited a damaged X chromosome from Margaret, as Zad did, he'd be a haemophiliac himself. Petra can have children, and they'll be normal (Fig. Y28).

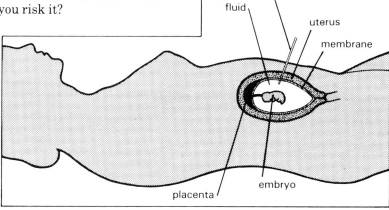

Y28

What about Jane? She could have inherited her mother's normal X chromosome, but equally she could have the damaged one. She can't tell without having children. If she is a carrier, half her sons are likely to be haemophiliac. Would you risk it?

Jane may soon have another choice, although for haemophilia the test is still being tried out. Cells from the fluid around an embryo can be sampled and checked for chromosome damage.

Y29 Amniocentesis

If the chromosomes are damaged, the parents might choose to have an abortion. The cell test gives clear accurate results in a case where the embryo has extra chromosomes – Down's syndrome. Down's syndrome children are mentally retarded. This condition is much more likely to happen if the mother is over 40.

Knowing the risk, an older woman might choose not to have a child, or to have a cell test and perhaps an abortion. Only the parents can make decisions like this, but it helps if they can be given clear advice about risks.

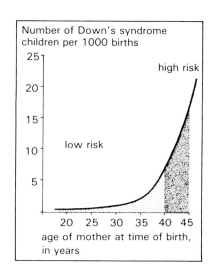

Y30

Even without genetic diseases in the family, genetics helps to avoid problems. Humans have many kinds of blood groups. The **Rhesus** group is important in pregnancy. Most people have Rh+ blood (Fig. Y31).

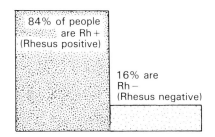

84% of people are Rh + (Rhesus positive)

16% are Rh − (Rhesus negative)

Y31

Occasionally a Rh− woman marries an Rh+ man. Half the children inherit Rh+ blood from him. If Rh+ blood cells from an embryo leak into the mothers blood, her body defence system is sensitized against Rh+ blood. The first Rh+ baby is all right, but the blood cells of the next Rh+ baby may be clumped together by the mother's blood system (Fig. Y32). A simple blood test can warn a couple of the danger. The mother can have treatment after each birth to prevent her system becoming sensitized.

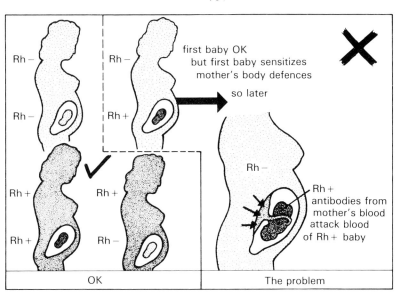

Y32

Genetics and legal tangles

The genetics of blood groups can help to sort out babies which are mixed up in hospital, or help to find the father. It works like this. The ABO blood system is important when transfusing blood. It is the result of one gene which is found in three different versions – **A**, **B**, or **i**. Figure Y33 shows the genotypes of the four blood groups.

Blood group	Genotype
A	AA or Ai
B	BB or Bi
AB	AB
O	ii

Y33

Ed suspects Marta has not been faithful. In particular he thinks weedy Mark is not his – unlike his favourite son Pete who is much more like himself. He insists on blood tests. Here are the results (Fig. Y34).

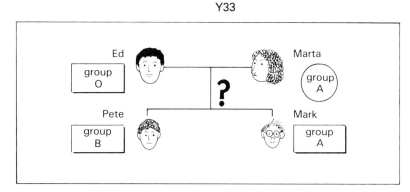

Y34

Oops – a pity he did that really. Ed has to be **ii**. Mark could easily be his son with an **A** gene from Marta and an **i** gene from Ed. But Pete! – he could have an **i** from Marta but never a **B** from Ed – Mark might well be Ed's but not Pete. What will Ed do? Write the next step in this drama yourself.

Using genetics - artificial selection

We do not breed people to order, but over the years we have made big changes in the animals and plants that are important to us. We have done it by selective breeding. Picking out the most promising varieties, we breed them rather than eat them.

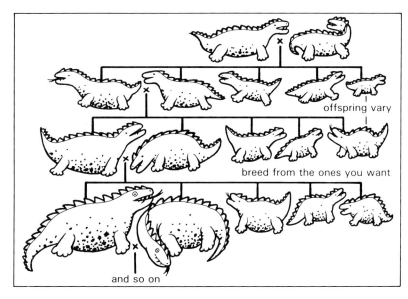

Y35 On breeding a better dragon

This is the way from wild pigs to pork pigs (Fig. Y36), from grasses to wheat (Fig. Y37), and many more.

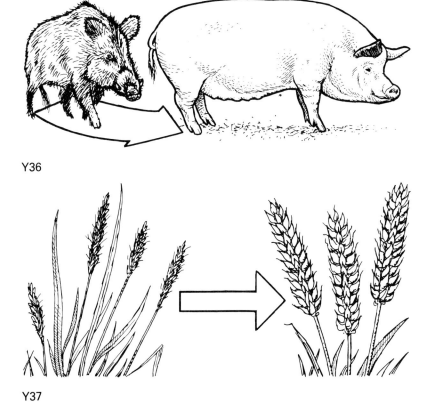

Y36

Y37

It can take many generations. Sometimes big advances have been made as the result of a rare useful mutation. Work continues – more productive rice, disease-resistant plants and faster-growing cattle may all help to provide the growing human population of the world with food.

Summary and questions

Summary
Completely new genetic material is the result of mutations or changes, such as loss of parts of chromosomes or changes in small pieces of DNA. A few changes are useful to the organism, but most mutations are harmful and in humans they may cause genetic diseases. Understanding the laws of genetics helps predict and so avoid genetic diseases. It can also sort out some legal problems. People have used genetic ideas for a long time (even if they didn't know it) to breed better plants and animals.

Questions

1. Explain what is meant by the following (with examples)
   (a) mutation
   (b) genetic disease
   (c) sex-linked genes
   (d) genetic counselling
   (e) artificial selection
   (f) a carrier (as in colour-blindness)

2. Explain why
   (a) a Rhesus positive (Rh+) woman does not have to worry about the blood group of the man she marries
   (b) people with sickle-cell anaemia get tired easily
   (c) in the haemophiliac family, it is reasonable to believe that Margaret inherited the damaged X chromosome from her mother, rather than that it happened as a mutation in her own ovaries.

3. The study of genetics is very important to humans, but it is often hard to understand human genetic patterns. Why?

4. A farmer would like his cattle to be hornless. Most of his herd are hornless but every so often a few horned ones are born. He guesses that the gene for horns is recessive to the gene for no horns, and that some of his hornless animals are heterozygous. What breeding plan could he follow to try and get a true-breeding (homozygous) hornless herd?

5. Huntington's chorea is a very rare and fatal disease of the nervous system. It does not develop until middle age. A man in his twenties learns that his father has Huntington's chorea. It is caused by a dominant gene (**not** carried on a sex chromosome).
   (a) What are the chances that he, the son, will also have it?
   (b) If the son does not develop the disease, what are the chances that his children will have Huntington's chorea?
   To work this out, choose a letter for the Huntington's chorea gene and for its normal version. Draw the family tree, then fill in the genotypes as far as you can.

6. A man who has slight sickle-cell anaemia marries a normal woman.
   (a) Can they produce normal children?
   (b) Can they have children with severe sickle-cell anaemia?
   (c) If they have four children, how many are likely to show some signs of sickle-cell anaemia? Explain your answers.

7. Two babies were born in hospital on a night when there was a blackout. It was possible that their identity bracelets got mixed up, so blood tests were done. Here are the results:

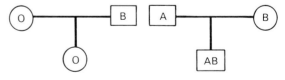

Y38

Are the babies with the right parents? Explain your answer.

Evolution-the theory

It has long been known that life on earth has changed as time has passed (Fig. Z1).

There have been many ideas about how this happened, but the theory that most biologists accept today is based on that of Charles Darwin.

Z2 Darwin in 1854

As a young man, Darwin travelled around the world in HMS Beagle as ship's naturalist. He was puzzled by many of the things he saw. For example, the Galapagos Islands each have their own species of giant tortoise. The animals are clearly related but slightly different. The same was true of the finches on the islands. How could this be?

Darwin's answer was **natural selection**. We now know more about genetics than Darwin, and as a result today's version of his theory is a little different from his own version. It looks as though this is what happens:

1. Organisms vary – even members of the same family.

2. The variations are the result of mutation (new genes) and sexual reproduction (new mixtures of genes).

3. Many more organisms are produced than grow up and reproduce. Most of them die.

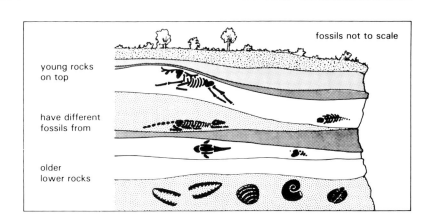

Z1

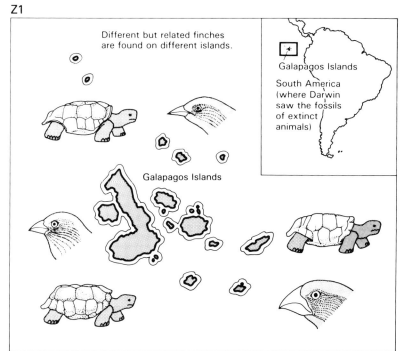

Z3 Different but related finches are found on different islands

Z4 Natural selection

4. Some variations are adaptive – they help an animal to survive and reproduce.

suppose living in an area there are

10 dark mice

10 light-coloured mice

half die for various reasons

and the owl gets some

the survivors breed

their babies are

16 dark mice

4 light mice

light mice will get rarer and rarer

Z5 Natural selection and mice

5. Organisms with the best adaptations survive and have offspring, which inherit the adaptations. These useful characteristics become more common in a group of organisms. The group changes as it adapts to its environment, because the less well-adapted die, or do not produce as many offspring as the others. This is natural selection.

Question

Which mouse is more likely to surive in Fig. Z5? Explain your answer.

Once a group is adapted to its environment, natural selection means it does not change much, unless the environment changes.

These odd piles are produced by mats of blue-green algae (Fig. Z6). Fossils of these simple algae have been found which are millions of years old. There are living ones in Shark Bay, Australia, where conditions haven't changed much in that time.

Z6 Stromatolites in Australia

Normally, environments do change – though it may take a long time. Organisms may take millions of years to evolve, but if they cannot keep on adapting they die out (become extinct) if their environment changes. Natural selection has no favourites.

Darwin used the term 'natural selection' because he knew about 'artificial selection' where people select the next generation to breed 'better' pigeons or whatever. He saw a connection with what happens in the natural world where the selective force is something like weather or predators like the owl. There were many objections to his ideas because they meant that the pattern of changes in living things was the result of chance and the physical laws of nature – that there was no plan in nature and humans were not special but animals. Some people still do not accept the ideas of evolution, but today there is more evidence for it than there was in Darwin's time.

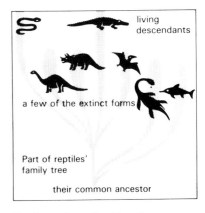

living descendants

a few of the extinct forms

Part of reptiles' family tree

their common ancestor

Z7 Part of reptiles' family tree

Evolution - the evidence

The theory of evolution suggests that living organisms are descended from a common ancestor (Fig. Z8).

There is quite a lot of evidence for this. You might expect related organisms to show similarities inherited from their common ancestors – and they do.

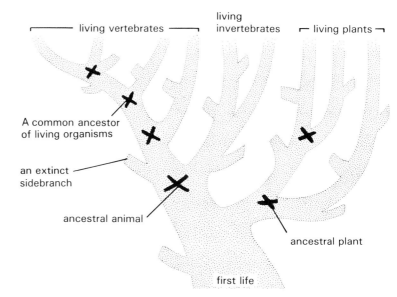

Z8

1. **Similar body plans**
   For example, vertebrate leg bones are based on the same pattern, though it is adapted for different situations in different animals (Fig. Z9).

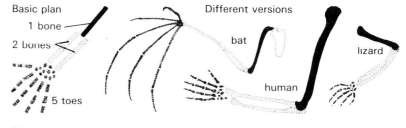

Z9 Basic plan

2. **Similar embryos**
   It is often hard to tell which vertebrate embryo is which when they are very young. As they grow, differences appear (Fig. Z10).

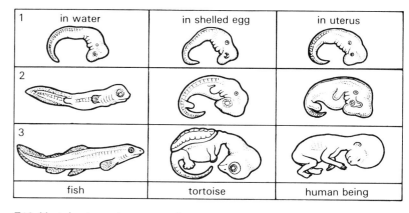

Z10 Vertebrate embryo growth

3. **Similar chemistry**
   Related organisms have inherited similar proteins. Unrelated organisms have rather different proteins, even if they look alike. (Fig. Z11).

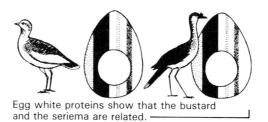

Egg white proteins show that the bustard and the seriema are related.

The secretary bird is not.

Z11 Proteins give the game away

Fossils are the remains of long-dead organisms (Fig. Z12). They include the ancestors of living organisms. You might expect to find fossils of organisms whose descendents are different because of natural selection. These should include common ancestors of animals that are rather different from each other today. We do find such fossils, but there are big gaps. Perhaps this is not surprising. Most dead organisms rot away completely. Few of them are preserved – most are lost. Evolutionary change, when it happens, may be fairly rapid. Few organisms from 'in between' stages are fossilized. We can, however, follow the evolution of some animals – including some monkeys and a sea urchin.

You might also expect to **see evolutionary changes happening** – though only small ones, because evolution takes a long time compared to our life span. Here is one example.

There was a time when **peppered moths** in England were mostly pale. The pale ones were hard for birds to see against tree trunks covered in lichen. The dark ones were not hidden, and were mostly eaten by birds.

After the Industrial Revolution, the trees in towns had dark sooty trunks. The pale moths were easy to see on these trees, so they were eaten. In towns, the dark (melanic) form of peppered moth increased in numbers.

The map (Fig. Z14) shows where the two forms of peppered moths are now found. Since the fifties, when the Clean Air Act was passed, there has been less air pollution in some areas, and lichen has been able to grow on trees again. In these areas, the melanic moths are becoming fewer compared to the pale form.

The moth population has changed in the last 100 years, because of changes in the environment.

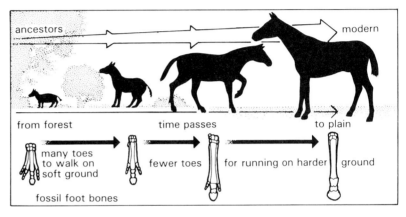

Z12 The evolution of the horse

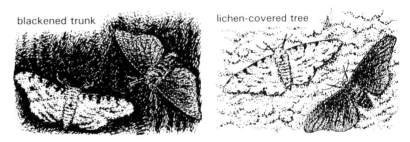

Z13 Peppered moths and camouflage

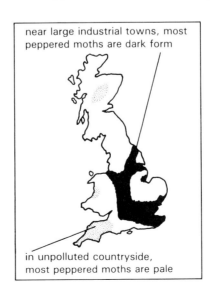

Z14 The distribution of peppered moths

Some evolutionary explanations

The theory of evolution helps explain some puzzling facts.

Vestigial organs

These are organs with no obvious use. 'Hip' bones in snakes seem pointless since snakes have no legs. But if snakes evolved from four-footed ancestors, these traces of their heritage make sense.

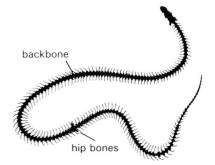

Z15 Snakes have vestigial hips

Faulty genes staying in a population

Sickle-cell anaemia is an example. A surprising number of people carry this gene – up to a fifth of the population in some parts of Africa. Why? It seems to be a harmful gene and it should disappear as the result of natural selection. It turns out that people with one sickle-cell gene are less likely to suffer from malaria than people with normal red blood cells. The advantage is great enough to keep the gene going – even though children who inherit two sickle-cell genes are likely to die young.

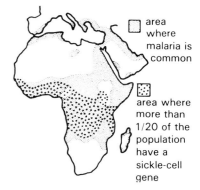

Z16 People in other parts of the world whose ancestors come from Africa may be carriers too

Life forms on islands

These are often unusual, and fit in well with the theory. The Galapagos finches were a great puzzle for Darwin without an evolutionary explanation. The story is probably this – a pair of finches were blown to one of the islands from the South American mainland (Fig. Z18).

On the island there was less competition than on the mainland. The descendants of the first pair evolved differently from mainland finches. They changed so that they could make use of the food available – fruit and insects as well as seeds. Some flew to other islands where conditions were slightly different and more types of finch developed.

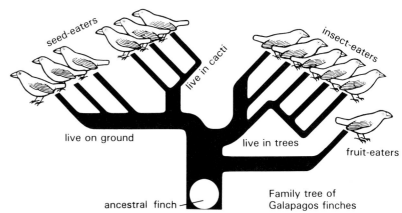

Z17 Island finch family tree

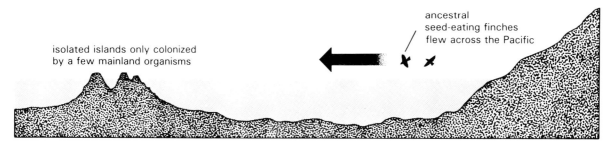

Z18 The arrival of the ancestral finches

Species

The word 'species' comes up often in biology. It is used to describe organisms which are related closely enough to breed successfully (Fig. Z19).

Z19

'Successfully' means that the offspring must be fertile (able to reproduce themselves). All humans belong to one fertile group – one species.

Horses and donkeys can have offspring – mules. But mules are sterile – the line stops there. So horses and donkeys are separate species (Fig. Z20).

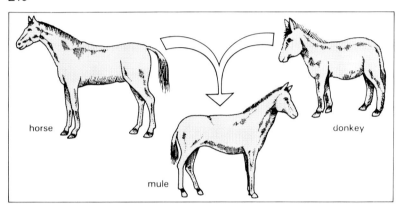

horse

donkey

mule

Z20

During evolution new species are formed. There are several possible ways this can happen. One is isolation. One group gets divided into two by something like water. The two groups are in slightly different conditions and evolve differently. Eventually they are so different that if they happen to meet again they cannot breed – they are two species, not one. This is probably what happened to the animals on the Galapagos. Water is not the only barrier.

ⓐ To begin with

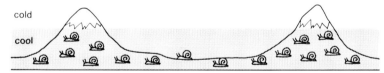

cold
cool

ⓑ The climate changes

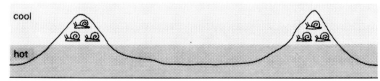

cool
hot

ⓒ The climate changes again. The two groups can mix but are now too different to breed – they are two new species.

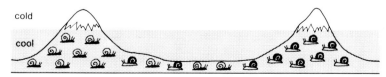

cold
cool

thousands of years

a) A species of snail does well in cool areas.

b) The climate changes. The valley is too hot for the snails, and they live only on the mountains.

c) The two groups on the mountains evolve separately, and over time they become different.

Z21 New snail species develop as climate changes

Grouping organisms

The end results of evolution are millions of living things in thousands of breeding groups or species (more about species over the page). Species are given names – mainly so that we can talk about them to each other. Putting species into groups of various sizes makes it easier to look at relationships and to understand how bodies work. This is known as **classification**.

Living organisms all
1. respire
2. grow
3. feed (this includes making their own food)
4. respond to stimuli
5. excrete (get rid of) wastes
6. move
7. reproduce

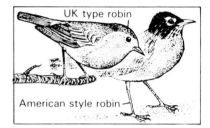

OUCH!

A crystal grows in a concentrated salt solution – is it alive? No, because it does none of the other things on the list.

Z22 Living things checklist

Naming species
Common names won't do. A robin, for example, is not the same bird in Europe and in the United States – or in Australia for that matter. A Swedish biologist called Carl Linnaeus devised a system of scientific names. Scientific names come in two parts – the **generic** name (which genus it is) and the **specific** name (which species it is). A genus is a group of closely related species.

Organisms with the same generic name but different specific names are closely related but cannot breed successfully. Only man has the generic name *Homo*, but in the past there have been at least two other related species, *Homo erectus* and *Homo habilis*.

If *Homo habilis* and *Homo erectus* were alive today, *Homo sapiens* could not breed with them but they would be more like us than, say, chimps are. Chimps have a different generic name.

UK type robin

American style robin

Z23 A robin is a robin is a . . .

Nepenthes

N. bongso

N. ampullana

N. gracillis

N. sanguinea

Homo (genus bit)
sapiens (species bit)

Z24 Another genus. In the genus Nepenthes there are several species of pitcher plants (insect-eating plants). Here are just four.

Larger groups
Even with species grouped into genera (plural of genus), there would still be far too many groups to deal with easily. Related genera are grouped as a **family**; families are grouped into **orders**, and so on (Fig. Z26).

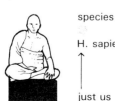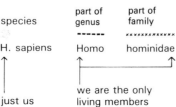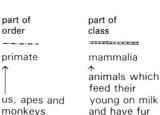

	species	part of genus	part of family	part of order	part of class	part of phylum	part of kingdom
		------	xxxxxxxxxx	–·–·–·–	☰☰☰☰☰	....	————
	H. sapiens	Homo	hominidae	primate	mammalia	chordate	animal
	just us	we are the only living members		us, apes and monkeys	animals which feed their young on milk and have fur	animals with backbones	

Z25 Homo sapiens' place in nature

We classify organisms by their similarities. The greater the number of similarities two organisms have, the smaller the group they can be put into. In larger groups the similarities become fewer and more basic. Backbones came before feeding the young on milk – they are more fundamental.

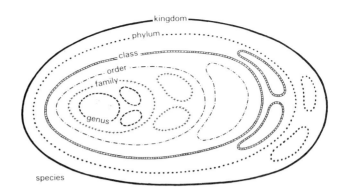

Z26

The largest groups are the **kingdoms**.

There are 5 (probably) kingdoms

– plants
– animals
– bacteria
– viruses
– fungi

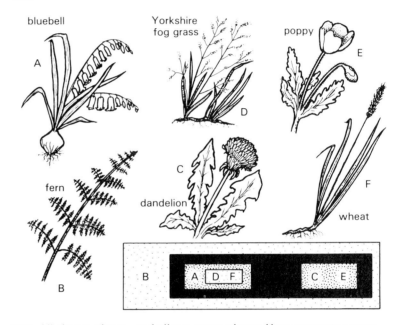

Z27 All six are plants, and all are green plants. How are we to group them? What characteristics count? Based on whether they have flowers, and the type of leaf veining, we get the boxed result. D and F are more closely related (have more similarities) to each other than they are to A or any of the others.

Questions

1. Here are some invented animals. They belong to different species, but are all members of the order Mugwumpida. Group the species into genera and give them scientific names. Group the genera into families. You can have a genus or a family with only one species in it if you want. Give your reasons for the way you have grouped them.

2. If you were given a small group (say six) of animals or plants how would you decide whether they all belonged to the same species or not? Give as many details of what you would do as you can.

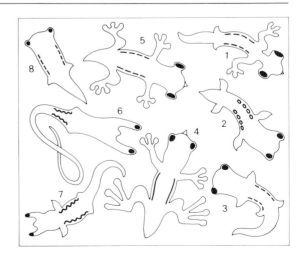

Z28

The making of Homo sapiens

Homo sapiens – us – has been around for a tiny fraction of the time that there has been life on Earth. The earliest fossils come from about 3 thousand million years ago, so life must have begun before that. Humanoids related to modern human beings were around 3 million years ago. That's less than a thousandth of the time we know there has been life on Earth.

We have fossil clues which give us the broad outline of the story of our evolution.

Each dot is a place where important human fossils have been found.

Cro-magnon

early man-types in Africa

Z29 Ancestral homes

The earliest ancestor we know of is a small ape type called Ramapithecus who lived 15 million years ago. All we have is bits of jaw but they are clearly more like us than modern apes.

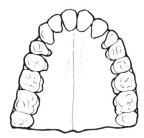

Z30 Ramapithecus had a rounded jaw like us – feel the shape of your jaw

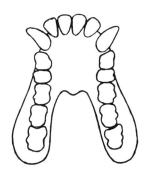

Z31 Gorilla jaw

Z32 An Australopithecine

Some of Ramapithecus' descendents evolved into the Australopithecines around 4 million years ago. They were two types – stocky five-footers and slimmer four-footers. They stood upright but probably waddled when they ran.

Between 2 and 3 million years ago, *Homo habilis* (handyman) joined the Australopithecines on the African plains. These people had larger brains and made simple tools.

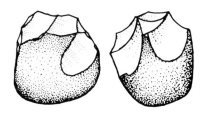

Z33 Pebble tools – 2 million years old

264

Homo erectus (upright man), who followed, was more of a traveller. Fossils of these people appear in Africa, Asia and Europe. They made more complex stone tools and used fire for cooking.

Homo erectus

and two views of one of his tools

Z34

The Neanderthal people had brains as big as ours, but they shared heavy brows and a lack of chin with *Homo erectus*. Neanderthals cared about the dead. The bones of a Neanderthal child have been found surrounded by animal horns in a specially dug pit.

In one group, not only brain size but also skull shape was changing. People very like modern man were around in Europe 100 000 years ago – *Homo sapiens* (wise man!) had arrived.

By 25 000 years ago, people like those at Cro-magnon in France were doing well enough to have time for cave painting, carving small statues and burying their dead with care. Changes in people since then have been less biological and more social. Ideas have been passed on as people talk and write. Over the years knowledge has grown and its use has changed the way we live.

Z36 Fertility goddess

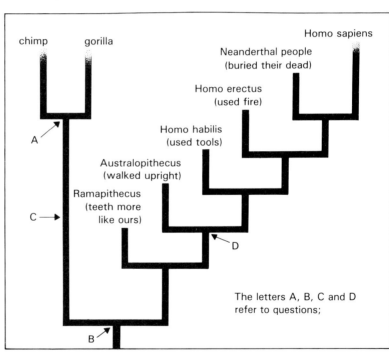

Z35 The relatives of Homo sapiens

The letters A, B, C and D refer to questions;

Questions

1. Africa is sometimes called 'the cradle of mankind'. Why do you think this name is given? Do you think it is an accurate description?

2. Choose **one** of these ancestors or near-ancestors of humans and explain how it differed from (a) its own ancestors and (b) us: *Homo habilis, Homo erectus Australopithecus*

3. Explain what is meant by
   (a) species
   (b) extinct

4. Imagine you are a reporter. You have interviewed Charles Darwin and asked him about his theory – especially where he got his ideas from. Write a short article called 'Great Naturalist Says Young People Should Travel'.

Summary and questions

Summary

We are beginning to understand the story of the evolution of life on earth. The end result of evolution is a wide variety of life, which we divide into groups for convenience. This is called classifying. The smallest groups are breeding groups – species.

Life on earth has evolved or changed over millions of years from simple organisms. Most organisms die before they reproduce. Those with adaptations which help them survive and find a mate are more likely to have offspring, and the offspring may inherit these adaptations. This is natural selection. If the environment changes, organisms which happen to be adapted to the new conditions will be the ones to survive and to breed. There is evidence from fossils, from the embryos and structure of living organisms, and (on a small scale) from examples of evolution happening over the last 100 years.

Questions

1. This is a cartoon borrowed from a science magazine. How do you explain it?

2. On the diagram of the human family tree (page 265) there are letters A–D.
   (a) One of these represents a common ancestor shared by humans and modern apes — which?
   (b) Which letter represents the common ancestor for modern humans and the Australopithecines?
   (c) On the map showing where human type fossils have been found there are big gaps where none have been found. How do you explain the gaps?

3. (a) Humans have an appendix – a small bulge from the wall of the large intestine. It does not seem to have a use, and if it becomes infected it can make people very ill. How do you explain the fact that we have an appendix?
   (b) Mauritius is an island in the Indian Ocean far away from the mainland of Africa. On it evolved a very strange bird. It was large, moved slowly and could not fly. When man came to the island and brought mainland animals it soon became extinct. How do you explain the dodo's story – how could it evolve in the first place and why did it disappear so fast?

4. In this book, the theory of evolution is illustrated by mice. Explain how the theory works using another organism to illustrate each point.

5. Bacteria are normally killed by antibiotics like penicillin. Chance mutations in some bacteria make them completely or partly resistant to certain antibiotics. If a group of bacteria is exposed to an antibiotic, the resistant forms may survive and breed while the non-resistant forms die.
   (a) Make up an experiment which would show whether a sample of bacteria included any resistant forms.
   (b) Anna and Kay are ill and are given a course of penicillin tablets to take (say for a week). Anna takes all of hers but Kay only takes half, because she feels fine after a couple of days and can't be bothered. Which girl is more likely to be carrying bacteria which she could pass on to someone else? Why?

6. Copy out and fill in the blanks.
   _____ worked for many years on his theory of evolution, in which he tried to explain how organisms _____. He said that huge numbers of organisms are born and most _____. Because organisms _____, some are better able to fight for _____ or hide from _____, and so on, than others. They are likely to have more _____ and the result is that a group of organisms gradually _____ as their _____ changes. A modern example is the _____ _____ which once was _____, and lived on light _____ covered trees. Pollution means that town trees have _____ trunks and in towns today a _____ form of the _____ is common. Selection is by _____ who eat animals they can see easily on the tree trunks.

1. The figure below shows two soil organisms, X and Y.

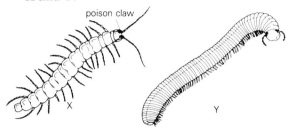

poison claw

X

Y

(a) Using the figure, list *three* differences between the two organisms.

	X	Y
1		
2		
3		

(b) *i* Which is likely to move faster?
ii Suggest *one* way in which the differences observed indicate differences in speed of movement.

(c) *i* Which of the two is more likely to be a carnivore?
ii Suggest *one* way in which the differences observed indicate this type of feeding.

(MEG)

2. The figure shows an animal cell.

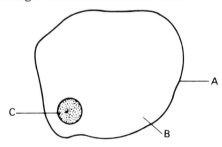

A

C

B

(a) Name the structures A, B and C.

(b) Which of these structures contains the genetic information?

(c) What is the function of structure A?

(MEG)

3. Vertebrates are animals with backbones. Name the GROUP of vertebrates which

(a) feed their young on milk,

(b) have bodies covered with scales and lay eggs which have no shells,

(c) have bodies covered with scales and lay eggs with shells.

(NEA)

4. (a) Name *one* parasite which affects Man.

(b) Describe *two* effects this parasite has on human health.

(c) How is this parasite spread from one person to another?

(MEG)

5. From the list of terms below choose *one* which best fits each description in the table. Write your answers in the spaces provided.

CONSUMER   NUTRIENT CYCLE
COMMUNITY   BIOMASS
COMPETITION   HABITAT
POPULATION   DECOMPOSER
PRODUCER

Description	Term
A group of individuals of the same species	
An organism which breaks down leaf litter	
Interacting populations within the same habitat	
An organism which changes light energy into stored chemical energy	

(LEAG)

6. The figure represents a sealed aquarium placed in natural light and containing plant and animal pond life.

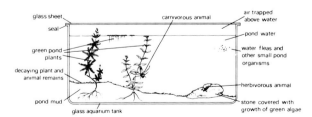

glass sheet
seal
green pond plants
decaying plant and animal remains
pond mud
glass aquarium tank
carnivorous animal
air trapped above water
pond water
water fleas and other small pond organisms
herbivorous animal
stone covered with growth of green algae

All the living organisms in the aquarium must obtain energy to survive.

(a) What is the source of energy for the green plants?

(b) What is the immediate source of energy for the herbivorous animals?

(c) What is the immediate source of energy for the carnivorous animals?

(In parts (d), (e) and (f) of this question you are expected to write several *sentences* to explain your answers.)

(d) In what ways would the aquarium be changed if all the animal life were removed and then the aquarium resealed?

(e) In what ways would the aquarium be changed if all the plants were removed and the animals were sealed in on their own?

(f) Would it be possible for the plants and animals to live indefinitely in the sealed aquarium as it was originally set up? Explain fully the reasons for your answer.

(MEG)

7. The figure below shows the processes involved in the water cycle.

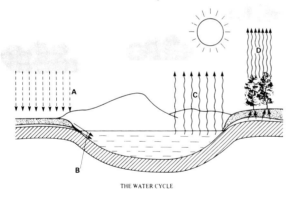

THE WATER CYCLE

(a) Name the processes labelled A, B, C and D.

(b) Name two substances which pollute water.

(c) Name two substances which pollute air.

8. The figure below shows the Nitrogen Cycle.

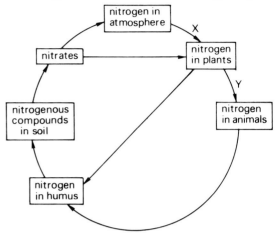

(a) *i* Name the process X.
ii Of what benefit is this process to plants?

(b) In what chemical form is nitrogen transferred by process Y?

(c) A gardener built a compost heap of plant material. After several weeks he observed that the heap had produced heat.
i What organisms were present in the plant heap to account for this observation?
ii What process, in the nitrogen cycle above, produced the heat?

(MEG)

9. The diagram shows the carbon cycle in nature.

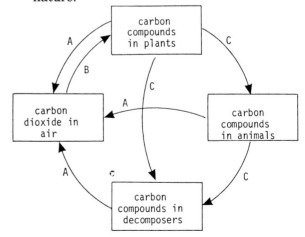

(a) Name the process shown by the three arrows marked A.

(b) Name the process shown by the arrow marked B.

(c) Name the process shown by the three arrows marked C.

(SEG)

10. The diagrams below show a small part of the lung from a healthy person and from a person suffering from the effects of air pollution. Both are drawn to the same scale.

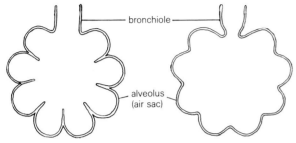

(a) Copy the table and write down on it two differences which can be seen on the diagrams between the healthy lung and the diseased lung.

	Healthy lung	Diseased lung
Difference one		
Difference two		

(b) Suggest why the differences you have described would make the diseased lung work less well.

(NEA)

11. The diagram below shows two cells found in human blood.

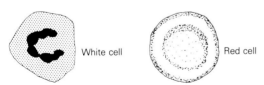

(a) What is the function of a red cell?

(b) Describe what the white cell would do if it met bacteria in the blood.

(c) *i* What must a doctor find out about a patient's blood before giving a blood transfusion?
ii Why does the doctor need to know this?

(NEA)

12. The figure above right shows the structure of a single villus.

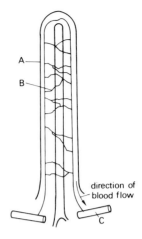

(a) Where would you expect to find this structure in the gut?

(b) Name *two* chemicals passing through part C after a meal.

(c) *i* What is part B called?
ii Why is it important in the villus?

(d) Name the blood vessel connecting structure C to the liver.

(e) Suggest *one* advantage of blood going to the liver from the villus before going to the whole body.

(MEG)

13. The diagram below, labelled A to K, shows a ventral view of a mammalian heart and blood vessels

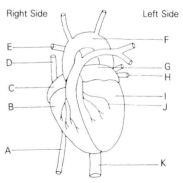

(a) State *precisely* where the blood in D and E would go to next.

(b) Write the letter of the part which contracts to send blood to the brain.

(c) *i* What effect may heavy smoking have on J?
ii How may this affect the heart as a whole?

(LEAG)

14. Complete the following statement about breathing using one word in each of the spaces:

When you breathe IN the _____ muscles contract resulting in the ribs moving _____ and _____. The diaphragm muscle contracts at the same time, moving the diaphragm _____. As a result the volume of the chest _____, the pressure of air inside goes _____ and air flows into the lungs.

(MEG)

15. The diagram below shows a section through part of a green leaf.

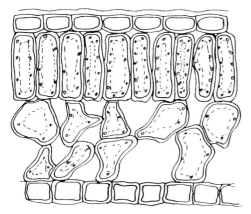

(a) ON THE DIAGRAM,
   i label the palisade layer with the letter X,
   ii label a vacuole with the letter Y.

(b) State two ways in which tomato plants growing in a greenhouse could be made to photosynthesize more quickly.

(NEA)

16. The diagram below shows a section through the elbow.

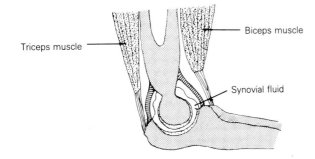

(a) ON THE DIAGRAM,
   i label a tendon with the letter X,
   ii label a ligament with the letter Y.

(b) Why does the joint have synovial fluid?

(c) Explain why we need a triceps muscle as well as a biceps muscle.

(NEA)

17. Which of your sense organs would be sensitive to each of the following?

(a) Music on radio.

(b) A red traffic light.

(c) Salt solution.

(LEAG)

18. A gardener has three plants of the same kind.
Plant A has red flowers,
Plant B has red flowers,
Plant C has yellow flowers.
The gardener carried out the crosses shown below.

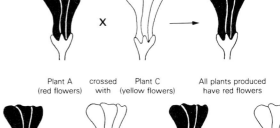

Plant A   crossed   Plant C   All plants produced
(red flowers)   with   (yellow flowers)   have red flowers

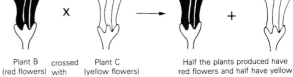

Plant B   crossed   Plant C   Half the plants produced have
(red flowers) with   (yellow flowers)   red flowers and half have yellow
                                   flowers

(a) *i* Which flower colour is dominant?
   ii Explain the reason for your answer to *i*.

(b) Explain what the gardener would do
   i to get plants which all have red flowers,
   ii to get plants which all have yellow flowers.

(NEA)

19. The diagram shows the human female reproductive systems

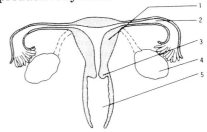

(a) Name the parts 1, 2, 3, 4 and 5.

(b) Give the *number* in the diagram where each of the following takes place.
   i fertilization (= fusion of egg and sperm)
   ii insemination (= deposit of semen in female)
   iii ovulation (= release of egg)
   iv implantation (= embedding of fertilized egg)

(SEG)

20. The diagram below shows the offspring of crosses between pure bred Aberdeen Angus bulls, which are black, and pure bred Redpoll cows, which are red. The ratio of the colours of the offspring of the first generation is also shown. Coat colour is controlled by a single gene which has two forms (alleles): one for black and one for red colour.

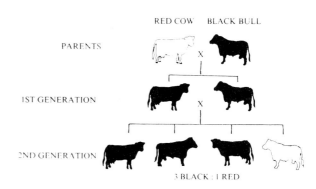

(a) What letters are suitable to represent the two forms (alleles) of the gene?
   i for black coat colour
   ii for red coat colour

(b) *i* Copy the diagram and draw a circle around each animal which is definitely homozygous for the gene for coat colour.
   ii Draw a square around each animal in the diagram which is definitely heterozygous for the gene for coat colour.

(c) Explain why some of the animals in the diagram could be either homozygous or heterozygous for the gene for coat colour.

(LEAG)

Index

A adaptation, 25, 230–231
adrenalin, 151, 153
albinism, 78, 246
algae, 16, 88
alveolus, 102
amino acids, 51, 69, 73, 74, 76
Amoeba, 18, 67, 98, 112
amphibians, 20
anaerobic respiration, 96
annelids, 19
antagonistic muscles, 114
antibodies, 167, 171–173
anus, 75
artery, 160
arthropods, 18, 20
asexual reproduction, 236

B backbone, 20–21, 120–121
bacteria, 13, 33, 34, 38–39, 66, 88
balance, 141
behaviour, 141
Benedict's test, 52
bile, 73, 76
biological control, 40
biomass, 42–43
biome, 24
birds, 21, 122–123, 147, 198
birth, 211
Biuret test, 52
blood, 154, 160–170
blood cells, 166, 167
blood group, 171, 253
bones, 115–122
Bowman's capsule, 175
brain, 131, 141, 144, 148–149, 150
breathing, 97, 105
bronchus, 102, 104
butterfly, 62, 199

C calcium, 58
cancer, 106, 167, 186–187
capillarity, 155
capillary, 102–103, 160, 161, 164, 175
carbon cycle, 94–95
carbon dioxide, 77, 82, 93, 94, 97
carnivore, 64
cartilage, 102, 116, 117
caterpillar, 199
cell, 79, 96, 126, 180–187
cell wall, 79, 182
cellulose, 51, 79, 182
Chlamydomonas, 16, 18
chloroplast, 77, 79
cholera, 75
chromosome, 183–185, 237–241, 251, 252
cilia, 105, 113
classification, 262–263
climax community, 226–228
coelenterates, 19

colon, 71, 75
colour blindness, 251
conifers, 17
contraception, 206–207
control experiments, 6
courtship, 27, 197
cuticle, 51, 79, 83
cytoplasm, 79, 112, 158, 182

D Darwin, 256–257, 260
decomposers, 9, 33
deficiency diseases, 61, 212
diaphragm, 73, 103–104
diarrhoea, 75
diffusion, 67, 97, 101, 154–156
digestion, 68, 74
disease, 13–14, 75, 167–171, 208, 232–233
dispersal, 110–111
DNA, 13, 14, 238–239
dominance, 245–247
duodenum, 73, 74

E ear, 136, 137, 141
earthworm, 18, 34, 35, 70, 114, 199
echinoderms, 18, 19
ecosystem, 24, 43–44, 220–228
egg, 189, 196, 198–200, 202, 205, 207, 210, 258
embryo, 116, 148, 196–197, 210–211, 258
endocrine glands, 150–151
energy, 42–43, 45, 80, 90–92
enzymes, 50, 67, 68–69, 73
epidermis of leaf, 79, 82
excretion, 173–175
exoskeleton, 129
exponential growth, 218
eye, 133–135

F faeces, 75
fallopian tubes, 205, 206, 210
family trees, 247, 257, 260
farming, 35, 45, 228
ferns, 17
fertilization, 190, 191, 196–197, 202, 204, 205, 206–207
fibre, 55
fish, 20, 100, 124–125, 162, 173
flagella, 113
flowering plants, 16, 17
flowers, 190, 192–193
fossils, 256, 259
frog, 148, 150, 200
fruit, 191
fungi, 15, 33, 67

G gametes, 190, 196, 236, 240
genes, 240–251, 260
genetic disease, 250–253, 260
genetic engineering, 239
genotype, 246
genus, 262
germination, 194
gestation, 210
gills, 100, 200, 201
glands, 71, 73, 150–151
glomerulus, 175
glucose, 51, 52, 77, 83–84, 192
goitre, 58
guard cells, 79, 82–83, 128

H haemoglobin, 166
haemophilia, 168, 251, 252
heart, 160, 162–163
herbivore, 64–65
hibernation, 27
hormones, 150–152, 206, 213
horse evolution, 259
human evolution, 264–265
humus, 32
hybrids, 248
Hydra, 88, 236
hyphae, 67

I ileum, 73, 74
immunity, 169
insects, 20, 51, 101, 131, 199
instinct, 147
insulin, 150
invertebrates, 18
iodine, 58
iron, 58, 62

J Jenner, 172
joints, 116–117, 129
joules, 80

K kidneys, 173–175

L labour, 211
lacteals, 74
large intestine, 75
lateral line, 131
leaf structure, 79
learning, 147
legs, 120–121
leukaemia, 167
lichen, 89
life cycle, 89
life span, 215
liver, 76, 169, 173
long sight, 135
lungs, 102–106, 173
lymph, 74, 76, 164, 167

M mammals, 21, 60, 144, 197, 202